SUBVERSIONS

Nancy Ellen Batty is an independent researcher living in Canada. She has published essays on Shashi Deshpande, Salman Rushdie, M.G. Vassanji, Arundhati Roy, William Faulkner, Toni Morrison and Nalo Hopkinson. With Dr Heather Marcovitch, she co-edited a collection of essays on the television series *Mad Men* (2012). Her monograph on the works of Shashi Deshpande—*The Ring of Recollection: Transgenerational Haunting in the Novels of Shashi Deshpande*—was published by Rodopi in 2010.

Dieter Riemenschneider obtained his Ph.D. with a thesis on *The Modern Indian Novel in English* in 1971 and taught Commonwealth literature/English Language Literatures at Goethe-University, Frankfurt (1971–1999). His main research areas are Indian English and Aotearoa New Zealand Māori literature and culture. Among his book publications are *The Indian Novel in English: Its Critical Discourse 1934–2004* (Rawat 2005); *Essays on Indian Writing in English* (Rawat 2016); (ed.) *Postcolonial Theory: The Emergence of a Critical Discourse: A Selected and Annotated Bibliography* (Stauffenburg 2004 & Rawat 2006); *Wildes Licht*, a bilingual anthology of poems from Aotearoa New Zealand (Tranzlit & Puriri Press, 2010 & 2012); and *Mediating Aotearoa: Essays on Māori Culture* (Tranzlit 2021). Website: tranzlit.com; tranzlit.de; email: kaitui80@gmail.com

ESSAYS ON LIFE AND LITERATURE

SELECTED AND COMPILED BY
NANCY E. BATTY AND DIETER RIEMENSCHNEIDER

cntxt

First published by Context, an imprint of Westland Publications Private Limited, in 2021

Published by Context, an imprint of Westland Books, a division of Nasadiya Technologies Private Limited, in 2023

No. 269/2B, First Floor, 'Irai Arul', Vimalraj Street, Nethaji Nagar, Alapakkam Main Road, Maduravoyal, Chennai 600095

Westland, the Westland logo, Context and the Context logo are the trademarks of Nasadiya Technologies Private Limited, or its affiliates.

ISBN: 9789357764605

10 9 8 7 6 5 4 3 2 1

Typeset in Adobe Text Pro by Jojy Philip, New Delhi - 110015
Printed at Saurabh Printers Pvt. Ltd.

‘Some of my favourite opinions are dissenting opinions.’

– Ruth Bader Ginsburg

Contents

Section III
Writers, Readers, Critics and Reviewers

Section IV
Texts and Genres

Section V
Places Recalled and Writers Remembered

Acknowledgements

I would like to acknowledge the very major role of Professor Dieter Riemenschneider and Dr Nancy E. Batty in compiling this collection. Both of them are deeply interested in Indian Writing in English and have published works on Indian writing. Prof. Riemenschneider has been a long-time authority in the field. The contribution of these two scholars has been immense, from selecting the essays, making suggestions that drew my attention to vagueness and discrepancies, asking me to amplify what they considered 'important ideas'—all this with the constant declaration: 'The final decision is, of course, yours.' Their encouragement and belief that these essays mattered sustained me throughout. In short, without their critical and appreciative minds, this collection would have been wholly different—if it had come into being at all. Working with them has been a wonderful experience. This three-continent collaboration helped me to get through the dark months of the pandemic in 2020. I have no words to thank them, so I will just say I am hugely grateful.

I would also like to thank Karthika V.K. for leading me, with her comments on the essays, to the title—always, for me, so hard to find. And for giving me, with each book, not just solid support, but also a sense of comfort. Rare, I should imagine, between an author and an editor/publisher.

Author's Note

Some of these essays originated in articles for newspapers, magazines and journals. Some others have come out of lectures and keynote addresses delivered at different venues. Many have been revised, some entirely rewritten. Nevertheless, I would like to acknowledge, with gratitude, the sources of these essays.

Keynote addresses: National Institute of Advanced Studies (NIAS), Bangalore; Indian Institute of Science, Bangalore; the Bangalore Literature Festival; the Goa Arts and Literature Festival; the Sahitya Akademi National Seminar on the short story; International Seminar held by Gujarat University; IACLALS conference held at Karnatak University.

Lectures at: the Thunchan Festival at Tirur, Kerala; the Munich Festival; Select Book House annual talk; Jaipur University.

I would like to thank all those who invited me to these events.

The essays began as articles in: *The Times of India*, *Indian Express*, *The Wire*, *Scroll*, *Guftugu*, *Biblio*, *First City*, *Outlook Travel*, *Little Magazine*, *Miloon Saryajani* (a Marathi magazine), and a volume that came out of a conference on Shakti.

'Mapping Bangalore' appeared in *Multiple City: Writings on Bangalore*, edited by Aditi De.

'Gulkand and Rose Jam' appeared in *Indian English and Vernacular India*, edited by Makarand Paranjape and G.J.V. Prasad.

The essay on Prof. Lal was written at the instance of his family and was published in a tribute to him brought out after his death.

Memory fails me and I am unable to locate the dates of some of the essays. I cannot identify the academic journal in which 'How to Read ...' was published, and I have no idea when and where 'Measuring Novels' appeared. I apologise for these lapses and for any other source I may have failed to mention. I am grateful to them and to all those mentioned here.

'A Short Personal History of Reading' was commissioned but has never been published before.

Introduction

Best known as a fiction writer, having published over a dozen novels and several collections of short stories, as well as a recent memoir, Shashi Deshpande is also a prolific non-fiction writer and one of India's most important intellectual voices. Her interests, expressed in dozens of essays published in newspapers and journals, range from observations on her own writing and that of others, to the state of literary criticism in India, and, importantly, to the state of India itself. Deshpande's long career has been devoted, in particular, to drawing attention to the status of women in India and to the status of Indian women writers. As the title of this collection indicates, Shashi Deshpande has never been afraid to intervene critically in the important political and literary controversies of her time, such as the perennial debate over the status of Indian Writing in English, even as she has sought to remind her readers of the infinite possibilities for a more equitable, just, and inclusive India.

It has been eighteen years since the publication of Deshpande's first collection of essays, *Writing from the Margin and Other Essays*. Since those essays were collected, she has published dozens more essays and reviews and given many public addresses, of which only a selection appear in the current volume. In compiling these essays for publication, we have considered both their ability to shed light on current times and their significance in terms of documenting the perspectives and attitudes of one of India's most important and celebrated writers.

The essays are presented in five sections, assembled thematically around the author's recurring concerns: the role and identity of the writer; women, writing, and empowerment; writers, readers, critics, and reviewers; texts and genres; and places recalled and writers remembered. Many of these essays have been previously published, and some of them have been updated during the editing process for the purposes of currency and brevity. It is appropriate—and entirely characteristic of Shashi Deshpande's humility and generosity—that the collection concludes with a reflection on the importance of Professor P. Lal to Deshpande's career, and to the career of so many other writers in India.

For more than forty years, Shashi Deshpande has—as a novelist, short story writer, essayist, memoirist, and public figure (in short, as a concerned and engaged citizen)—audibly contributed to the lively public debates on the role of the writer and writing in India and to an understanding of India's contemporary social, literary, and political issues. She has not been reluctant to insert critical and dissenting notes into the public discourse of her nation. We are reminded constantly by the essays collected here that Deshpande is, first and foremost, a reader and a listener, actively and compassionately engaged in dialogue with others. The present collection invites its readers to enter that fascinating dialogue.

Nancy E. Batty
(Red Deer, Canada)

Dieter Riemenschneider
(Kronberg, Germany)

Section I

THE ROLE AND IDENTITY OF THE WRITER

The Writer as Activist

Of what use is creative writing? The general understanding is that it comes under the heading of culture—something you enjoy when you have time, money, and nothing more important to do. On the other hand, there is also the idea of the writer as a thinker, an intellectual and a shaper of opinions. In India, specially, because of the ancient connection between literature and religion, writing was imbued with a special aura and writers with greater wisdom. So here we have two completely different pictures of the writer's work and role. But the writer looks at herself differently. For one thing, writers, like all artists, find great joy in their work, something denied to most people, for whom work is a drudgery. And, therefore, there is a sense of guilt, which brings up the questions: *Why am I so privileged? What makes me deserving of such a privilege?* But it is during times of crises, of national or international turmoil, that writers find themselves seriously confronted by the question: *of what use is my work?* There is then a sense of being like Tolstoy's Pierre (*War and Peace*), a bumbling amateur among soldiers, who knows his curiosity and questions are futile and foolish in the midst of savage suffering and death. At such times writing seems a self-indulgent activity. I am then forced to ask myself the question: *Of what use am I? Do I have any role to play in society?*

When we talk of the writer's role, we have necessarily to bring in the intent, because you can't have a role unless there is an intent to play the role. The question '*Why do you write?*', very often addressed to writers, is difficult to answer, since the urge to write comes from an unknown source. When writers try to explain themselves, various interesting reasons emerge: that they write out of anger, out of curiosity, from a desire to create order out of chaos, to escape from this world, to create a world over which they have more control, etc. When I look back to the beginning of my own writing, I see that it came out of both anger and confusion. Something, I felt, was not right with the world, with *my* world. It was hard to get a clear sense of what was wrong. It was only much later that I was able to connect my anger to the sense of denigration I was made to feel about being a female, about the roles that my gender identity seemed to have locked me into, roles I often chafed against. Worst of all was the idea that this gender identity, and the roles that came with it, seemed to deny my intellectual self, a self which was as important to me as my emotional self. It was out of this turmoil that my writing was born.

While different writers speak of different factors that propelled them into writing, a few common threads run through the fascinatingly diverse and contradictory statements of writers. Almost all refer to the mystery of the beginning of writing: they don't really know where the writing comes from. Writers speak of receiving an order, of an unknown force within propelling them into writing, even of hearing voices—the last, not a mysterious Joan of Arc kind of feeling, but something more literal. In fact, at times I have the sense of being an instrument, of having a finger in my back, prodding me, telling me, 'Now write!' Writers also speak of finding meanings, of learning things in the course of writing; the word 'discovery' resonates in most accounts. In other words, you don't start off from a position of knowledge; writing is a process of discoveries, often serendipitous ones, a groping in the dark, during which unexpected gifts fall into your hands. And since, most often, you write to make things clear to yourself, it is mainly a process of self-learning. One begins with questions; in fact, sometimes, even the questions are formulated only when you start writing. The questions are then pursued, not theoretically, but through human lives.

The third commonality is a love of words, something that is inextricably linked to the urge to say something. Ideas and words are yoked together in a symbiotic relationship. There is a desire to communicate, but as aesthetically as possible and always with a need for the right words. When you look for the right word, you are in fact examining the soul of the word itself. Only by discovering this will the writer know whether the word is appropriate and conveys exactly what she wants to say.

Now, what place is there for the social role of a writer in all this? If, when you begin writing, you don't know where it comes from, if you don't know where you are going, how can a purposeful role be a part of writing? In fact, amazingly, writers very rarely speak of wanting to play such a role. It seems an entirely self-contained activity, work pursued for its own sake; writing, it seems, *is* the thing. Nevertheless, the fact remains that writers *have* written to express their anguish about social evils and human problems. In our country, writers in the latter part of the nineteenth and the early part of the twentieth century were preoccupied both with social evils and the enslavement of the nation by a foreign power. Religious orthodoxy, the problem of child marriage and widowhood, our enslavement by a foreign power—these formed the subject of the literature in most Indian languages. Coming into contact with another nation, with another culture, one which believed in individual liberty and individualism, sparked off a great deal of introspection about what suddenly appeared like flaws in our own social structures.

Undoubtedly, a writer writes not only out of herself, but out of the society she is living in, as well. But the basic focus is always the human being; it is the individual's response to society, what society does to the individual, that the writer is really concerned with. People are both complex and complicated, and therefore writing, good writing that is, ultimately provides a complex, complicated picture, not the simple picture that would emerge if the writer's intent were to pinpoint social evils, or speak of social reform. In Tagore's *Binodini*, for example, even if Tagore gives vent to his views on the unfortunate plight of widows, Binodini is not portrayed wholly as a victim: she is manipulative and flirtatious, she is a temptress, using her charms, very skillfully, on men; she almost destroys a marriage. Ultimately, this is not a novel about widows, but about one woman, Binodini. And, like it always is with creative writing, characters take over the story, bringing in complexities which have no place in a merely moral narrative. In a novel, human truths emerge, and artificial constructs fall by the wayside. Almost no creative writer is interested in conveying a message, whether political or social. Nadine Gordimer, whose work is so closely connected with apartheid, says that politics influences her work only as it influences the lives of people. Tolstoy too disdains the idea of writing a novel to express his views on social questions. The truth is that the writer is expressing something intensely personal. It is difficult, almost impossible I would say, to control the flow of creative writing between the narrow banks of political and social reform, or of any message at all.

Where is the reader in all this? Surely, even if the writer is not thinking of reforming society as a whole, perhaps she is thinking of a reader whom she can influence? But most writers deny that they have a specific reader, or a species called 'readers', in mind when writing. For some reason, this seems difficult for the world to understand. The writer writes to communicate; surely, then, she is thinking of someone who will receive the communication? But as I see it, the reader enters the picture only *after* the writing is complete. Before that, I am my own reader. When I write, I split myself into two: there is the writer who is writing and there is the other self who is the reader. In fact, when I am writing,

I am telling *myself* things. But to say 'I am my own reader' is not enough; the matter is slightly more complicated than that. Since an important aspect of the urge to write is the desire to communicate, it presumes someone who will receive this communication. It is only with this connection that the writing becomes real. Borrowing Shankaracharya's terminology, there is a chain: *vak* (speech), *sphota* (apprehension) and *dhvani* (meaning).[1] Without the apprehension, there is no meaning and without meaning, speech has no existence. In fact, again using Shankaracharya's idea, words are transient and ephemeral; it is the meaning which makes them eternal. And, therefore, the enormous importance of the reader, because it is only when the reader apprehends the word that it is invested with meaning.

But, if writing is to communicate with a reader, the question is: communicate what? No, not a message; what the writer is trying to do, rather, is to make sense of life—for herself and, incidentally, for the reader. It is a kind of self-communing, of which the reader becomes a part. What is ultimately communicated is a picture of the world as the writer sees it, a picture that comes out of somewhere deep within, often taking the writer herself by surprise. It is almost like hypnosis: things one didn't know were there, things one wouldn't have expressed in ordinary life, emerge. It is also a little frightening, being almost like an emotional and intellectual striptease; there is a sense of standing exposed under the spotlight.

Once again there is nothing in this picture that speaks of the writer as one who wants to play a positive role in society. Clearly, the writer rarely sets out to achieve something. What the writer is doing, instead, is to set out on a very personal quest, one that leads her on to wholly strange and unknown paths. It's a solitary quest, involving, at least in its intentions and its beginnings, no one else. Nevertheless, the idea of the writer as some kind of an

---

[1] I have this from Ganesh Devi's *After Amnesia*.

activist, as a social reformer, is very strongly entrenched in our minds. It is because of this belief that the writer is often criticised for not performing such a role adequately. I myself have often met with disapproval for not adhering to some standards of feminism—the message I am supposed to be conveying through my novels. The presumption is that I am writing to solve women's problems, or, at the least, I am dealing with these problems. And therefore, my novels need to be faithful to the feminist agenda. Whereas, as a writer, I am interested above all in an individual human being, and her understanding of herself is, to me, the real goal. In our country, the idea that the writer should adhere to a cause is, actually, a pointer both to the importance of the writer and the need for social reform. Certainly, no one, least of all a writer, who is supposed to have a greater sensitivity, can ignore the social and political realities of our lives. And most writers, good writers, that is, do not ignore them. But once again, I have to emphasise that it is the effect of these things on a person that interests the writer.

Apart from this, there is a deep suspicion in our country of what is called 'art for art's sake'. Of what use is art if it is not wedded to a social purpose? To my mind, this whole argument does not understand that the artist is committed to the art itself and that a purpose will be achieved only if it is good art. Good art is powerful and can communicate much, whereas bad writing, even if carefully structured for a purpose, will fail to move a reader. To me, the writer's integrity is far more important than any avowed purpose. The word 'integrity' as applied to writers and writing has a special meaning. Virginia Woolf expresses it best when she speaks of '... integrity for the novelist, the conviction that the writer gives the reader that this is the truth'. In other words, it means believing in what one is saying. Clearly, if I do not believe in what I am saying, how can I convey any conviction to the reader?

It is important, I think, to understand the way a writer works before giving her the role of a social activist. As I have said earlier, it is not the events *per se* that are of interest to writers; it is what events do to people that really interests them. Secondly, writers need to distance themselves from events before they can write about them. Facts are stored, they are sifted through memory, transformed by the creative imagination and articulated in a way that expresses best what the writer wants to say: this is how the writer works. Certainly, there is a problem if writers do not take note of major events, like the partition of India, for example. But I would rather be interested in knowing why writers have failed in this, than see this lack as an accusation. And in any case, the accusation may only mean that the writing has not dealt *directly* with the event. Because, even in the course of my own severely limited reading, I have come across excellent creative writing which deals very skillfully with contemporary issues: a Hindi story which brings in the issue of reservations for women in the village panchayats, for example, or a Kannada story that centres round the Babri Masjid demolition. Nowhere in these stories is there a direct comment on these events; they are concerned, rather, with the involvement, or even the chance or tangential connections of people to the events.

One needs to understand that basically the creative writer works very differently from the historian or the social or political analyst. The writer explores the gaps, the silences, the ambiguities, the complexities, the contradictions—and this, not to get to any kind of a conclusion, because often there is no conclusion. As far as a writer is concerned, what matters is understanding and reconciliation; this is what human life is all about. When it comes to activism, I am on the side of those who declare that writing *is* the writer's form of activism. As a dramatist named Kalidasa declared centuries ago, 'drama is not a popular method of preaching. Drama is the study, not the moral of life'.[2]

---

[2] Adya Rangacharya, *Drama in Sanskrit Literature.*

However, there is no doubt that writers can play a role in another way: they can make an impact on social and political life through their ideas, because their reputations as thinkers and writers give them a privileged place. Have our writers done this? Have we made any impact as thinkers and opinion makers? I have to admit that writers in our country are, unfortunately, not playing the role that they should. There are many reasons for this, some of which are outside the writers' control. One of these is that there are too many voices speaking out today; the voices of politicians, journalists, celebrities, the media, of the many specialists in each field are loudly audible. There is nothing wrong with this; but it does mean that it is hard to hear the writer's voice in such a cacophony of voices. There's this too, that the mystique surrounding the writer has all but disappeared. This is inevitable in an age of enormous media coverage; it is, in fact, the flip side of publicity. By making the writer a celebrity, the media has weakened the writer's role. In fact, the media has also taken away, to some extent, the writer's freedom. For fame brings about its own pressures which are hard to cope with. Virginia Woolf's words about Shakespeare say it beautifully: 'Now I think Shakespeare was very happy in this, that there was no impediment of fame, but his genius flowed out of him.'

But the media is not the only instrument that puts pressure on a writer; there are many more. Yet, the myth of the writer's freedom is as strongly entrenched in human minds as that of the pen being mightier than the sword. 'Behold there is no calling without a director except that of the scribe and he is the director': these words from ancient Egypt tell us that the idea existed even then. However, I am sure it was as little true then as it is now. Freedom comes only with money—and no writer can be free if she has to depend on someone for money. In earlier times, patrons helped writers to survive. A small acknowledgement, a salaam, was enough to keep the patron happy and the writer could go on with her work. But, today, the writer has to please many more people—publishers, readers, journalists and reviewers, etc.—for writing has become a market-driven profession. In addition, there is also an urgent need to be on the right side of the government. For to write, to be published and to be read is not enough; these are no longer the only ambitions of writers. There are prizes and awards to be won, committee memberships to hanker for, political appointments, possibly travels abroad—all these benefits depend on pleasing the right people.

But a problem greater than all these external pressures is that writers are themselves often stricken by doubt and at their most cynical and despairing moments might think of literature being, as a dissident Russian writer Sorokin called it, 'just letters on paper'. I remember my own anguished helplessness after what happened in Gujarat in 2002. What could I say? Who would listen? But Sorokin himself, in spite of knowing the dangers of being a dissident writer in Soviet Russia, continued to write. The truth is that the doubts are almost always only momentary; one would not be a writer if one did not believe in what one was doing.

What is sad is that there seems to be no place for the reasoned balanced opinion in a democracy. A single voice has no value; only numbers matter. Appealing to passions works; reason and sense stand no chance. In our own country, we are seeing how gradually and insidiously the fabric of our society is being damaged by dividing people on the basis of caste, religion and language. What have writers been able to do about this? I am frightened by the way the idea of this country as one of multiplicities is being eroded, of how slowly the idea is being circulated of a country of one ideology, one religion. I am frustrated too by the inability, by the impotence of writers and intellectuals to contest this idea.

In any case, I sometimes doubt whether writing—creative or otherwise—can have an immediate impact on anything. For example, after so much has been written about feminism, even today many people still equate feminism with hating men, abandoning families, lesbianism, etc. The truth is that writing by itself, one writer by herself, can achieve very little. Virginia Woolf, speaking of masterpieces, says, '... masterpieces are not solitary births; they are the outcome of many years of thinking in common, of thinking by the body of people, so that the experience of the mass is behind the single voice'. I know how true this is when I think, once again, of the feminist movement. It was the effect of the voices of writers, academics, journalists, lawyers, doctors, activists, scientists and ordinary women, all speaking together, that finally made some impact. One Simone de Beauvoir, one Germaine Greer, could never have done what was achieved by so many coming together. The writer matters as part of a group and, in the group, the writer's is a very important role, because the writer can spearhead a movement. By articulating ideas with great clarity, she makes it possible for others to identify with what she is saying. And often, the writer, by first articulating an idea, builds a platform on which others can stand. For example, twentieth-century writers such as de Beauvoir and Greer stood on the shoulders of Mary Wollstonecraft, whose eighteenth-century *A Vindication of the Rights of Woman* remained largely unheard until her voice fell on fertile ground. The world was ripe for a change and therefore feminism gathered strength.

A writer's major role, then, is to work as part of a community, to be part of a body of voices. It happened in our country in the Dalit movement, where the writing kept pace with the general trend of feeling; it happened with the women's movement, where writing by women became part of a whole movement. But these are rare examples. Writers have not been able to use their stature as writers and thinkers to form a collective voice and speak on important issues.

However, I do believe that there is a role which writers continue to play, a very important role which is not connected to society as a whole, but to an individual human being. Alexander Solzhenitsyn's *One Day in the Life of Ivan Denisovich,* while giving the reader a vivid picture of the cruelty and oppression in the Stalin work camps, is mainly a story of human endurance and survival which most humans can identify with; perhaps, they may even be inspired by it. It is through giving expression to such universal human feelings that the writer can become part of a movement for social change. Very importantly, a writer gives voice to the voiceless and speaks on behalf of people who are unable to articulate their ideas, their thoughts, or their fears the way a writer can. I don't think a book can change a person's life, though blurbs often make this grandiose claim. But sometimes a book can spark off an understanding of herself in the reader which becomes part of the process of healing, of moving on. If writing is a quest, the reader is part of the quest, a partner who travels with the writer. The reader may diverge at some point; nevertheless, that book is what started the reader off on the journey.

I have no doubt that no writer sets out to actively play a role in society through her writing. For a writer, as I said, *writing* is the only thing. But in exploring ideas, in teasing them, in stretching them and trying them on, the writer helps others to open their eyes to what they have not been able to wholly glimpse on their own. The writer's imagination is a very powerful tool; it has both muscle and vision. I would compare it, not to the butterfly's flitting, but to the eagle's swoop and soar in flight. There is something daring about imagination, about the way it can go into the dark, leap over a yawning abyss and make connections which never seemed to be there. It is imagination that allows the artist to get to the inner truth, which goes beyond the facts, behind the presumed reality.

How do we live? This is the question which, above and beyond all questions, has plagued the human mind. We have found answers to a great many questions, but this one continues to elude us. This is the question all serious writers address; there is little hope of getting an answer, but to pursue the question itself is to understand a little more of life, to get some glimpses of possibilities. To me a writer's main role is in providing these glimpses. And there is this too, that a writer is different from all others in that at the moment of writing, she steps out of the room, so to say, stands at a distance, a little away from her own humanity and sees the world from this vantage point. This gives a unique perspective, the larger picture which is closer to the truth than anything else. This perspective also allows for much to fall away—our accepted ideas about ourselves and the world, for example. It also lets us see clearly our strengths and weaknesses, our flaws and follies, our dreams and nightmares. This is what the writer has to offer a reader; this, perhaps, is truly the writer's role.

(2003)

Catching the Truth of a Nation

When I began collecting my thoughts for this talk, I realised I faced a dilemma: how do I steer my way between the sentimental and the coldly intellectual? The problem is that the nation is both an abstract idea, a symbol that touches us emotionally, as well as a reality in which we live. To think of the nation in the abstract, as a symbol, is to get a set of images, some of which evoke strong emotions in us. To see the national flag being hoisted, to hear the national anthem, even to watch a cricket match of India against Pakistan, say, makes us extremely, sometimes embarrassingly, emotional. It is like the idea of the mother in the abstract, which, as a symbol, is more powerful and more emotional than the reality of one's own mother. If we think of it dispassionately, the reality of the nation can irritate and anger us the same way our mothers can at times. But when I look at the nation as a writer, it becomes something more than a vague emotional symbol, or an irritating reality. For one thing, it is connected to my identity. Of course, many other factors go into one's identity as well, like gender, religion, language, caste and so on; but the nation is an important part of this identity. Yet, it is not something which the writer consciously writes out of. In fact, it is an unstated, taken-for-granted, implicit foundation of our lives and our writing.

At a recent conference I attended, the issue of 'who is an Indian writer?' found almost every writer saying 'I do not think of myself as an Indian writer'. Surprisingly, even those writers who live abroad, and with whom in mind this question was presumably framed, had the same answer. What we meant was, that we do not ever *consciously* think of our selves as 'Indian writers'. Nevertheless, the nation is part of our selves and the fact that we are Indians informs our writing. The nation in this context does not mean only the geographical location or the territorial limits; it means the culture, the history, the civilisation in which we live. These are closely intermeshed with the idea of the nation, in the same way that our personal histories are part of our personal identities. Therefore, to understand my identity, I need to get hold of the idea of the nation.

It is rare that anyone, even a writer, sets out consciously to discover what her/his idea of the nation is. The idea comes to us gradually in the course of our lives—indeed it seeps into us from the moment of birth. And each one of us will have a different idea about the nation. It is like the story of the blind men and the elephant; what you get hold of is, for you, the shape of the nation, My idea of India encompasses stories from the Upanishads; the two great epics—the Ramayana and the Mahabharata; the magical stories of the Buddha; King Ashoka; Akbar; and a man of our times, Mahatma Gandhi. As also the men and women who tried to question the terrible inequalities of their society through their 'bhakti' (devotional) poems, which are alive and part of people's lives even today. The picture would not be complete without images of the world I have lived in: Tibet and the lonely figure of a boy, the Dalai Lama, escaping to India. The cries of '*Hindi Chini bhai bhai!*' and the shocking betrayal that followed. The wars with Pakistan and what they did to our psyche; the paranoia that entered the nation. The religious, caste and linguistic divides in the country which were exploited by unscrupulous politicians. The ruthlessness and the corruption of unprincipled rulers. The Emergency. These pictures clashed with the others and the conflict disturbed and troubled me. And, like it is for all writers, the turmoil contained the seeds of a novel which embraced all these things, with the nation being the backdrop to human lives. The novel I had in mind would take in what happened to the country in the decades after Independence, something which had begun troubling me greatly in the Indira Gandhi era: the corruption, the sycophancy and the autocracy that came into the politics at the time. The sight of schoolchildren in Mumbai's Shivaji Park singing a patriotic song, a song that spoke of war, became the central point of my troubled feelings. To listen to children's voices singing in a chorus is always a deeply moving experience. Here, when they were singing of the nation, of their determination to fight for the nation, of either winning or dying, it made me even more emotional. To think of a nation which had believed in Gandhi's idea of *ahimsa* teaching children to sing songs of aggression seemed a symbol of what was wrong with our nation. This would be part of my novel, *That Long Silence*, too.

But, as often happens in the course of writing a novel, it changed its course. And instead of focussing on the nation, it became a novel that concerned itself with the man-woman relationship, it became an intensely personal novel of a woman's exploration of her relationship with the world. And so, while I had wanted to write a novel in which I actively engaged with the nation, I wrote instead what is slightingly called, specially because it was written by a woman, 'a domestic novel'. I did have a sense of failure. I thought I had failed, not in the novel which I finally wrote: no, I had no regrets about that, but in not having been able to write the novel I wanted to, one which articulated my troubled feelings about the nation.

But had I really failed to do that? Some years later I came across a statement by a Polish woman who had emigrated to Sweden, and had married and raised a family there. Speaking of her contribution to Sweden's social and economic life, she said that she considered she had made a sort of contribution to this, because 'after all, I have established and cultivated that smallest cell of social life, a family ...'

I agree with her. The nation is an abstraction and it is only through the reality of human lives that you can approach that idea. Even *War and Peace*, that epic novel about Russia, speaks through the lives of people. Its epic qualities come not only from its telling the story of a nation at war, but also from the vast number of individuals, the variety of people it embraces in its scope. Written of Russia during the time of Napoleon's invasion, the author's focus is the nation. Yet, throughout the novel, speaking directly to the reader in his author's voice, Tolstoy is openly critical of the historian's method of taking only the events and the principal actors. He talks instead of using an 'infinitesimally small unit' for understanding—the ordinary individual, the family. And it is through the lives of a few families that Tolstoy has given us a picture of the chaotic, shifting and tumultuous state of the nation at that time. To me some scenes evoke the Russian people and the times more vividly than anything else could. This is the method of the creative writer: evoking, through a phrase, a line, a scene, a much larger picture, something that crystallises an entire world. It is the creative writer's imagination that enables the writer to make the leap into dark unknown areas, to make the connections, to go beyond the façade into complexities and ambiguities, without which the picture is never complete. By bringing out the various shades, including the uncertain grey, the writing presents a picture closer to the truth than a bland 'this is how it was'. Like Hemingway said, 'you make something through your invention that is not a representative but a whole new thing, truer than anything true and alive'.

Truer than anything true and alive—these words say it all. The fact is that the creative writer captures the living breathing soul of a nation, as well as its living breathing body. As Tolstoy has done in *War and Peace*. So too George Eliot in *Middlemarch*, though this novel presents us with a picture of a nation in times of peace, not in times of war.

However, even when the writing comes out of a genuine concern about the nation, it does not necessarily follow the path of patriotism. An Indian novel written by a writer considered a great nationalist has many surprises in store for the reader. This novel is Rabindranath Tagore's *Gora*. In this novel, Gora, the main character, is a fervid nationalist, his whole life and identity contained in his feelings about India, in his hostility to foreign rule and the rulers. Yet, at the end of the novel, it turns out Gora is not even an Indian. He is totally shattered by the discovery: he feels himself a man without an identity. 'The only thing left for me is a vast negation', he says. But it is out of this lack of identity that he moves on to an identity beyond nation and religion and sees a clearer picture of India, an understanding of what the nation really is. In Tagore's *Home and the World*, which is again about nationalism, one of its characters, Nikhil, says, 'to worship our country as a god is to bring a curse upon it'—the same idea which is touched upon with greater subtlety in *Gora*.

It seems, then, that even when the writer is actively engaging with the nation, when the writer takes the nation as a subject, the writer cannot and does not write to an agenda which gives the nation a place beyond and above humanity. Like it is in all writing, the writer has to follow her/his own truths, some of which go uncomfortably against this idea of 'my nation right or wrong'. I think of the great nationalist leader Lokmanya Tilak who lived and worked in the late nineteenth and the early twentieth century. Fanatically nationalistic, rejecting everything that the foreign rulers did, he was against a move to raise the age of consent (to sex in marriage) of girls to an age beyond ten. The issue blew up because of the death of a child of eleven who had been forced into sex by her husband and had bled to death. While the British and many Indian leaders like Ranade, Gokhale and others argued for raising the age of consent, Tilak thought that the British could not and should not meddle with our culture and customs. His nationalism was greater than his concern for little girls who were married to men double their age and had to become their sexual partners. How would a writer deal with this? After all, Tilak was one of the most respected and revered leaders of his time. In my novel, *Strangers to Ourselves*, one of the characters, Ahalya, speaks of her husband's opposition to Tilak and how he was maligned and hated for it.

So how then does the writer look at the nation? A plethora of literature was produced at the time of our freedom struggle and many of the poems, songs, plays, novels which were written at the time have entered our national mythology. But these were written about a dream: it was the writers' homage to an ideal of a nation that was still a dream. This writing had its role to play at that time. But when the writer looks beyond the dream, when the writing goes beyond the idealised abstraction to the reality, it becomes something quite different. Like Tolstoy and Tagore did, the writer stumbles upon something closer to the truth than the ideal. Even if it is a love for one's country that stimulates the writer into writing, in the course of the writing, something happens that takes the writer beyond this idea of patriotism to something more timeless.

We have another problem in India which is that the idea of a nation as we see it today is not a very old idea. In fact, it came into being during the freedom struggle. Even today, most of us do not immediately think of ourselves as Indians; Tagore spoke of himself as one who was 'firmly grounded in Bengali history and culture'. Most writers in our country would think the same way, as being grounded in their own specific regional culture. The regional identity is twinned with the language identity. Later, the religious and the caste identity emerge. It is only when we go out of the country that we become Indians above and beyond all these other identities. But today, in this global world, how important is this identity? The truth is that the idea of the nation has become even more important in a world in which boundaries seem to be giving way, as happened in Europe, for example. Paradoxically, the sense of being threatened, of being swamped by a global culture, has made nations and cultures even more aggressive and jealous of their individual identities. Boundaries were drawn and redrawn after the two world wars in the last century. Later, many countries had breakaway groups who considered themselves as having an identity quite different from the country they actually are a part of. I remember meeting two professors of English at a conference who told me, as soon as they introduced themselves to me, 'We are Kurds, we are Christians'. This was their identity.

Globalisation has also given writers another problem to contend with, which is the fact that globalisation of literature has meant that English books have a global market. This has a very great impact on writing in this country—on the writing in English as also, to a smaller extent, writing that is translated into English and is able, therefore, to go outside the country. The place of these books in the global market is that of 'an Indian book', or even 'a book *about* India'. But creative writers don't write 'about India'; that is for travel writers, it is for tourist brochures. But this is what globalisation has done to literature. While globalisation seems to be erasing many distinctive cultural signs, ironically, it has become more important for literature to highlight these signs. So that, while most writers would, as I said earlier, take the fact of their writing being located in India as an unstated, a taken-for-granted, in the global market it is important for this fact to be proclaimed, to be presented with a flourish. Which means that, while the nation is important to the writer, both because it gives the writer an identity, as well as being, at times, the subject of the writers' text, it has now taken on a new importance: the nation is a selling point and is used to sell the book. In other words, Mother India has become Miss India.

But there is a problem in selling things. The goods have to be suited to the buyer's needs. And therefore the creation of an India which the reader needs—an exotic, mystical country of poverty and spirituality. A country in which people live ordinary mundane lives, where they are individuals, not Indians, does not go down very well. Even Tagore, speaking of the Western response to his post-*Gitanjali* poems, complained, 'they have labelled me a mystic and when I produce something that is not mystical they are offended'. This apart, there is a need to spell out things, to simplify them, to emphasise what is Indian in the sense of being not-Western. It has also to be an idea of India that the world is comfortable with, an image that conforms to the world's idea of India. Surprises are not welcome. And therefore it is possible that writers will re-form the nation, making it what the outside world wants it to be: a neat picture of an India that is comfortably acceptable as India, instead of the chaotic, confused one that would be closer to the truth. E.M. Forster's much admired and lauded book, *A Passage to India*, never appealed to me, because I felt it was constantly highlighting the fact that this was India, this was not-England. Perhaps it was exactly this quality that made Western readers comfortable with it. I consider Forster's *Howards End* a vastly superior novel, being very English, without this fact being spelt out anywhere.

The fact is that the idea of a nation cannot be simplified; it cannot be fitted into stereotypes, clichéd images and known attitudes. It is a complex thing which can never be approached directly. How a writer can evoke a nation without actually referring to it, is, for me, exemplified by a Kannada short story (*A Piece of the Wall* by Bolwar Mahammed Kunhi), which effectively, subtly and artistically provides a picture of the Ayodhya-Babri Masjid crisis. The complex truth of what that event really meant is brought out with an amazing clarity through the lives of people living in a small town in coastal Karnataka. I'm sure many writers in various languages have dealt with this event. In this Kannada story, however, Ayodhya never enters directly into the story. The event happening far away from this little town, is brought out through the interaction between Hindus and Muslims *there*. By showing, through small details, what impact this event has on their ties and their relationship, it presents a real living picture of what that event meant for the people in this country. Presenting the nation to the world is easy; as long as the picture conforms to known images, it works. But, for us to understand it ourselves is much harder. And this is what writers really do through their writing, this is why they essentially write: to get some glimpse of an understanding of the world we are living in, of which the nation is a part that immediately concerns us. This understanding is presented to the reader, not as a certainty, but as something which will be the starting point for the reader of her/his own journey of understanding.

Today, when there is a greater interference with writers and their writing, when a certain idea of the nation is being regarded as the right view and any other view condemned, when books are burnt and publishers threatened, when attempts are made to glorify the nation at the cost of all else, when history is being distorted and being rewritten for a purpose, it is essential that writers write their own narratives, narratives which will comprise these ugly attempts as well. For, as Toni Morrison said, writers bear witness to an age. War times are not the only critical times. Today the nation is being threatened, not by any outside force, but by forces within the country, forces which are trying to change the very idea of our nation. If writers do not write with honesty and without fear, it will be their tragedy as well as a tragedy for the nation. If some writers have succumbed to a sense of frustration and despair, there are others who have forgotten their role, because they are too busy promoting themselves. Writing has become a self-indulgent and self-promoting business. Writers seem to be totally involved in their own little world, in their petty rivalries and squabbles. It is a splintered group, caste-ridden and gender divided. It seems to me that there is a desperate need not only for individual voices to speak up on issues, but for a body of opinion to be created which will matter, which may make a difference to the nation. I remember my father, a writer of stature in Kannada, campaigning during the elections after the Emergency, addressing street meetings at the age of seventy. He was heard, not only because of his individual stature, but because he belonged to a body, a group that had validity and was respected.

Some time back I heard a young Tamil poet speak with great anger and sorrow about the lack of any political movement in Tamil poetry. Now I know the importance of what she was saying; I know what she meant when she said that they lacked a movement like the Dalit movement in Kannada. Such a movement made it possible for voices that would otherwise have been suppressed to be heard. Writers should be able to be the bridge between intellectuals, politicians and the people; they are well qualified to do this, being able to embrace abstract ideologies as well as human realities. We have to believe that ultimately the voice, if it is selfless and has integrity, will be heard. We need to speak, to go on speaking, to reclaim our role in the nation before it is too late.

(2003)

A Short Personal History of Reading

It has become almost a professional hazard now for a writer to be asked the question: Do you think the habit of reading is dying out? Are fewer people reading today? Undoubtedly there are many more distractions than there were earlier: mobile phones, computers, TV, social networking, e-books, and so on and on. Besides there is the problem of too little time due to the long hours of both working and commuting, as well as the pressures of modern living. Jobs are demanding and even students have to face the problem of intense competition. To add to these woes, libraries have become scarce and bookshops are steadily closing down; these facts—the most visible proof of the threat to the reading habit—are staring us in the face. Can we then deny that the reading habit is in peril?

However, I see it differently. Reading has always been a minority interest; there never was, at any time, a large majority of people reading. Today, increased literacy means that even if readers are still very much in a minority, the actual number of readers is more than it was earlier. Bookshops and libraries are rapidly closing down, not because people are not reading, but because, in urban areas, bookshops can no longer afford the high rents and other overheads. In any case, book lending and selling has never been a highly profitable undertaking. What has really changed is the kind of reading people are indulging in. More people read newspapers and magazines, they read on the internet, and there's Kindle and e-books as well. And, strange fact, a great many people are writing today (sometimes it seems we have more writers than readers), because of the internet; and writing is, after all, closely akin to reading. So perhaps, if we presume that those who write also read, it's not a completely dismal situation.

In any case, I am not talking about reading in general, but about the reading of fiction, very specifically of the novel. Here, too, the prophets of doom and the cawing crows are at work, announcing, whenever they get a chance, that the novel is dead. Or, if it is not dead, it is in the ICU and soon it will be all over. This theory of the impending doom of the novel has many votaries. For example, V.S. Naipaul, a distinguished novelist himself, said that after 9/11, 'soft fiction' had to yield to what he called 'hard facts', while societies struggle with the forces of terrorism. In such terrible times, he says, why would people want to read novels? There's also the argument that in this world of information, works which provide information and knowledge, non-fiction, that is, are valued way above the novel which, after all, is 'only a story'. Yet, can we forget that humanity has always loved, told and listened to stories? All cultures, all civilisations, have their own store of stories which were orally passed on from generation to generation, some of which were, at some point, written down. These stories are national treasures today. All religious works are full of stories, for it is through stories of people like ourselves, rather than through dry abstract statements, that we can grasp what is being told to us. And novels are, primarily, stories about people.

Not surprisingly, novelists themselves have strongly defended the novel. I myself have been a passionate reader of novels all my life and would fiercely defend novels against anyone who predicts its doom or extinction. I began reading as a very young child; in fact, I can't remember a time when I did not read. There were no bookshops in Dharwad, the small town where I grew up, nor did many people have books at home in those days. And if they did, they were mostly Kannada books. Whereas I, because of the accident of studying in an English school, read only English books. Where did I get the books from? I suppose I read any book that came to hand, most of them borrowed from my school and college libraries and from wherever I could find them. There was no one who told me to read, or what to read, nobody who guided me into reading; I read anything I could get. It was an adventure, trying out new books, new authors. If I were to try and list all the books I read as a child and girl, I would feel like Ernest Hemingway, who told an interviewer, when asked about his literary forebears, that it would take him a day to remember the names of books and people who had been an influence on his life. And, he added, 'then it would sound as if I were claiming a credit I do not possess'. To avoid the same danger of being called a show-off, I will speak only of a few books that I remember and some that influenced me.

Now that I look back, I think it was a most curious conglomeration of books that I read: from *Alice in Wonderland* and *Arabian Nights* to *Treasure Island* and schoolgirls' stories by Angela Brazil, from Jane Austen, Dickens, the Brontë sisters, Thackeray and Mrs Gaskell to Daphne du Maurier and Nevil Shute, from E.M. Forster and Virginia Woolf to Agatha Christie, and Dorothy Sayers, D.H. Lawrence as well as Georgette Heyer. And so on and on.

But the earliest books I read that come to my mind are: a children's book called *The Rambles of Three Children, Pride and Prejudice*, the plays of Leo Tolstoy and the Sanskrit drama *Svapnavasavadatta* by Bhasa, which I read in the English translation.

The children's book was one I could identify with because, like the characters in the book, we were three siblings: two sisters and a brother. I identified strongly with the younger daughter and through her entered the book with such pleasure, that, even now, decades later, I can remember the book. *Pride and Prejudice* was a book that came by chance to my hand in the house of a family friend we were visiting. I was absorbed in the book and it was only when my parents were leaving that they searched for me and found me reading. I was fascinated by the book for some reason and read it as a whole a few years later. When I found it was a text in my first year of college, I thought—oh, but this is *my* book—and didn't want to share it with a whole class of indifferent, uncaring students. The third book, Tolstoy's plays, happened to be at home and for some reason it became a great favourite. I still have the copy with me, a dirty, smudged copy, much read, but again I wonder how well I understood the plays, because I was only about twelve when I read it. Yet, I read it so often that I knew some of the dialogues by heart, knew exactly where a particular dialogue would take place. The Sanskrit play *Svapnavasavadatta* by Bhasa spelt high romance to me; I thought it was as romantic as Daphne du Maurier's *Frenchman's Creek*, which I read a little later. Indeed, a most eclectic bunch of books, with nothing in common between them.

What did I get from these books? An escape from the world around me which often did not please me. A story. And one about people who were like me and yet unlike. Entertainment. A love of words and of the language. An identification with some characters. But, unfortunately, my reading was not much appreciated. 'She's showing off, she can't understand the book', our host said when they found me lost in *Pride and Prejudice*. 'You're neglecting your studies', I was told. 'Of what use is all this reading?' I was asked. 'You're wasting your time', my father said. Unforgivably, he told my teachers I could no longer borrow books from the school library. And he, a writer himself! But I have realised something only now, when I am nearing the end of my life: some of the books I read have so shaped and influenced me that I would not have been what I am today but for these books. (I am not speaking of having become a writer, that is a different matter altogether.) Coincidentally, two books I recently read speak of the power and the influence of novels, in fact, strangely enough, of the same novel—George Eliot's *Middlemarch*. One of them, Rebecca Mead's *My Life in Middlemarch*, is entirely about *Middlemarch*. In this book, the author speaks of how the book and her life impacted on each other, how the experiences of her life made her understand the book better, while the book in turn made her understand her own life much better. The other is an essay by the British writer, Zadie Smith, in her book, *Changing My Mind: Occasional Essays*, for which the starting point is Henry James' review of *Middlemarch*. After reading these, I thought: what is it about Eliot's novel, a Victorian novel set so firmly in its age and its values, that makes us still feel the need to discuss it and to find in it some relevance to our lives?

Rebecca Mead writes: 'Reading is sometimes thought of as a form of escapism and it's a common turn of phrase to speak of being lost in a book. But a book can also be where one finds oneself. When a reader is held and grasped by a book, reading does not feel like an escape from life so much as an urgent crucial dimension of life itself.'

The theme of *Middlemarch*, 'a young woman's desire for a substantial rewarding meaningful life', is one that resonates in every age in at least some thinking young women. In the life of this young woman, Eliot's Dorothea Brooke, we see the questions which trouble such women. Like (I'm now quoting Rebecca Mead): 'How on earth might one contain one's intolerable overpowering yearnings? Where is a woman to put her energies? What in the end, is a young woman to do with herself?' (Apart from getting married and having a family, of course.) These were the very questions and problems that troubled Rebecca Mead at the time she read *Middlemarch* and it is through her experiences in life that she began to understand the book better, just as the book helped her to understand her experiences in life better. The point is that what we get from a novel, or what we don't, depends on what or who we are, it depends on the time of our life when we first read it. For example, it was George Eliot's *The Mill on the Floss*, which I read as a girl that I responded to, not *Middlemarch*, which I read much later. (Fortunately, perhaps, because Virginia Woolf calls *Middlemarch* 'one of the few English novels written for grown-up people'.) At the age I was when I read *The Mill on the Floss*, I could identify with Maggie Tulliver, a bright, smart and confident girl, who is constantly being put down and told that her intelligence is of no use because she is a girl. And later, while she is growing up, she is made to feel unattractive compared to her conventionally good-looking cousin, which can be very troubling for a young girl. I so identified with Maggie, that her death still remains like a knife in my heart.

> The only effect I ardently long to produce by my writings, is that those who read them should be better able to imagine and to feel the pains and joys of those who differ from themselves in everything but the broad fact of being struggling erring human creatures.

These words of George Eliot not only give the writer's point of view, they point out what the novel does to the reader. To enter into another's life, another's feelings, is to experience life to a greater extent, it is to extend your own person. To be contained only in your own self seems a poverty-stricken life in comparison. And since the novelist never sits in judgement on her own characters, we learn to accept, more sympathetically, people who might at first seem to be repellent. Lear's grandiose ego, his foolishness, become, in the course of the drama, something we weep over. Shylock, so vengeful and grasping, arouses our softer emotions when he tells us what it is to be a Jew. Heathcliff, in Emily Brontë's *Wuthering Heights*, is an impossible-to-like, rather frightful man. And yet, Catherine loves him. In fact, the love between Catherine and Heathcliff is one of the most intense in literature. One of the finest passages in the book is of

Heathcliff standing the whole night under Catherine's window when she is dying, standing so still through all the dark hours that, the author tells us, a pair of birds made a nest very close to where he is standing.

I also strongly believe that the novel teaches us to live better with our own selves. Reading about all kinds of people, we realise that we are not abnormal, that we are not unnatural, and that the thoughts and fancies we sometimes have, which seem to us abnormal and unnatural are, in fact, very natural and normal in humans. We learn what it is to be human, we recognise that humanness in our own selves and can therefore live more comfortably with ourselves. This is specially true for the young who, sensitive and ignorant as they are, are often afraid that there is something wrong with them. Even to have lofty ideas and ambitions, even to aspire to goodness (like Dorothea Brooke does) is often ridiculed. Reading, when it gives us a sense of identification with characters, with thoughts and ideas which seem to echo our own unspoken ones, assures us that we are not alone—a most strengthening thought. And there are books which go deep into you and pluck out thoughts you were afraid to acknowledge even to yourself—truly a very cathartic experience. We need fiction in our lives, whether or not we are writers, because we often feel the need to recreate our lives, our very selves, and find ourselves more comfortable with this life, this self, than with the reality.

To move from the abstract to the particular, I know, from my own experience, how some novels leave their mark on you forever. In Charles Dickens' *David Copperfield*, a big novel in every sense of the word, Dickens has, on a very large canvas, given us the journey of a young boy through a life of hardship, grief and struggles, and his gradual growing up. Like in all of Dickens' novels, there are a large number of unforgettable characters. The novel and the people in it entered my life, became a part of me, a point of reference in my life. Some sentences are unforgettable.

Listen to this: 'From Monday morning until Saturday night, I had no advice, no counsel, no encouragement, no consolation, no assistance, no support, of any kind, from anyone that I can call to mind.' These are the words of the ten-year old David. Even today, to read these words brings a lump in my throat. Many writers have written about the poignant joys and sorrows of childhood—something most of us will identify with, for all of us were children once. And when we read, we remember what we have perhaps forgotten since we became adults: the power that adults have over children; the helplessness of children in their dealings with adults. This is equally true with Jane Eyre and her relationship with her vicious aunt. But Jane fights back, a splendid fight-back against injustice.

Another novel, which too I read as a girl and which has remained with me, is *The Bridge of San Luis Rey*. I still have a copy of the book, a slim book of just 124 pages, tattered and aged now. And even today I read it with the same awe, the same admiration, even today it remains for me the almost perfect novel. Written by Thornton Wilder, an American writer, it begins with the fall of a bridge in Lima, Peru. Five people were crossing the bridge at the time and all of them died. The scene was watched by a priest who begins to wonder: Why these five people? Were they marked in some way? Was there something in their lives which brought them to die together? He investigates their lives and is left more confused than ever. None of them, it seems, deserved to die, though to the world they were flawed human beings. This was the time of the Spanish Inquisition (and Peru a colony of Spain) and so his questions about whether there is any pattern in human life, or any plan in the universe, his final understanding that there is none, are considered heretical and he is burnt at the stake. He dies, innocently wondering where he went wrong.

What is there in the book that so enchanted me that I read it even today over and over again? The profound question raised by the priest, whether we live by accident and die by accident, or live by plan and die by plan, is casually abandoned when the priest goes to the stake, puzzled and bewildered. The death is not heroic, either. So what makes the book great? It is the stories of the five people who died. Their relationships with others. The intensity of their emotions. The complexities within them. And what people they are! The foolish aristocratic old woman who loves her daughter to a frenzy, a love which is not returned. The little girl, who wants to be good, but has to live as a companion to the rich woman, a duty imposed on her by her beloved Abbess. A manager of a drama company, admirer and passionate lover of an actress who has turned her back on him and on the theatre. The actress's little boy who suffers from fits and is being taken away by the manager to be educated. And a young man, whose acute and dumb suffering at the recent death of his twin remains for me the most tragic, the most unforgettable part of the novel. The novel ends with the words: 'There is a land of the living and a land of the dead and the bridge is love, the only survivor, the only meaning.'

It is hard to analyse the effect of a book on a reader. I can only say that this book entered into me and became part of my life, part of my self. To read this book was for me a great never-to-be forgotten experience.

Dostoevsky's *Crime and Punishment* is perhaps one of the greatest novels ever written. A novel which has for its main characters murderers, pimps, prostitutes and evil people, it is perhaps the most moral story ever written. A searing, harrowing novel, to read it is to go through all the experiences that life has to offer, it is to learn that in love lies redemption, that to atone is to overcome the evil done. 'A book must be an axe to break the frozen sea within us.' Kafka's words state the truth of what a novel like *Crime and Punishment* does to a reader.

In Zadie Smith's essay on Henry James and *Middlemarch*, she says: 'For Eliot ... people are still all that people really have; our knowledge of, and feelings for, one another.' This, in effect, is the reason why we read novels, the reason why they affect us so much. Because, ultimately, they are about *us*. In them, we learn things about which we perhaps have had a vague idea, but which we have never been able to articulate clearly, even to our own selves. *Middlemarch*, Smith says in her essay, tells us that love enables knowledge, while Mead adds that George Eliot elevates experience above information, that to her it is human experience that is sacred and matters. Whether it is an epic novel, like Tolstoy's *War and Peace*, or a quiet, contained one like Jane Austen's *Emma*, it is because of the human experiences we read about in the novel that we are influenced, that we are shaken, that we see the world differently. Blurbs on books bravely claim that this book will change your life. No single book can do that. It is through reading a large number of books, through entering the worlds the authors have created and through living with the characters that we get glimpses of something. An idea of what life is about, perhaps.

How do we live so that this life makes some sense, is a question that has plagued humankind. Even today we don't have an answer to the question; but novels, good novels, great novels specially, give us a glimpse of an answer, because these are the questions all serious writers of fiction address, the questions they pursue through the lives of seemingly ordinary human beings. As long as humans survive, the human story will continue to fascinate us and novelists will go on writing their stories, trying to make some sense of life. Readers and writers are co-travellers on the same journey and the reader is bound to share whatever the writer learns in the course of writing the novel. As a writer I have realised that a writer never starts writing with knowledge. On the contrary, it is through doubts, questions and uncertainties that the writer works; there are, often, serendipitous discoveries that the writer stumbles across in the course of writing the novel. And the reader, who is the writer's companion, gets some glimpses of these discoveries. Incomplete, vague, though the glimpses maybe, they illuminate some of the shadows within us.

In today's world, art, in which I include writing, is given an important place. This is in theory, specially when we call it 'culture'. Sadly, in practice, art is a luxury; other things in life have priority, art comes way below. Books that give you facts, like those that speak of politics, economics and history, are way above novels, which many people not only don't read, but which they vehemently and proudly deny reading. But the novel works in a very different way from the way non-fiction does. It is not concerned with giving facts or nuggets of information. As I said, it works through questions, doubts, ambiguities, uncertainties. It embraces the shadowy area in the wings, as also the darkness backstage along with the brightly lit stage.

All events, all people, are central to themselves, but peripheral to others. This is indeed a great truth—one that fiction understands very well. To scorn reading fiction is to deny art any place in our lives. And to live without art is to live an incomplete life. I remember a few years back I came across *Bel Canto*, written by Ann Patchett, an American author I had not read until then. I was struck by the way it placed art and the love of beauty in the centre of our lives. The truth is that humans have an inherent love of beauty and of creating beauty. We have been given two great gifts—intellect and imagination. There is no doubt that we need both.

Finally let me answer the question: Is the novel dead? Has reading lost its charm? I can do no better than quote yet one more novelist who speaks up for the novel. This is A.S. Byatt reviewing Neel Mukherjee's *The Lives of Others*:

> I think there is a long way to go—an unimaginable way—before we can do without an art form that combines language and story ... we still tell stories, and we still think with language.

(2014)

An Open Letter to the Congress Party

In a democracy it should be possible for a citizen to meet her elected representative. But for various reasons, citizens never get to see an elected MP or an MLA in person. Hence this letter. I am sure that what I am going to say will be considered too basic, too simplistic, too often said by political pundits and veteran journalists. I am equally sure that your party has enough learned men (I use the word 'men' deliberately) who know all these things. However, at times, specially during times of crisis, we need to go back to what we have taken for granted, we need to reiterate some facts, ideas and beliefs which may become invisible in the haze of political debates and loud arguments.

This letter comes to you from an ordinary citizen who has lived eight decades in India, who has watched the birth of an independent India, who saw the Indian tricolour go up and the Union Jack come down, one who has voted in most elections since attaining adulthood. And, yes, a citizen who has, through the years, seen your party move from nation-building, to power-grabbing, to money-amassing. You need to know what such a citizen thinks. Besides, as a writer I believe what an American author, Ursula Le Guin, said—that there are matters on which one needs 'to stand up and be counted, lest silence collude with injustice'.

To get to the point: While you are being criticised, ridiculed and humiliated after the 2019 elections, I think of you as our most valuable asset at the moment, since you are the only national party which can provide the country with an opposition. Now that the Communist Party is only a shadow of its earlier self, and Lohia's Socialist party splintered, you, however poor your performance in these and the last elections were, still remain the only national party, apart from the BJP. To have two strong parties is the ideal situation for a democracy. But yours has been a swift and steady decline, your numbers in Parliament are abysmally low and with a poor leadership and skewed priorities you have lost contact with the people. You knew, even before the 2019 elections, that you had no chance of getting enough seats to form a majority. You hoped to align yourself with some regional parties, but you bungled even that. The regional parties were confident that, together, they could form an opposition. That, too, did not work out. I am glad the regional parties have not been able to become a strong force. Regional parties will never be able to coalesce into a single force. They are committed to the interests of their states; a conflict of interests, which is always possible, will divide them sharply and decisively. And a splintered opposition is a gift to the ruling party. Alexander Hamilton, one of the founding fathers of the United States, whose influence on the making of the American Constitution was great, believed in a strong centre. The greater the powers given to the states, he said, the weaker the Union would be. This is so much more true of India, which has never been a single entity until Gandhiji came and knitted the country together. We have a long history of satraps, who rebelled against their masters and became independent powers themselves. And therefore, though our Constitution had wisely maintained a balance of powers between the Centre and the states, I strongly believe that we need both the ruling party and the main opposition in Parliament to be national parties. We need a national party as the main opposition even more at this time when the ruling party has such a huge majority. Which makes it possible for the party to impose its ideology on the country with nobody to stop them. It can make changes in the Constitution, some of which can have frightening consequences. The party is now free to implement its ideas, of which we have already had a disquieting glimpse. They are raring to go. Democracy itself is likely to be threatened when the ruling party can roll over citizens like, yes, an appropriate phrase, the chariot of Jagannath.

Not many people believe you can pick yourself up and come back. You are considered a lost cause. But surprisingly there are a great many, even those who opposed you and voted against you, who hope you will make a comeback. You cannot go into hibernation (which you call introspection!); you have to come out of it. Look at what happened on the first day of Parliament. It was as if the Battle of Panipat was being fought all over again with opposing cries of '*Har Har Mahadev!*' and '*Allah ho Akbar!*' Is this going to be our future? Will we never hear an *Indian* voice in Parliament again? Do you think you are capable of giving us that?

I wonder if, during your introspection, you realised that it was your policy of 'Muslim appeasement' that drove many voters away from you and into the Hindutva fold? While you mull over this, you should also think of how little you have helped the Muslim community and how shallow and false your policy of helping them was. If they have progressed, it is because of the men and women in their own community, not because of any one of the political parties. You also brought words like 'secular' and 'liberal' into disrepute, both of which came to mean being pro-Muslim. Words have remarkable power. At the same time, they change meaning according to the times. Look at the words 'secularism' and 'socialism' which have become heavy with the contempt they have gathered through the years. This is because to you they were just words; you did nothing to make the words a reality. The word 'secular', whatever its dictionary meaning, in our country meant, or was supposed to mean, not bringing religion into politics. Now religion is everything in politics.

Sadly, you have succumbed to the idea that religion matters; you have begun speaking of 'soft Hinduism'. Your leader visited as many temples as perhaps the BJP leaders did. There is no such thing as 'soft' Hindutva. In any case, Hindutva was never what your party believed in. Stand by your convictions; abandoning them to gain some votes will backfire. Hindutva worked for the BJP because it was always at the core of their ideology. If you wear saffron today, even if it is only a loincloth, you will lose all the credibility you have left. You badly need to ask yourselves: What is our ideology? What policies will we follow in pursuit of this ideology? You have to be clear about this before you face your voters again.

Your sycophancy has made you the target of your opponents, yet, amazingly, you don't seem to understand how dearly it has cost you. Even today, after your debacle at the polls, in spite of Rahul Gandhi declaring, not once, not twice, but often, that he does not want to lead the party, you still cry out for him. In Rahul I saw, I see, a reluctant politician. He did his best. Now he says he wants to go. Respect him by believing him and let him go. Failure is no shame, but failing to see the truth is. And the truth is that Rahul is no leader. So move on. The family has had its chance. Now elect a leader. Electing a leader is one of the basic tenets of democracy. To elect a non-Gandhi as leader of your party is not lèse-majesté. By holding an election, you will prove to us that the country matters more to you than an individual, more than a family. Until now you showed us that your loyalty to a family was greater than your loyalty to the country. The country cannot forgive you for this. Louis XIV, that most powerful monarch, he who said when he was young and arrogant, 'I am the State', was the same man who told his courtiers when he was dying, 'I am going but the State remains'. Yes, the Gandhis may go, but the country remains. We hope you will think of this and elect a new leader: the best woman or man you have. Be assured some leader will emerge. And you never know from where that leader will come.

You need to do more than this: you need to reinvent yourself. You have become structurally rigid and ideologically dithering. Shuffling the same tired old faces around, including some who have a stain on their record, won't help. Holding out empty promises, criticising other parties and their leaders will put off the voters. Tell us what *you* are going to do. Right now, we can see that you are bankrupt of ideas. You need fresh blood. You don't need to ask where it will come from. Look around, look at the large number of young people in the country, young people exploding with energy and talent. Use these qualities for the good of the country. Think of the huge hunger of the young for opportunities, for a chance to prove themselves, to find their place in the world. Feed that hunger and give them opportunities in politics. Get more women into the party, not because they are connected to a man, or because of political correctness, or just because numbers make you look good; choose women because there is a huge potential waiting in them. Women are eager to prove themselves. Make use of their talents, use them for the good of the country. This is the century of the young. It will also become, I am confident, the century of women. Accept these two facts and shape your party accordingly. Let me be frank—the country is tired of old men for whom lying, hypocrisy and chauvinism have become a habit. Give us better leaders, both women and men. And a manifesto, perhaps the shortest in India's political history, which promises us just four things to start with: health, education, justice and freedom. Many lifetimes will be necessary to make these four simple words into a reality, but a start in earnest has to be made. Why not by you?

Remember that you can offer the country something which the ruling party cannot. Your history, if we ignore the past few decades, tells us that you do not believe in dividing the country into Hindus and Muslims. Which the ruling party, despite its soft words after the elections, does. We have heard the words of women and men in their party, we have seen them acting on this belief. My generation remembers the bloodshed and carnage of Partition; many more will remember the killing of Sikhs after Mrs Gandhi's assassination in 1984, the brutal planned violence in Gujarat in 2002.

I go back to Alexander Hamilton, who said that what works during a revolution does not work after the revolution succeeds. Gandhiji too had advised you to disband after Independence. Perhaps it is good that you did not heed his advice then. The country needed the leaders who had fought for freedom to help the nation get over the trauma of Partition, to set us on the path to a mature democracy. This moment, now, seems to be the right time to take Gandhiji's advice. You need not disband, but you have to remake yourself. Make yourself into a party which gives voters an alternative choice. If you do not, you are doomed. Unfortunately, without a strong opposition, the country we fervently believe in may also be doomed. Come out of your closed room. Listen to us. You can find no better teachers than the people you claim to represent, the people who rejected you in the last election, but who wait for you to give them what they want—a strong opposition. An alternative.

(2019)

At the Crossroads

In the past week or so, I have had a number of calls from journalists asking me whether I would be attending the Bangalore Literature Festival. Everyone here knows how charged the atmosphere in our country is today. The killing of Prof. Kalburgi, a respected scholar, stirred writers like never before. While many writers returned the awards given to them by the Sahitya Akademi, I decided to resign from the General Council of the Sahitya Akademi; I realised that I could not be associated with an institution which, while being the highest literary body in India, did not even make a statement condemning this killing. That the killing may have been done by an extreme rightist group which has arrogated to itself the 'right to protect Hinduism' made things much worse and resulted in a schism between pro-government writers and writers who believe in the freedom of expression. Obviously many writers opted out of this festival. It made me realise how political even attending a festival has become. I myself had absolutely no hesitation in saying that yes, I would be attending the festival. I had committed myself to this more than a year back and saw no reason to back out. I also believe that this is a festival of and for the people of Bangalore, it is for the readers of Bangalore and for writers everywhere; this is a festival of my city. Above all, by coming here, I will be able to talk to fellow writers, to readers, and to others interested in literature.

So much has been happening in the country and the world that the conflict between some writers and the government in our country may seem a small issue. This is often the problem for writers—there are times when you doubt yourself, when you wonder why you are writing an imaginary story when the world is in such a fragile state. But the doubts don't last. You know that for a writer, everything is important, or nothing is important. Our lives always run on parallel lines, on the small issues of our own lives and the line of greater issues which lie outside our lives; we live and write taking account of both.

One of the problems of this debate about the writers' protest has been that there are too many misunderstandings about the writers' intentions. Following these misunderstandings, the discussions have moved along totally irrelevant tracks. The emphasis throughout has been on writers returning their awards and the questions flung at writers often begin with 'Why didn't you do this earlier? Why now?' What was never understood was that returning awards was not the main issue, and there never was any coercion on writers to return an award. Besides, people who returned their awards, those who resigned from positions, and those who signed statements—all of them were equally part of the protest.

The other disturbing thing is that what began as a writers' movement against some developments in the country and against the silence of those in power, has now, in some inexplicable manner, turned into a confrontation between two opposing sets of writers. We now have an ugly atmosphere, which is not only disturbing, it is distressing. One has to wonder whether this is the result of some very clever manipulation of politicians, or whether it is a natural consequence of writers talking *at* each other through the media and not *to* each other. Obviously, there were going to be writers with different views; no one expected all writers to converge into a single group. But one did not expect the personal animosity, the bitterness that has crept into the discussions. The English writer Margaret Drabble once said to a reviewer who had made some unpleasant remarks about her or her work, 'Look me in the face and say that'. It is true. To talk to each other makes it impossible to demonise the other.

I will begin with the personal, because, since each writer took her/his own decision, I can only speak of my experience.

It was a great shock to me when Prof. Kalburgi was shot, not only because I knew him a little, but also because I was born and grew up in Dharwad where he lived and was killed, a town which was always known as a gentle and civilised town. That a scholar, who had only expressed his honest opinions about certain matters in religion, could be shot in broad daylight in his own house, and in a place like Dharwad, was incredible. He was a member of the General Council of the Sahitya Akademi, he was on the Advisory Board and he had received a Sahitya Akademi award as well. For all these reasons, I was sure the Akademi would make a statement expressing shock, not only at his death, but at the manner of his death; I thought the Akademi would support the right of writers to write without fear. Nothing happened. A little later, I heard from a friend that the Akademi had held a condolence meeting in Bangalore, in which, she told me, except for two persons, all the rest spoke as if nothing untoward had happened and Prof. Kalburgi had died a natural death. It left me baffled, uneasy. What was going on? Were we going to brush this matter under the carpet and ignore the serious implications of the killing of a man because of what he had written? And then two senior writers, Nayantara Sahgal and Uday Prakash, returned their awards because of the killing of a poor Muslim on the suspicion that he was eating beef. This was also a protest against the murder of two rationalists, Narendra Dabholkar and Govind Pansare, and of Prof. Kalburgi. At this moment, I knew that my uneasiness came out of the thought of being part of the Sahitya Akademi, which had failed the writers it represented so dismally. Let me make it clear: I have always respected the

Akademi for being the one institution which brought all Indian languages under one umbrella; I admired the work they did in getting translations done and in publishing books which no commercial publisher would publish. But now I knew that I could not work with an institution which treated writers' lives and their rights in so cavalier a manner. I could not understand the reason why it had ignored something that impacted writers' lives and their work so much. And so I resigned from my position on the General Council of the Akademi and the two boards I was a member of. Much happened in the following days, with more writers either returning their awards, or resigning from positions, or signing statements. Suddenly it was a flood and a few gestures became a movement. That so many writers followed the first few has been described as a herd mentality; writers have been compared to sheep. I think of it as one spark igniting another. If this is a herd mentality, then indeed all those who were part of the French revolution, or the freedom movement in India were also sheep.

Can a writer be an activist? There have always been divided opinions on this subject. I felt that in recent times writers had lost the stature they once had, that their voices were no longer listened to, or even heard. In fact, it seemed that writers had abnegated their position in society, that they rarely raised their voices, as if they knew that their opinions no longer mattered. Now, suddenly, the time seemed to have come when writers were reclaiming their voices, the time seemed to have come when writers were coming together in a spontaneous movement, each writer's act an individual and independent one. For the first time since India's independence, there was a community of writers' voices speaking. Writers from different languages, from different regions of India, senior writers, younger writers—all of them came together to voice their fears about how slowly, insidiously, threats to writers' freedom were growing. How writers had to be careful about what they wrote, specially if it was about religion or caste. How the government was trying to invade or take over cultural institutions, the FTII (Film and Television Institute of India) being a prime example.

One would have thought that the Akademi and the government would have taken this seriously. That the fact of so many writers speaking in one voice on an issue would have made them sit up and take notice of the issue, that they would say something, do something. Instead there was a running down of both the protests and the cause and of writers themselves. Writers are—no, I will not use the word 'intellectuals', the word has been debased by the wrong use made of it; I prefer to call writers 'thinkers'. Yes, writers are thinkers. The very act of writing compels thinking; it brings up questions and doubts. Which is why the world has always given them some regard and respect. Now, on the contrary, both the government and critics of the protest spoke of writers in a most derogatory manner. Just this week, I read a conversation between President Obama and the American writer Marilynne Robinson in *The New York Review of Books*. It was a one-to-one conversation about serious matters, about reading and writing, about politics, about the United States and what was happening inside and outside it. When I read the conversation, I envied a country in which the head of a state would have a discussion with a writer; it showed his respect, not for that writer alone, but for all writers and for their opinions. And I thought with distress of how the writers' protest had been greeted in India with ugly accusations, with derision. Stop writing, a minister said. Manufactured revolt, another said. 'Political stooges', 'intellectual mercenaries', 'mafia' were other terms of abuse. They are doing it to get some publicity, many said. The protest was belittled, the issue trivialised in many ways.

This belittling, this contemptuous trivialisation, has saddened me more than anything else. It is a sad day when a government cannot respect its artists and scholars (for there are others too in this movement, film-makers, artists, as well as scientists and educators). A sad day for the country when the government takes the lead in vilifying its creative people. No country, however, economically developed, can call itself a civilised country if its artists, writers, scholars and thinkers are treated with contempt.

Not many writers responded to these attacks; many of the charges were too absurd to be taken seriously. But two points need to be made.

Firstly, about the charge that writers were insulting their awards by returning them. Not a single writer will say that the award did not matter to her/him. When an award is given for your work, it is precious. To return it does not show a disrespect for the award; on the contrary, it is a sacrifice. The awards were returned to draw attention to something that was happening in the country, a threat to independent views, to different ways of living and thinking. Secondly, most of the authors who started the movement are senior authors, men and women who, through decades, have earned their name through their work; they do not need the publicity. This may not be true of all writers; there are always exceptions. But it is true of most of those who began the protest; these are people who are respected in their own languages. As for doing it for political considerations, there could not be anything more ridiculous. Writers are rarely political beings; a search into backgrounds will show that very few would ever have been members of a political party. There was talk of the protest being manufactured solely to impact the Bihar elections. If it was true, I would be pleased, because it would mean writers have immense power in this country! My own connection to politics is confined to voting in each election; I must have voted in every election in the last forty years. A most dismal record, nevertheless, for each individual, each party I voted for, lost. With this kind of a record, I am sure political parties will go down on their bended knees, praying that I do not support them. More seriously, why would a political party patronise writers? They have nothing to offer politicians. In the kind of democracy we have today, only numbers matter, only vote banks count, appealing to passions and fears works. Reason and sense have no place at all. We only have to look at how the word 'intellectual' is regarded to understand what place thinking people have in the power structure of our country.

The questions the writers were asking were missed in all the noise that followed the protests. The questions were: What kind of a country do we want? A country in which people of different religions, castes, languages, cultures live together, in harmony and mutual tolerance? Or a country in which one religion dominates, one idea of how we should live is imposed upon everyone, allowing no room for differences, not even for arguments and debates? Do we allow some people to impose on others the idea of what our country is? Do we put up with the derogatory statements that are made about women? Does anyone have the right to define to others what patriotism or nationalism is?

It seems to me that there is a dreadful resemblance in what is happening now to what happened in the USA during the McCarthy era. This was during the fifties of the last century, at the peak of the Cold War, when the Republican Senator Joseph McCarthy, playing on the fears of Americans about Communism, decided that there were many Americans who were Communists and that they needed to be got rid of. Therefore, people whose pasts included a contact, however brief, with the Communist party were called for interrogation and asked the question: Are you, or have you ever been, a member of the Communist party? Nobody was exempt from questioning if the House Committee on UnAmerican Activities felt they should be investigated. The entertainment industry was specially targeted, for artists are often mavericks; they are known to be people of independent views. Charlie Chaplin, Danny Kaye, Dashiell Hammett, Elia Kazan, Arthur Miller, Lillian Hellman were among those who were brought in for questioning. People were encouraged to inform on colleagues and friends, which would make their own punishment lighter. Lillian Hellman, the playwright, in her letter to the Chairman, the House Committee of Un-American Activities, wrote: 'To hurt innocent people whom I knew many years ago in order to save myself is, to me, inhuman, and indecent and dishonourable. I cannot and will not cut my conscience to fit this year's fashion.' Arthur Miller refused to answer. Writers and actors were blacklisted, which meant they could not get work. Obviously, there were many who informed on their friends and colleagues. And, equally obviously, there was a deep divide among writers.

Today, I am deeply distressed by the divide I can see between writers in India. It is difficult to understand, because most writers were, until now, just writers. Now we realise, to our bewilderment, that we are either for or against the government, we are either leftists/intellectuals/liberals, or we are rightists. Writers who returned their awards were on the receiving end of hate mail. But when Amitav Ghosh said that he would not return his award, he got a lot of hate mail as well. Which is disturbing. For, how can those who believe in free choice deny others the right to make their choice? Obviously, this is not the work of fellow writers, but of those who use, or misuse, the easy access that social media allows, to abuse others. This is deliberate mischief and writers must learn to ignore these attacks. There is no coercion on anyone to show solidarity with the movement. The policy of dividing writers is not a new one. It has been done on the basis of language, on the basis of caste, on the basis of ideology. But writers need to understand, specially now when the atmosphere is so vitiated, that literature is inclusive, not exclusive; that each writer is free to write what she/he wants, that the only curbs are those that the law imposes. We need to stop the name-calling, the abusing. All writers need to remember that the writers' movement is about the writer's right to freedom of expression. This right, a constitutional right, has been given to all citizens, but it means something more to writers. For writers to be forced to write according to any ideology is untenable. Creative writing abhors ideology; no writer can write a story, a poem, a play, or a novel according to an ideology. Besides, the writer's freedom is important for society as well. As Boris Pasternak, the Russian writer, said, '[I]t was my duty to make a statement about our epoch'. Which he did in *Dr Zhivago*. Which Alexander Solzhenitsyn did in *Cancer Ward*, *The First Circle* and *One Day in the Life of Ivan Denisovich*. Writers bear witness to an age: Toni Morrison's words. Through the stories writers write, the future will know how people lived at any time, what were their hopes, their dreams, their fears, their nightmares, what they held sacred and what they hated. While history gives the larger picture, fiction, or any creative writing, gives the micro picture. Svetlana Alexievich, the Russian writer who won the Nobel Prize last year, has written, not about events, but about people's response to events, how people feel, think, etc. She calls her writing a 'history of human feelings'. A history which will obviously contain as many different feelings and views as there are people. To look at the regimented writing that came out of Soviet Russia is to understand how dull, how deadly it is for writers to follow an imposed view, to have a homogeneous view, how important it is for many narratives to be told. There is no place for conformity, unanimity or the majority view in any art. Each piece of art, whether it is a painting, writing, music or anything else created, is unique. Creativity means uniqueness, it means no sameness, no duplicates. At present, homogenisation is only a possible threat, but the threat continues to lurk in a society where people are condemned for holding different views. An artist must be a reactionary, Evelyn Waugh said. Resistance is the heart and soul of literature; it means asserting one's own version of life. We need many views and opinions, we need to agree to disagree, we need arguments and debates; we need to talk *to* each other, not *at* each other, we need to support any writer who is threatened by force, for, who knows? The next writer threatened could be me. We have to speak, for as I said in my letter of resignation to the Akademi, silence is a form of abetment. Writers who are speaking of what is wrong with our country today are being called 'unpatriotic'. We must not wash our dirty linen in public, we are told. What do we do with dirty linen then? Keep it until it stinks? And, we who are writers know that we can write with the greatest knowledge of our own people, we can be critical of our own.

Very few men or women can change their society, even fewer can change the world. Writers too can't change much. I remember a letter that two writers, Harold Pinter and John le Carré, wrote to President Bush when he was on the point of embarking on the first war with Iraq. Of course, President Bush took no note of that letter, he went ahead with the war. The letter changed nothing. But the writers had spoken; they had made their point. And though writers cannot change the world, their writing, their opinions, may help in creating an awareness, in rousing people to asking questions, to debate. Montesquieu, Voltaire, and Rousseau are credited with having started the French Revolution, Abraham Lincoln called Harriet Beecher Stowe, who wrote *Uncle Tom's Cabin*, the little woman who started a great war. But this is not entirely true. A great many factors go into any happening, whether it is war, revolution, or some smaller event. But ultimately, what these other factors do is to arouse the great hunger for justice that lies dormant in all humans. The writer's response to events is, most often, to write. Arthur Miller wrote *The Crucible*, a play about the Salem witch trials, which paralleled the McCarthy investigations. It showed how people could be driven to cruelty by fear, how a mob could sway others. But there come times when writers feel the need to do something more, to speak openly, to resist what is wrong. This is not a crime; it adds to the richness of a democracy.

Finally, what do writers want? They want to write, to write what they want to without fear, they want to be published, to be read and, hopefully, to earn some money from their writing. Nothing more, nothing less.

(2015)

Why Read?

What place do the creative arts, like music, painting, literature, etc., have in our lives? How much do the creative arts matter in this utilitarian, science- and technology-oriented world? No doubt the creative arts are looked at with respect and the creator with some awe, for the magic of creation is still acknowledged by most human beings. Yet, one sees a kind of subtle denigration of the arts in the tone of condescension with which they are sometimes spoken of. A common response is: 'It's okay, but it's not for me. I don't have the time for such things.' And very often, when it is a man, he will add, 'I leave these things to my wife'. The fact that the arts are regarded as a female preserve is a significant pointer to the way they are looked at! Anything connected to women becomes a minor matter.

Art matters, but if one is to be candid, it is a very low-priority interest in most people's lives. At the best, artistic pursuits are regarded as a 'time-pass' (as we Indians say) and at the worst, an elitist activity, something which the common person has no need of and use for. This idea comes out of the notion that art is not a basic need like food, drink, sleep, sex, etc. I, however, question this. I think that the love of beauty and the urge to create is innate in a human being, if a little lower on the priority list than urges like hunger, sleep and sex. If the instinct to create were not an intrinsic part of a human being, why would humans have expressed themselves through poetry, songs, pictures, sculptures, and so on, instead of just functional speech and straightforward communication? If a cup were created purely for the utilitarian purpose of drinking water, why was it necessary to make it beautiful, to give it a graceful shape and a more elegant look? There is nothing elitist about a love of beauty and of creating something beautiful. And, if I may use a scientific term very unscientifically, I would say that by now love of beauty and the urge to create beauty have become part of our genetic store. They may be suppressed for a time when survival itself is in question; but we don't always live life on the edge of survival.

I, however, am going to speak of literature, which differs from the other arts, because it works through the medium of words. And therefore, to have access to it, you need to be literate, which means it is not for everyone. On the other hand, all human beings use words to communicate. Words are the most direct means of communication, though we do admit the eloquence of silence, of the sometimes greater power of pictures. Words are also the most difficult—they can become weapons, they can become links, they can hurt, they can heal and so on. Above all, they are tricky, for words are loaded with a baggage of meaning acquired through years of use and often get a connotation that cannot be divorced from them. J. Krishnamurthi, the philosopher, speaks of thought as being 'extraordinarily slavish to words'; what he means is that the idea, or the emotion, takes on a certain form *because* of the word. But does the idea create the word, or the does the word give birth to the idea? This is something that can be debated endlessly; it is like the 'Which comes first: the chicken or the egg?' argument. Whatever it is, words have a power that cannot be denied.

But this power seems to have somewhat faded in our era of information and knowledge. SMSs and WhatsApp, which are the most important means of communication today, rely on abbreviated language, emojis and emoticons. Politicians too have debased words, forcing them to mean what they want them to mean. In India, for example, the words 'patriot' and 'nationalist' are now being used to mean not love of one's own country, but hatred of another. Ideas themselves are at a discount unless they are connected to a definite function. There are also the problems of changing trends in literature. Poetry, so revered at one time, is much devalued today; it is considered of no 'use' to anyone, not even to the poet, since poetry earns no money. The novel, too, which at one time had lorded it over the other genres, is now under attack as being unable to cope with 'real life', and therefore futile, specially in times of crises. An example of this is novelist V.S. Naipaul's comment that, in the post-9/11 world, what he calls 'soft fiction' must yield to hard facts. Faced with such threats and danger as we are, Naipaul says, people no longer want to read 'made up stories about made up people'. That this is not an isolated comment or opinion is made clear by an increasing number of writers who use both real people and real events in their fiction, by the increasing number of movies that deal with real people and real-life incidents and by something truly bizarre, the reality shows on TV. In India, too, if we look around, we will see that fiction has all but vanished from the pages of magazines and the Sunday newspapers. Reviews of non-fiction get more space than fiction. I also hear an increasing number of people say, 'I don't read fiction' in a tone of smug self-satisfaction, as if it makes them superior. On the whole, fiction is considered lightweight, mere entertainment and often escapist. 'You write stories?' someone asks me and I wonder whether the questioner realises how insulting and condescending the tone in which the question is asked is.

Has the novel no place in our lives then? Fiction writers are themselves often stricken by doubt and ask themselves, 'What am I doing?' At the same time, I am sure that anyone who is a novelist is primarily a great lover and reader of the novel. Jane Austen, for example, in her novel *Northanger Abbey*, spoke of the novel as 'some work in which the greatest powers of the mind are displayed, in which the most thorough knowledge of human nature, the happiest delineation of its varieties, the liveliest effusions of wit and humour are conveyed to the world in the best-chosen language'. And another great novelist, Henry James, called the novel 'the most independent, most elastic, most prodigious of literary forms'.

But this is a novelist's point of view. And the novelist is not the person we can rely on when we look for an answer to the question 'Of what use is the novel?'—no more than we can expect a mother to speak in an objective manner about her child. We have to know what it does to a reader, to society, we have to ask what a reader gets from a novel and why we should give it a place of importance in our lives. And therefore I will answer these questions as a reader who has found great joy in novels all her life and whose life has been greatly enriched by them. But before I marshal my arguments and speak of how important the novel is to human life, I need to clear up a few wrong ideas about the process of writing. The idea that a novel is only a story, a 'made-up story', as Naipaul calls it, gives rise to the idea that it does not belong to the real world, which consists of more important things, like economic and political matters and so on. And therefore 'soft fiction', as opposed to 'hard facts'. And therefore, 'only a novel', as Jane Austen said, caustically repeating the generally held idea of the novel. But how does this novel, this story, come into being? While there are various ideas about creation and an infinite number of theories floating about, one thing that they all have in common is that there is a thing called inspiration and, once it appears, abracadabra, a novel is ready. Or a picture, or some beautiful music.

Now, inspiration is certainly a part of writing, like it is of all creativity, including the sciences, and I don't intend to run it down. But it seems wrong to emphasise one part of the whole process at the cost of all else that goes into the process of creation. Imagination is just as important a part of the creative process. Whether it is a book, or a painting, or Galileo's or Copernicus's idea of the universe and of our place in it, whether it is Newton's discovery of gravity, we can be sure that a daring leap of imagination has taken place. Added to imagination is faith in what one's imagination gets hold of. And then follows a great amount of hard work, often years of it. More importantly, something that is rarely taken note of by the general public, there is an intellectual rigour to the novel, which, apart from underlining the work, holds in leash ideas, emotions, craft, language, etc.

Creative writing really begins with the desire to communicate. However, the novelist rarely knows what exactly it is that she/he wants to communicate. Ask the novelist and the answer will be: 'I have a vague idea. I will know what it really is when I start writing. And when I come to the end, it may be quite different from what I thought it would be when I began writing.'

The fact is that writers are explorers—explorers of new worlds which they create. And during the course of the exploration they may stumble upon serendipitous discoveries. Novelists are not learned or wise people; they are curious, questioning people. It is this curiosity, this questioning, that leads them into writing a novel. The novelist's way of working is very different from that of the scholar or the researcher. Firstly, the writer needs to distance herself from what she is writing about. Even if it is a personal experience, the writer has to move away from it, get outside of it, before it can be written about. Nor is the novel an instant response, because immediacy is not an essential part of fiction. Facts are stored, sifted through memory, transformed through the creative imagination and then articulated in, as Jane Austen said, the 'best-chosen language'—which really means the language which can best convey what the writer wants to say. Moreover, what the novel really offers is not only a story. Coded within it are various things that make it go beyond the story, beyond that particular situation, those particular people, so that it vaults over them and becomes universal. In Anne Michael's *Fugitive Pieces*, for example, the holocaust is seen through the story of one Jewish boy whose parents were killed by the Germans. But it is, above all, a story of an ability to heal and survive.

What the novel creates is not a mirror image of society, but a picture that goes beyond the façade, beneath the surface. A tentative, questioning picture, offering the reader no certainties. And, in the process, unearthing hidden truths and complexities that mere facts can never get at. What the novelist really does is to create an alternate world, which gives a reader a glimpse of other possibilities. And once it enters the human consciousness, that which was only a possibility can become real. In this connection I would like to quote some words, words which I think very accurately express what I am trying to say:

> I think democracy exists in the West because the West has had the novel. And despotism reigns in the East because the East has had poetry. The novel develops the democratic imagination because it offers various paths, various destinies, while poetry is despotic. (Sorour Kasmai, Iranian writer)

I think these words, though very generalised, are worth pondering over.

Equally remarkable is a tribute which comes in a Foreword to a book of sociology: M.N. Srinivas's *The Remembered Village*. Professor Sol Tax in the Foreword compares what he calls the 'relative failure' of the ethnographer to capture a human cultural tradition, to a 'poet or novelist who brilliantly catches the truth of a nation, a civilization, an era'. The major disadvantage that the ethnographer suffers from, he says, is that he has 'to collect ... the mundane data ... from which any eventual interpretation can be made. This process itself fogs the mind—the forest is lost in the trees'.

The way I see it is that facts, specially for a novelist, give only a tunnel vision. Meeting events head on makes it possible to miss out everything that happens outside that range. Beyond and outside the world of facts lies another world. These few lines from Auden's 'Le Musée des Beaux Arts' brilliantly encapsulate the way art embraces the shadowy peripheral areas, areas which one is not even aware exist. In the poem he is speaking of the paintings of the Old Masters and how:

> About suffering they were never wrong
> ...: how well they understood
> Its human position: how it takes place
> While someone else is eating or opening a window or just
> walking dully along;
> How, when the aged are reverently, passionately waiting
> For the miraculous birth, there always must be
> Children who did not specially want it to happen, skating
> On a pond on the edge of the wood: ...

Auden goes on to speak of a painting of Icarus by the Flemish painter Brueghel. Icarus, according to Greek mythology, tried to defy gravity and fly. And failing, plunged to his death:

> In Brueghel's *Icarus*, for instance: how everything turns away
> Quite leisurely from the disaster; the ploughman may
> Have heard its splash, the forsaken cry,
> But for him it was not an important failure; the sun shone
> As it had to on the white legs disappearing into the green
> Water; and the expensive delicate ship that must have seen
> Something amazing, a boy falling out of the sky,
> Had somewhere to get to and sailed calmly on.

These lines capture the connection between art and life perfectly. They show how art makes the tangential connections which create a truer picture. In fact, the argument that literature can no longer cope with this terrible post-9/11 world seems flawed to me for this very reason, because creative literature is not directly about events, but about the effect—and not always the direct effect—that events have on human beings, on human lives. Tolstoy's *War and Peace*, for example, or Dickens' *A Tale of Two Cities*, go beyond Napoleon's invasion of Russia or the French Revolution to some human truths. To say that fiction cannot cope with this terrible world is to deny the truth that the world must have often seemed terrible to the people who lived in it. Yet, some great books have been written about terrible times, terrible events, about human agony.

Recently my attention was drawn to an article on the internet by an American academic, Professor Richard Rorty, titled *Redemption from Egotism*, in which he comments on a book called *How to Read and Why* by Harold Bloom, another eminent academic. This book, and Professor Rorty's own comments on it, propound some very interesting ideas about literature. Harold Bloom's book deals with the reading of 'novels, plays, short stories and poems', which he calls imaginative literature, as opposed to argumentative literature, which would include books of philosophy, political economy, etc. He says that imaginative literature confers autonomy on a reader; by which he means that it 'liberates one from one's own previous ways of thinking about the lives and fortunes of individual human beings'. He goes on to explain this by saying that 'all writing that is not merely a matter of conveying information offers, explicitly or implicitly, a context in which to put many propositions we have previously believed, many of the people we have known, *parts of our own life-stories* (emphasis mine), and many of the books we have previously read'.

To elaborate on this in my own words and with my own understanding of these statements, I would say that to read a novel is to go through a whole gamut of human experiences, it is to see the randomness of life, the unexpectedness of events, the multiplicities and complexities of human ways of thinking and action. To do this is to become more open to other people, to different kinds of people, to different ways of living, different predicaments, different ideas. This leads to what Bloom calls 'redemption from insensitivity or egotism'. In other words, partaking of a variety of human experiences expands the reader's experiential and emotional world, which is, if one were to look at it logically, as valuable as the world of information and facts. In the novel *Bel Canto* by Ann Patchett, one of the characters tries to tell an opera singer through an interpreter that he loves her. He begins fearfully, hesitantly, with the story of his childhood in post-war Russia when his family had lost everything. His grandmother, however, held on to a book of paintings which she allowed the children to look into every evening. It was through that book that he got access to the world of art and beauty. He concludes by telling the singer, 'I have a right to love you because I have been taught to love beauty'. This marvellously illuminating statement says that love of beauty and creation gives us an entry to a richer world. That it allows a quality in us to emerge, a quality that all of us possess, but which we suppress in the interests of being practical people, of coping with the necessities of daily living. To see the novel merely as entertainment, escapist, as lacking the substance of factual documentation, is to ignore this.

I spoke earlier of novelists being curious, questioning people; I also referred to there being an intellectual rigour to a novel. Both of these lead to an aspect of the novel which is very important to a reader—which is that a good novel has no place for stereotypes. Stereotypes are the result of intellectual laziness, an unwillingness to think for oneself, a willingness to accept what has been given to us. A good writer, on the other hand, will take nothing for granted, will put aside all that as already been said and begin afresh. My own writing began with my dissatisfaction with the picture of women I saw in most of the literature I read. Women are such and such, one was told. And most of the women I read about in books seemed to conform to this picture. But I knew this was not a true picture, I knew that there was much more to women than what these stereotypical images showed. It is not just women, because one day I almost literally 'saw' Duryodhana entering into a lake after his defeat in the battle. This vision was the beginning of a story which gave me a glimpse into the mind of a man who is regarded as the archvillain of the Mahabharata. The way I saw him and then wrote about him surprised even me, because suddenly there was much more to him than just a wicked man. Again in the Mahabharata, there is a scene between Bhima and Draupadi, when they are living out their year of disguise in the court of King Virata. Draupadi, who is being harassed by Kichaka, the Queen's brother, visits Bhima secretly and ask him to help her. And Bhima, the practical man, the angry and violent man, takes Draupadi's hands to his face, a gesture of such reverence, tenderness and sorrow for Draupadi's troubles that it does away completely with the usual stereotypical picture of Bhima.

What does this do to the reader? In the words of Harold Bloom and Richard Rorty, reading imaginative literature not only liberates a reader, it often increases our tolerance for strange and initially repellant people. To read Tolstoy's *Anna Karenina*, for example, is to get a glimpse into the mind of a woman who commits adultery and deserts her husband and child. We may not appreciate what she does, but we don't condemn her, either, because we see why she does it. So too the murderer Raskolnikov in *Crime and Punishment*. The whole point is about making choices. Certainly, people make the wrong choices, and the greatest literature has been about such wrong choices. Yudhishtira, for example. Or King Lear. But the writer, the creator, takes no sides. Actually, it is because of not taking sides that the writer can present a picture with so many shades in it, not only the black, white and the grey, but other colours as well. I think of all writers as being like that original storyteller in the Mahabharata, Sanjaya, who is engaged in telling the story of humankind to a blind king.

Does literature, the novel specifically, change the world? Does the writer base the novel on any ideology? Certainly, no novel can change the world the way a work like Marx's *Das Kapital* did. But there is a perception that an ideology-linked novel is weightier and more valuable. Intrinsically, however, the novel is incapable of carrying the load of any ideology and writers themselves rarely write with the aim of changing the world. There is a troubled feeling about the state of the world, some discontent, which is then channeled into the act of writing. But the writing is mainly to express these disturbed feelings, this anger. According to me, the value of the novel lies exactly in the fact that it is not pegged down to an ideology, that it is unfettered and not tied to any 'ism'. This leaves the novelist free to explore, to go on to unknown little paths, even those that reach a dead end. And, as I said before, the writer does not make a didactic statement, saying that this is right, and this is wrong. The writer does not condone the wrong, either. For a moral vision is very much part of a good novel. In Dostoevsky's *Crime and Punishment*, for example, the hero is a murderer, the heroine a prostitute. It is peopled, besides, with all kinds of murky characters—pimps, drunkards, liars, bullies, cruel people, idlers. Yet, one never has a sense of debased human life. For through all of it, shines the light of what could have been, what should have been. And in the end, the hero Raskolnikov's act of atonement redeems not only his life, but our vision of life itself.

Summing up, the value of the novel lies in creating an alternate world in which we see the human predicament. We can rarely, I may say never, see ourselves clearly; but the novel, in showing us people who agonise over choices, over tortured relationships and the direction their lives are taking, gives us a glimpse of our own selves. To see these people coping with these things, to see how they deal with them, how they succeed, or how, more often, they fail, helps us to see our own selves differently. We enter their world, identify with them and come out enriched.

The writer and the reader meet in a book that can spark off an understanding that could be the beginning of a process of healing for the reader.

Ultimately what place the novel—or indeed any art—has in our lives depends on us, the readers, the viewers, the listeners, it depends on the place we give it. It depends on what kind of people we are, what we are prepared to become. There are different words in different languages for the lover of the arts. *Rasik,* for example, which I prefer to 'connoisseur' or 'aesthete', because it brings in a sensory response rather than a cold judgement. But the word that describes the perfect response of a person is, I think, *sahrudaya.* This word speaks of becoming one with the creation, of entering into it completely. If a person has this quality, then even what seems like an ordinary lamp, will, when rubbed, have a genie emerge from it, asking, 'What can I do for you?'

I would not dare to claim, like publishers' blurbs do, that a single novel can change a reader's life. I would not say that even about the greatest novels. However, a lifetime of reading can make a reader a different person from what she/he would have been without this reading. What a reader gets from reading novels is, in effect, the experience of humanity. Through reading novels, we see not only the variety of humans, human behaviour and motivations, we see the shadowy links that connect us to other people, to our pasts.

I would like to end with a quote from Joyce Carol Oates, a contemporary American writer:

> Life is energy, and energy is creativity.... And even when we as individuals pass on, the energy is retained in the work of art, locked in it and awaiting release if only someone will take the time and care to unlock it.

The person who will unlock the work of art is the reader, the listener, the spectator.

Section II

WOMEN, WRITING AND EMPOWERMENT

I Believe ...

A recent issue of *Time* discusses a book by Susan Faludi, who examined the issue of why 63 per cent of American women reject feminism. The answer, according to Faludi, lies in a backlash against feminism, 'a highly effective, often insidious campaign to discredit its goals, distort its message ...'

My reaction of disbelief when I read this was directed against the number (63 per cent of American women?), not the theory that Faludi propounds to explain the phenomenon. It seems very plausible to me, because in recent years I have been noticing with anger and dismay an increasing number of women in our country too making the comment, whether it is relevant or not: *'Thank God, I'm not a feminist!'* Unfortunately, one cannot dismiss these statements as being of no significance, because the women who make them are, as is obvious from the fact that their statements are being reported, women who matter. It was an activist, for example, who explained in a lengthy article why she refuses to call herself a feminist, one reason being that feminism is a Western concept. An actress who said that she is not a feminist because she has no desire to desert her family and go out on the streets screaming for women's rights. A columnist who says that she stopped calling herself a feminist because she is not anti-men and does not hate men. To the uninformed who read and may be influenced by these comments, feminism will mean these things: a Western concept, rejecting the family and home, hating men and waging a war against them. After three decades of feminism being written about, discussed and practised in this country, is this what intelligent women make of feminism?

It took me years to say even to myself—'I am a feminist'. It was the culmination of a voyage that began within myself and went on to the ocean of women's place in the world. Today, when I call myself a feminist, I believe that the female of the species has the same right to be born and survive and to fulfil herself and shape her life according to her needs and the potential that lies within her, as the male has. I believe that women are neither inferior nor subordinate human beings, but one half of the human race. I believe that women (and men as well) should not be strait-jacketed into roles that warp their personalities, but should have options available to them. I believe that Nature, when conferring its gifts on humans, did not differentiate between males and females, except for the single purpose of procreation. I believe that motherhood does not bar everything else, but is a bonus, an extra that women are privileged to have. Would the anti-feminists deny all this?

What saddens me is that the women who make such statements are themselves splendid examples of what women can achieve against many odds. What naming games people play with themselves is no concern of mine; but when they give a wrong colour to feminism, these women are grievously wronging all those men and women who, through the years, have spoken and worked against the injustice done to women. I have no doubt at all that it is the women's movement which has made it possible for an increasing number of women to have more space to breathe. I know that as a writer I am privileged to be living at a time when the women's movement has, hopefully, made it possible for my voice to be heard, for the things I write about to be taken seriously, looked upon as issues that concern all of society, and not just dismissed as 'women's stuff'.

Is to be a feminist to want to be like a man? I don't think so. On the contrary, to me it has meant an acceptance of my womanhood as a positive thing, not as a lack. An understanding that I am different, not inferior. And how can feminism be anti-men when it is really working for a better, a more meaningful and companionable relationship between men and women, instead of the uneasy relationship between tyrant and oppressed? When women can fulfil themselves, when they are not suppressed and do not have to sacrifice themselves, it will obviate the need to play power games within the home, to thrust ambitions on husbands and children, to work out frustrations on them. Cage in the self for too long and it becomes a dangerous, snarling animal. Go on sacrificing and you create monsters of selfishness. Sacrifice, except for a helpless, dependent infant, has no role in Nature's plan. (I am convinced that the wholly sacrificing Ma of Hindi movies is a male fantasy.) I believe that the family is not a divine, sacred institution, but one created by humans for the benefit of all society; and therefore, it should be built, not on the sacrifice of some, but on the cooperation and compromises of all of its members. The loud cry of the new-born is a triumphant assertion of being—I AM. Does a baby girl cry less loudly?

As for feminism forcing women to have careers, to be dissatisfied with being housewives, to desert husbands and families and rush for a divorce at the smallest pretext, it is not just absurd, it is a great injustice to all the activists in this country, who, it sometimes seems, are the only people who care about dowry/rape/desertion/cruelty/slander victims. And I am always annoyed when women speak of themselves as 'only a housewife'. Only a housewife when you work all day, seven days a week, twelve months a year? Many women do enjoy housework and find fulfilment within the home. They have every right to do so. But there are the hazards of not being able to support yourself when it may be necessary to do so; glorifying the wife and mother roles sometimes hides this ugly reality. To be dependent means to be a burden on another, at times to be forced to endure violence because there is no choice. 'Violence at home is better than violence on the streets', a woman columnist says. An obnoxious statement. It implies that women must submit to some violence. Obviously, she has no idea of the years of systematic physical cruelty that many women endure. 'Women are not mentally equipped to make the right choice', she adds. But does the solution lie in depriving them of choices or in giving them a chance to learn to make their own choices? And which one of us can ever be certain that we have made the right choice?

Feminism, I read somewhere, is a movement that has grown out of and built upon prevailing social needs. I can see how true this is in India, where it has grown out of our own society, out of local specific issues and has addressed them directly. The truth is that we cannot go back. That a great number of people now live within nuclear families, that many women have to go out and work, that stresses are making relationships more vulnerable: these are facts. It is in the context of this reality that changes are required in the man-woman relationship. And therefore, the issue of gender equality, which embraces everything from female foeticide and equal pay to dowry and rape, has to be faced. Those who are afraid that women will turn freedom into license forget that the needs of daily life impose their own restrictions on human liberty. But often there are no limits to human cruelty. And cruelty has to be opposed. To be silent is to abet it.

Whether we admit it or not, most of us who are adapting to this changing world, gracefully or otherwise, are practising feminism. We don't have to sport any labels. Ask any woman, 'Do you believe in gender equality?' and she may retort, 'What's that?' But ask her instead—'Do you think your daughter is a lesser human being, that she should not be educated, should be married early, to anyone, at any price, that she should have nothing in her life apart from her family and home and should stay within the family at all costs, even if it is to suffer or die, getting no support from you once she gets married'—will she say 'yes'? Or will it be a 'no'? But why do I say 'she'? Most men, I have no doubt, will say 'no' too. A world without frightened, dependent, trapped, frustrated women is a better world for all of us to live in.

(1992)

Is Shakti Woman Power?

'Empowerment' is a word of our times, a word that promises much to all those who have, until now, been kept outside the circle of power. It is a word that has entered the vocabulary of the women's movement and almost, one might say, been appropriated by it. The word and its use mark a movement forward; it means going a step ahead of the documentation, the analysis and the debating of women's problem, of the struggle to give women back their rightful place in human society. Empowerment is, in other words, part of the 'right'ing process.

Yet, there is a queer contradiction within the word which at times makes me uneasy. Applying the concept to personal lives, it becomes a rather troubling thought. A friend and I discussed this once and asked ourselves: Is it possible to empower ourselves without disempowering someone else? Can there be power for one without exploitation of another? The mother-in-law and daughter-in-law struggle, at once both a joke and a tragedy, spells this out most clearly. A woman gets power when she becomes a mother-in-law, only because she has the daughter-in-law completely in her power. This is a human phenomenon.

As a writer, these ideas have continued to trouble me. Initially, it was the revelation of women's powerlessness that set me on my path as a writer. I wrote, for example, of Amba, a woman whose story is almost an aside in the Mahabharata, a woman whose life, it seems, had place in the epic only because it was part of Bhishma's story. It was this woman's story that spelled out most clearly to me the powerlessness of women, as well as their illusion of having power. For the story begins with a *swayamvara*, a shining symbol of a woman's right to choose her partner. And so there is Amba, eager, ready to garland the man she loved, heady with the feeling of being in control of her own life. And then comes the horror of abduction by Bhishma, of being completely helpless. Worse is to follow when she is tossed between the man she wanted to marry, the man she was brought to marry and the man who abducted her and destroyed her life. I saw Amba's angry helplessness at being trapped in the web of male codes of 'honour', framed for the benefit of males and meaning nothing to her. I had Amba finally destroying herself, thinking that, if she had no power over her own life, she could at least have control over her death. This is a tragic story; nevertheless it is better than what happened to Amba's sisters, whose lives too figure in the Mahabharata as a 'by the way'. The two girls, abducted at the same time as Amba, are married to an impotent man, widowed and then raped to provide heirs for the kingdom. And there is the mother, their mother, who watched her daughters being abducted, unable to do anything to help them, and later, it seems, was totally alienated from their lives. All of these women with no control over their own lives, over each other's lives.

Yes, we need empowerment in the sense of being able to control our own lives, something we have never had. Instead, we have been offered Shakti, woman power, symbolised by the goddess Durga, an avenging fury. Who becomes, in human terms, the woman pushed to the limit, desperate, tapping this divine power and fighting back to defend, most often, her chastity, her child, her wifehood. Shakti is, therefore, the power allowed to women only in these cases, making women, even here, custodians of the values of the male world.

I have always had a deep mistrust of the idea of Shakti. I have considered it a sop thrown at women to give them the illusion of power, the dust thrown up to conceal the complete control of their lives by others. At the other end of this idea of the Trishul-wielding goddess is the reality of most women's lives, lives in which strength turns into endurance, into a struggle for sheer survival. Between these two extremes is a long line on which most women stand, women who need something very different from this extraordinary strength—which may never be theirs—and this constant struggle to survive. As a thinking woman, as a writer, I look askance at the idea of a divine strength which comes in at moments of desperation, at times of crisis; all humans are able to tap an extraordinary source of power in themselves on such occasions. What women need is the strength to deal with the problems of quotidian life, a sense of having the power to deal with everyday problems, as well as large ones. They need to have the power to take their own decisions, without being constrained by traditional ideas of honour or sacrifice, an ability to see beyond these ideas, to see things with their own eyes, to think with their own minds. This power can only come through knowledge; knowledge is to me the other meaning of power, of freedom. To have power is to know, it is to take responsibility, for oneself, primarily, then for others. Without understanding, without knowledge, there can be neither power nor freedom—the right kind of freedom and power, that is.

Words are important. The way they have been used, the context in which they are used, the meanings they have taken on through the years and what they stand for—all these things go into the meaning of a word. And therefore the word 'Shakti' makes me uneasy. To me, it symbolises much that is wrong. Not all myths are strength-giving. We need to know them, but knowing them, knowing their meaning for us, we need to move on and at times, to turn away from some of them. To hold on to the mythical idea of Shakti is to embrace the subtle subtext of the myth—that only extraordinary women can have power, that they can have this power only in extraordinary circumstances. What we need is for ordinary women to understand the possibility of power, of being able to control their own lives. And, to have this power, not as mothers, not as devoted wives, but as ordinary women, as humans. In other words, we need to see power in human terms and human terms only. It is human strength that matters, it is human strength that we need.

'Empowerment' too needs to be spelled out clearly, so that we know exactly what we mean when we use the word. We need to debate the meanings of these words, not just as part of an academic discourse, but for us to use in our ordinary everyday lives. For the way we use words can alter the concept itself. An anthology which brings together the various aspects, meanings and subtle ramifications of this concept is, therefore, a very welcome and valuable beginning to a better understanding of the whole idea of empowerment or Shakti.

What we want is an empowerment that does not disempower others, but instead, gives us control over our own lives. With this kind of power, perhaps, it may become possible to stop celebrating goddesses and survivors and find cause for rejoicing, instead, in the lives of ordinary humans.

(2003)

In the Beginning Was the Word

I would like to begin with a story which comes from John Steinbeck's *East of Eden*. This story shows the enormous power of words and how they shape our ideas about ourselves and the world. It is about the response of a character, Lee, to some verses from the Bible in the fourth chapter of Genesis which narrate what God said to Cain in the Garden of Eden. In the King James version, God tells Cain, 'Thou shalt rule over sin'. Whereas, Lee finds that the words used in the American Standard translation of the Bible are 'Do thou rule over sin'. He is intrigued by the different words used in the two versions, words which convey very different meanings, for if 'thou shalt' is a promise, 'do thou' is an order. And so, out of a curiosity to know what the original word, which had been translated so differently, was, he, along with four other scholars, starts learning Hebrew. After two years of learning Hebrew and after much reading and discussion with a Rabbi, they come finally to Genesis 4:6-7 and get 'the gold from our mining' as Lee calls it. They discover that the original Hebrew word was 'timshel'—which means neither 'thou shalt', nor 'do thou', but 'thou mayst'. 'Thou mayst rule over sin'—these words which, unlike the words in the other two versions, give humanity the choice; for, if thou mayst, it is also true that thou mayst not. Lee's words about what this revelation did to him are worth quoting: 'I have a new love for that glittering instrument, the human soul', he says. 'It is a lovely and unique thing in the universe. It is always attacked, but never destroyed—because "thou mayst".' Lee is right. To know we have the choice is to change our whole idea of ourselves and our lives. A single word can change everything.

I had exactly this kind of sense of revelation some years ago when I came upon a line from the *Bhagvad Gita* while I was editing a translation of my father's two books on the *Gita*. These words of Krishna's, which come at the end of his exposition to Arjuna, are: *Yathecchasi tatha kuru*. Do as you desire. These four words gave me a vision that was as exciting as the word 'timshel' was for Lee (or Steinbeck). They erased a philosophy very prevalent in India which put the whole responsibility for human actions and their consequences on God. Like 'timshel', these words, 'the choice is yours', confer adulthood on humans, they make humans responsible for their own lives, their own actions. To accept and to understand these words means to look at yourself, at the whole human race, differently. Truly, the power of words is great.

But words are powerful only if the listener receives them with understanding, for there are always two parties to any transaction with words—there is the speaker (or the writer) and the listener (or the reader). It is only when the receiver accepts the words that the communication is complete. It is only when there is an understanding of them that it becomes good communication. This does not always happen; in fact, it happens rarely. And perfect communication is, of course, almost impossible, though there is an example of this in the Upanishads. In this story, the Prajapati's children—gods, men and demons—go to their father for instruction. To the gods, Prajapati says the syllable 'Da' and asks, 'Have you understood?' 'We have understood', they reply. The word is *Daamyata*—control. Prajapati offers the same syllable 'Da' to the men who reply, 'We have understood. You say Datta—give'. And the demons, to whom he repeats 'Da', answer, 'We have understood. The word is *Dayadhvam*. You ask us to be compassionate'.

Such perfect understanding is rare. And enviable. It is a very unusual father who can make his children understand what he is saying through mere syllables. Most of us find it hard to be understood even when we use torrents of words! Sometimes, of course, we are deliberately trying to deceive others through the words we use; for, though words are the tools for communicating with others, the truth is that we use them for our own purposes. The question is: do words carry their own meanings within them, or do we infuse our own meanings into them? It is not that simple, actually, for there are many factors that influence not only the meaning, but even the existence of words. For one thing, language is not static; words drop out of use for various reasons and then become archaic. For example, the language of a feudal society has no place in today's world; we no longer need so many words with nuances of inferiority and superiority. In India there were different terms of address for different relationships, each spelling out the respective positions of the speaker and the person addressed in the family hierarchy. Now, the erosion of the joint family, considerably less interaction between extended family members, and the growth of individualism and democratic ideas, have made changes inevitable. But the loss of these words has meant that the fine nuances of the family and social network are lost; it means a kind of impoverishment of language, as well of family life.

Nevertheless, often there is also a gain to offset losses because new words are constantly entering the vocabulary in different ways, for example, through an interaction with other languages and other cultures. Words may also come in to meet new needs, and advances in science bring new words into a language. Sir Alexander Fleming calls words the missionaries of new ideas. 'Each advance', he says, 'signaled the invention of a new word'. Psychology, for example, has brought a great number of words into our everyday language—ego, libido, psychotic, neurotic, and so one. In our own lifetime there is the computer, which has spawned more new words than any other invention.

This apart, words may continue to exist, but their meanings may change. If the concept a word stands for is devalued, it may no longer be a feel-good word. Sir Ernest Gowers, in his *The Complete Plain Words*, gives the example of 'imperialism', once a good word, but now tainted by the way we see imperialism. Appeasement, too, is apparently no longer a good thing to do, for the word does not have a very good aura around it. I myself remember using the word 'gay' in a novel nearly two decades back, which my English editor replaced with 'joyous', for she said that the word 'gay' meant something entirely different now and no longer carried the sense of joyous. It seems sad to me that we should lose a word which conveyed a particular meaning with such clarity and evoked that particular feeling so well. But there it is! 'Gay' can never be 'joyous' again.

Never has the power of words been as well understood and so completely exploited as it is now by governments, who are very skilful in making use of words for their own purposes. Words, they have fully understood, are a very potent political tool, since propaganda is a major weapon in a democracy. If ideologies give birth to political parties, they are cradled in slogans, they survive because of them and often get power through slogans as well. Democracy itself began with the chant of the mantra 'liberty, equality and fraternity', and later the Communists worked through words with even greater skill; some words acquired a halo around them, while others like 'bourgeois' became almost words of abuse. In India, the word 'secular' has acquired a particular meaning in the political world. The dictionary meaning of the word is being concerned with the affairs of this world and not spiritual or sacred. But it has begun to mean something quite different: trying to please the minority community in order to get their votes. Politicians have grasped the fact that words can mask the reality; they can change the way we look at things. The word 'riots' can be a cover for mass killing and genocide can be called 'the final solution' to mask the ugliness of the deed.

But there is a positive side to rewording which comes from a new awareness of words and a conscious attempt to correct old wrongs. For example, we no longer speak, as the Bible once did, of the lame and the blind. We say the visually and the physically disadvantaged or differently abled. By which we hope to remove the way these disabilities were looked at, to take away the taint which the word conferred on the people. Racism is also countered by deleting some words and changing others. Gandhiji did it for a certain caste group by coining a new word for them. But this word 'Harijan' has also lost out and the words now used are: Scheduled Castes, Scheduled Tribes, Backward Castes, Other Backward Castes, and so on. Even these words have been reduced to SC, ST, BC and OBC, which makes them sound innocuous; but they are not. They still carry the taint that the earlier words had. The changes may be laudable attempts at not just refraining from giving offence, but at giving people back their dignity. Though, very often, it is political correctness and not good feeling that dictates these changes. But, unfortunately, the problem is not in the word, but in the minds of people and the taint on original words continues to cling to these new forms; neither racism nor casteism have been done away with. Nor has calling the poor 'the economically disadvantaged sections of society' changed anything for those who are poor. There is a point at which the change of a word becomes a mere cosmetic device, just a token homage paid to the god of political correctness.

To me the most significant attempt at rewording, a very deliberate and conscious rewording, has come out of the women's movement. For centuries we have been blind to the astonishing and rampant sexism in language. But with the new awareness of women's positions and lives has come a corresponding awareness of the gender bias in language and an attempt to change this. This is one change that I am intimately aware of and very much involved in, because, both as a writer who uses words and as a thinking woman, it has been impossible for me to overlook the bias against women in language. For long, like so many others, I accepted the words and the languages that gave women an inferior place, I took these things for granted. But once I became aware of the way language denigrated women, I woke up, like so many women did, to the fact that language is man-made and that sexism in language comes out of the way women are looked at. Inevitably, therefore, all the words associated with women get the fatal stamp of inferiority and triviality. Even the word 'suffragette', for example, which came out of a memorable, but now forgotten movement, and which was coined for those courageous English women who fought to get the vote, has the suffix 'ette', which transforms the word into a diminutive. The word 'feminism' itself has attained a rather unpleasant colour, which is why, perhaps, so many men, as well as women reject it emphatically and are hostile to it. I began using the term 'women's movement' instead of 'feminism' to set this right; but I wonder how much it helps. I know it will still convey a sense that includes bra burning, hating family, husband, and children and so on. In effect, radical and aggressive, but never reasonable.

The bias exists in the mind and not in the word; therefore it is a hard struggle to rid language of any bias. Worse, the attempt to free language of both the word and the bias is regarded as both trivial and unnecessary. Why, one is asked, when there are so many huge problems in this world, is it important to debate the question of whether we say 'he', or 'she', or search for a comprehensive pronoun?

But in truth, to reject gender-related words, especially when they are so inappropriate, does matter; chauvinism in language is an indication of chauvinism within ourselves. The word we use determines our view of that thing. By correcting the word, we are trying to correct the greater wrong that the word has done through what it meant. But this is never understood or taken into account. Often it seems the easiest thing to let things go on as they were. When for centuries 'man' has included 'woman', when we know that 'mankind' includes women as well, why not go on with these words? But when the pronoun 'he' is used, a woman cannot but have a sense of being excluded from the statement. In fact, as I was writing the story from the Upanishads, I noticed how, in spite of it being a universal story about the propensities of humans, there were only male characters in it: Prajapati and his sons. Which makes one want to ask: where were the women and why did Prajapati leave them out when he was giving instructions? If the answer is that gods, men and demons include females as well, the truth is that when one reads the story as it is, it is impossible to picture a female anywhere in it.

We have not got very far; in fact, we have scarcely begun this journey of rewording, a journey that began quite some time back. One of the earliest conscious attempts at rewording came to me from a story about a very young suffragette being comforted by an older colleague in prison with the words, 'Never mind, dear. God is there, she will look after you'. No, we have not yet been able to turn God into a woman. Yes, we have our goddesses, but above all the gods is the father, Brahma. And there are a huge number of semantic obstacles lying in our path. If Henry James can be called 'The Master', can we call Virginia Woolf 'The Mistress'? And do we say 'Post Mistress' and 'Station Mistress', knowing very well the guffaws and poor jokes that this term would invite?

However, in spite of the many problems which will confront us, it is important to make language gender equal. To quote Anne Fadiman, 'Changing our language to make men and women equal has a cost. That doesn't mean it shouldn't be done. High prices are attached to many things that are on the whole worth doing'. This comes from *Ex Libris,* one of the finest tributes to a love of books.

What comes first, the idea or the word? Do the ideas come because we have the words, or do the words emerge out of an already existing idea? I am no scholar and have no answer. I can only speak as a layperson who knows there are valid arguments on both sides. In fact, it is a 'which comes first—the egg or the chicken?' kind of debate. What does matter is that the two are closely related. And whether we change words to change our ideas, or use different words because our ideas have changed, does not matter. It needs to be done.

I would like to end by quoting a few lines from the last chapter, titled 'The Right Word', of my novel *Moving On*:

> *Friend, family, comrade, partner, lover*—I bring out all the words, consider the array and think: somewhere, between all these words, is the one that will define our relationship. The right word matters. I think of my grandfather speaking to Baba of his dead wife as 'your first mother'. Strange words to use for a wife. Yet, for him, perhaps, they were the right words. And for Raja and me? What is the right word for our relationship? And does a relationship have to be snagged on to a word? Raja would say it does.

So would I. When a woman of an earlier generation spoke of her husband as her 'yajaman'—that is, master—she was very accurately spelling out the relationship between the two. And therefore, when we try to set right this relationship, when we try to make it more equal, it is important that we change the word that is used as well.

(2005)

Even the Gods Raped

The recent rape of a young woman in Delhi, the tremendous violence with which this rape was accompanied and her subsequent death, have disturbed almost the whole country. Women, specially, have mourned her death as if it was the death of a family member. And ever since the news broke out, so much has been said, so much is still being said on the subject of crimes against women in general and on rape in particular, that there seems to be nothing left to say. For which reason I thought I would look at the issue of violence against women in the larger context of the relationship between men and women and the struggle of women against their subordinate status. I will therefore come to violence against women in a rather circuitous manner.

Decades back, when I was asked by an institution to lecture on any topic of my choice, I chose the topic of women's writing and how, through the years, it has been marginalised, always put in a slot labeled 'women's writing'. This, I had realised, was part of women's marginalisation in society and paralleled it. My own writing was always slotted as 'women's writing', perhaps more so because, not only was I a woman, I wrote about women's lives. I spoke on the subject, giving examples from women's writing all over the world. At the end of my talk, the chairman said, 'This lady seems to have a lot of complaints against men'. And I thought, isn't this exactly what I was saying? Is he not proving my point? In fact, his responses were an example of what someone once called the 'tone-deafness' of men, of their inability to hear women's voices, to listen to what they are saying. I had written a story, as well as a novel, which spoke of marital rape, at a time when the phrase was unknown. I had written about women's silences and the breaking of these silences, I had written of the dilemma of making a rape victim's story public. I wrote of two women, a woman artist and a Communist party member, who broke societal rules and lived the way they wanted to. All these were regarded as just stories and novels 'about' women and therefore not part of mainstream literature, but a sub-category labeled 'women's writing'.

What I was really trying to say simply did not register. Men and women, I have now come to understand, speak different languages. A great many years back, I came across some words of Karl Marx: 'The relation of man to woman is the most genuine relation of human being to human being.' Marx is right in saying the relationship is natural. But the relationship is never an easy or a simple one; it is difficult, complex, almost a minefield, which we cross with apprehension.

Both violence against women and the problem of women being regarded as subordinate human beings are part of the same disease, a disease which is and has been endemic in most societies in the world for centuries. All our societies are patriarchal, a word so much and so often used in women's arguments that I am rather uneasy about using it; it is, I admit, a tired word. But we cannot ignore the word, because patriarchy has shaped and impacted women's lives more than anything else, it is reflected in every aspect of human life: customs, beliefs, behaviour, laws, institutions. All these carry the imprint of patriarchy. Each declares that this is man's world. Not only has patriarchy allowed men to control women's lives for centuries, it has led to a great desire for sons, a desire that has harmed our society more than we know. It means that everything in a family, as in society, is based on a system of male domination. It means that property belongs to the males and that property will be passed only through the male line. Even the children belonged solely to the father; in fact, women were themselves the property of men. Each culture tried to soften this harsh truth by giving women some vague powers as goddesses or angels. But never any power as a human being, as a woman. And therefore, though there have been many changes in human lives through the ages, the one thing that remained unchanged has been the status of women. Laws, social rules, religion, customs, traditions—everything conspired to keep women firmly in their subordinate position. Margaret Mead, the anthropologist, considers that 'the suffering of either sex ... the sense of failure in an enjoined role is the point of leverage for social change'. However, change in this one particular matter of women's place in the family, or in society, has always been strongly resisted. For, to allow any change is to shake the foundation of the family, which means the foundation of society itself. The balance of power could not be allowed to shift.

Yet, throughout history there have been, if very rarely, women and men who protested against the injustice that permeated women's lives. In our country, strangely enough, it was colonial rule and exposure to the Western world that created this demand for change. And, even more strange, many of these pioneers agitating for changes in women's lives were men. There is Raja Rammohan Roy's crusade against sati, the earnest pursuit of education for women by Mahadev Ranade and his wife Ramabai Ranade, by Jyotiba Phule and his wife Savitribai Phule. Maharishi Karve not only advocated widow remarriage but married a widow himself and started a school for girls, which has now grown to be a huge institution. His son, Raghunath Karve, was determined to free women from the burden of endless pregnancies and childbirth and with his wife tried to teach women about contraception, about family planning; the couple was much reviled by an orthodox society. These are, even in today's context, amazing men and women who were intent on improving the lot of women. Their work encouraged women to fight their own battles, which itself became possible because a whole new generation of girls were able to go to school. My mother's family lived in Pune, one of the centres of social reform, and her father was a great advocate of educating girls. But this was an exception; the proclaimed goal of most girls' lives was marriage and children. Girls were married off very young, often to men much older than themselves; men who had lost a wife or two. The callousness towards women's lives can be seen in the fact that while a man married almost immediately after his wife's death, women who were widowed were condemned to a lifetime of deprivation of everything in life that could be termed a pleasure.

It was the freedom movement that allowed Indian women to come out of their homes and Gandhiji's magic that made it possible. Women like Sarojini Naidu and Vijaylakshmi Pandit became role models. After Independence, the Hindu laws of marriage, adoption, succession, etc., were codified for the first time. It was a great step. For the first time, bigamy became illegal, the age of marriage for girls was raised to eighteen, divorce became possible for Hindu women; they too could adopt, and daughters inherited property equally.

I studied law soon after the Hindu Act was passed and I must admit that, while studying it, I did not entirely realise its huge significance. It was only much later, when I saw the powerlessness of women, their lack of control over their own lives, their inability to get out of a bad marriage because of economic dependence, that I found myself questioning what I had been told, that marriage and children were the ultimate goal of a woman's life. When I began writing, for me it was a way of trying to understand these things. When my own children started school, I went back to reading and it was then that I stumbled, serendipitously, on the story of the Suffragette movement, a struggle of the women in England to be able to vote. It seems a very small thing now, but the opposition was fierce and the women very determined. The bitterness of the fight makes for strange reading today, though the arguments against giving women the vote seem very familiar. Arguments like: Giving women the right to vote would spoil the peace of the home, it would create division between husbands and wives and why did women want to vote anyway, they had enough power in the home and so on. Anyway, with the beginning of World War I, women stopped the movement, became part of the war effort and, as a reward they got the vote. 'The history of feminism', says the writer Margaret Forster, 'is one of stops and starts'. Women, she says, come together to achieve a goal, the goal once achieved the movement disappears.

But a movement that began after World War II promised to be different. It was diffuse and broad and demanded equality for women in all spheres. It was a movement based on an ideology, feminism, and rested, like the French revolution did, on the foundation of brilliant works written by women like Simone de Beauvoir, Germaine Greer, Betty Friedan, Kate Millet and many others. Patriarchy, feminism said, is responsible for the way women are seen; the ideas that we have about them are not absolute truths, but have come out of the needs of a patriarchal society. With this movement, it seemed that the idea of women's liberation had finally arrived.

I have always considered that there were three great movements in the last century: communism, the movement for democracy and the women's movement. The first two have been regarded as significant movements, whereas the women's movement was either ridiculed, or ignored. It is not surprising that the movement petered out. There are many reasons for this. For one thing, it was confined to the West and mainly to white women. For another, it seemed to most people to be anti-men and anti-family. Another major reason for its failure, if indeed one can say it failed, was that it tried to bring about changes in the man-woman relationship, to bring about changes within the family, in the home. People are more amenable to changes in the world, very resistant to changes within their homes. Betty Friedan, whose book *The Feminine Mystique* started the debate which culminated in the women's liberation movement, said that it was easier for her to start the women's movement than to change her own life.

Though the movement seemed to have failed, it left its mark on the world. An awareness was created, some things could no longer be seen in the same way again. A huge change was that the movement brought gender relationships from the domestic space into the public arena. Gender bias was no longer a domestic matter, but a political one. Much that had been taken for granted, now became suspect. It was a revelation to me to read in Siddharth Mukherjee's book on cancer, *The Emperor of All Maladies*, an example of how the movement impacted different areas of life. In the late sixties, according to him, 'medicine was turning out to have deep fallibilities—flaws that appeared to cluster pointedly around women's health'. Speaking of how some women had begun to resist radical mastectomy, then almost universally the one way to tackle breast cancer, he adds, 'Political feminism ... was birthing medical feminism ....' Ideas which feminism had spoken about moved into the working, lived-in world. This happened so gradually that the moment of change passed us by silently.

In time, some laws were changed, like a change in the laws of rape, new laws were brought in, like the one against domestic violence and sexual harassment at work. Added to this there was the fact that women's education had taken a leap, at least in urban areas and among the middle class. That women were working in varied fields, that contraception made it possible for women to control childbearing, made it seem that feminism had got somewhere. But strangely, at this very time there was a backlash against feminism. In fact, the women who had gained most from it, young urban educated women, rejected both the word and the ideas.

This was, of course, a miniscule minority. The majority was still struggling in a male-dominated world. There was also a rumbling underneath the surface which was beginning to make itself felt. Violence against women had increased, it was finding new ways, crueller methods. Female foeticide was rapidly increasing, in spite of the law against it, there were 'honour killings', acid-throwing, wife-burning, there was more domestic violence and in the kind of homes where one would have imagined it would never happen. One does not know how many cases were reported and how many remained hidden in homes, like the concealed bruises of domestic violence victims.

But for most of us, these things were happening *elsewhere*, it was happening to *other people*. And therefore, we took everything in our stride. Until the day a young woman was raped in a bus in Delhi and assaulted with such unimaginable savagery that she died within a few days. And the conscience of a whole nation was aroused. Why did this rape catch the attention of the country, of the world? Why did so many of us grieve so much when the girl died? And why did protests suddenly erupt in Delhi, so that women's issues, which had always been marginalised, were suddenly centre stage?

The protests made two things clear: rape was a human problem, not just a 'women's issue'. And, a very heartening development, many men joined women in their struggle; men and women were, for the first time, fighting together for justice for women. I also found it a very welcome change that the arguments of the earlier feminist movement, its very terminology, were brought back during the protests. The same women who had rejected feminism, ignoring the fact that their lives had changed because of feminism, now took to the streets in an outburst of anger. Listening to what was being said, reading what was being written, I had a sense of déjà vu.

Why did this rape become the flash point? 'Enough is enough!' some of the placards the protestors carried shouted out to the world. Were women finally going to fight back? Or was it just this one issue that had roused so many young women? In truth, rape is a crime that cuts across class, caste, religion and age; no one is spared. Women in burqas and ghungats are raped, as also women in saris, trousers, salwar kameez and skirts. Babies are raped, as well as children and older women; the rich are raped as also the poor. Women are raped in homes, as well as on the streets. There was also a question which haunted me, which still haunts me: Where have these monsters, who did these barbaric, savagely cruel things to the young woman, come from? Had they lived in our midst all this time and if they had, how come we did not know? Women were also asking themselves, with a sense of bewilderment: Where does this hostility to women, this immense hatred, come from? Is it because men, used to having power and control over women, don't know how to deal with women who do not recognise this power? Or are there simpler answers, like, it's happening because women are more visible in public now, because the media highlights some cases? Is it because the movies, advertisements, and pornography highlight the sexuality of women, make them out to be objects of enjoyment? Whatever it may be, the final and the harsh truth is that innocent girls and women are raped for no reason except that they are female. And this because men look at women's bodies as having been created for them to use, for their enjoyment.

After all, rape has a very ancient history. We have to remember that even the gods raped. Indra and Zeus, kings of gods, both of them, were famous for their raping of women. The story of Indra and Ahalya, the story of Zeus and Leda, Zeus and Europa are part of human myths. These stories also give a clue to the why of rape. It is an assertion of power by a man, an assertion of his right to claim the women he wants, whether they are willing or not. As a matter of fact, rape is but one of a long list of wrongs that men commit against women: stupid inane jokes about women, eve-teasing (abominable term with connotations of innocent mischief), domestic violence, sexual harassment, abuse and threats on social media, touching in crowds, stalking, flashing and finally the worst crime of them all—rape. Susan Brownmiller, whose book *Against our Will* is a graphic and disturbing account of rape, calls it 'nothing more or less than a conscious process of intimidation by which all men keep all women in a state of fear'. She writes of the rapes that have been a part of all wars from ancient times to today; the invading victorious army always raped women, regarding them as their rightful property.

Since the rape in Delhi, there has been a great amount of discussion on various aspects of this crime; there is an attempt to understand why there are so many rapes and what to do about it. As far as the 'why' is concerned, it is surprising that greater note has not been taken of female foeticide, of the large scale killing of girl babies, which has left some parts of the country with a very skewed sex ratio. Gang rapes remind me of a pack of hungry animals, prowling the streets, looking for their prey. When female foeticide became a major problem, there was an apprehension that this would, in a decade or two, lead to more rapes. Which has happened. But there was also a hope that, perhaps, with fewer women around, women would become valuable. Which has not happened. Women are brought from elsewhere, no, they are bought and obviously treated like chattel. Women it seems can never win; whatever happens, they are the losers.

The statements of some men, many of them in positions of power, have also revealed the canker in the heart of this country. Just as I wondered where the monsters who raped and killed the girl had come from, I watched in amazement as strange, repellent creatures crawled out of the woodwork, saying things like 'the victim is responsible for the crime'. That rape happens because of the way women dress, because they go out at night, because they use mobile phones. That women who go out of their homes, women who do not dress 'modestly' (modesty being defined by men) are immoral women and deserve to be raped. But the cause of rape is not the sight of a woman's body or face; the darkness lies within the heart of the rapist. And so little girls are raped, mothers as well as grandmothers. Rapes happen more often inside the home and cousins, uncles, fathers, brothers, even grandfathers rape. If a wife has not consented to having sex with her husband, his forcing himself on her is also rape. But even today marital rape is not recognised as a crime in India, for fear that it might damage the 'sacred' bond of marriage. In the outside world, rapists can be teachers, guardians, policemen, bosses, public figures, bishops and godmen. What connects all these men is power, the power of belonging to a superior caste, class or race. And finally, the delusion of power that a man holds within himself, the power he thinks has been given to him because he is a man.

There are men who cite our ancient culture and want a return to that culture, imagining that the past was a safe and cosy place, where men went out to work and women stayed at home, modestly covering their faces and bodies. And all was well with the world. The men who advise women to stay at home forget that it is only the upper middle class and rich women who can afford to stay at home. Most women have to go to work out of sheer necessity. And it is strange that these men do not seem to know that in villages women go out to work in the fields along with men, that the agricultural labour force consists of as many women as men. Men who invoke our culture forget that Sita was abducted by Ravana, and, later, like often happens even today, abandoned by her husband for having lived for some time in her abductor's home. These men forget that Draupadi was undressed in public, they forget that Amba, Ambika and Ambalika were abducted by Bhishma to marry his sickly brother. And when Amba refused (she dies for that act of courage) and the sickly brother himself died, the two surviving sisters were forced to sleep with a fearful-looking stranger in order to provide heirs for the kingdom. If that was not rape, what was it? They forget that Karna was born to Kunti when she was still a very young girl and that there is a possibility that she was raped by one of the men in the ashram; it was a frightened young girl who abandoned her illegitimate baby. No, let us not talk of culture, for all cultures have been hostile to women.

This one rape in Delhi has shown up how many things are wrong in our country: the flouting of laws and regulations, the apathy of the police and the public, the inadequacy of the law and above all, the uncaring attitude of the authorities. In this one rape, we can also see how much is wrong in the way women are looked at and treated in our society, in this country. Therefore, when we talk of prevention, where do we begin? At home, perhaps, with boys and girls being treated in the same way, with girls not being devalued. And though I am not sure myself if this will work, it seems to me that coeducation could help; perhaps, if boys and girls come to know each other at a young age and become friends, it could make the boys, when they are grown men, look at women differently. Adolescents, boys specially, need to know more about their sexuality, about how to deal with it. We need better laws, laws in which violence against women is recognised as a major crime, in which 'eve-teasing' is termed what it is, sexual harassment. We need what everyone has been saying: a better policing, a more women-friendly and gender sensitive police. We need more policewomen. We need a better and thorough investigation so that the guilty do not escape because of lack of evidence. The truth is that not all cases of rape are reported, that the police are not amenable to filing FIRs (First Information Reports), and the conviction rate is abysmally low. We need more judges, so that cases are swiftly disposed of. We need less leeway given to judges in punishing crimes against women, because there is always the possibility of a male bias, even in judges. What else but a male bias would make judges find being drunk an extenuating circumstance in a case of rape and murder? None of these steps will guarantee us a world free from crimes against women. Yet, it is necessary to do these things and much more, all of them simultaneously and with total sincerity.

Above all, we need more women in politics, more women in positions of power which is, according to me, the only thing that will really help. And, for this, women have to take some steps themselves. It is hopeless expecting male politicians to pass the Women's Reservation Bill, hopeless to expect political parties to give women one third of the seats (let alone one half which is the right thing) in Parliament and the State Assemblies. They will never do it, they will never share their power. I think that women need to realise that they are a vote bank, the largest vote bank in the country and make full use of it. Will this ever happen? Will the flame lit by that nameless faceless woman who died such a cruel death continue to burn until these things are done? Or will it be slowly snuffed out and finally die?

I wait in hope.

(2013)

We, the People of India

When, decades back, I had to study the Constitution of India as a law student, it was in its infancy, scarcely a decade old. For us students, the chapter on Fundamental Rights mattered only because it was important for the examinations. It took the Emergency for many of us to understand the real importance of these rights. Today, I look at the rights differently, perhaps with a greater understanding. Article 14, which promises all citizens equality before the law, seems remarkable when I think of what it meant to a people who, ruled by a foreign power, had been second-class citizens in their own country for two centuries. What it meant to a people who lived in a rigidly hierarchical society in which people could never hope to move up the social ladder, because caste pinioned them to their places. Where you were born, there you lived all your life. Caste was certainly no believer in equality.

But before I talk of the right to equality, I will go back for a moment to an earlier and a personal story. Many years ago, I was in Cambridge for a seminar on British literature. There were five of us from the subcontinent at that seminar, three Indians, one from Bangladesh and one from Pakistan. During a casual conversation, one of these two said to us Indians, 'We envy you. You can stand in the middle of the street and criticise your Prime Minister'. The other heartily concurred. I imagine we patted ourselves on the back then for being a mature democracy. We had the splendid example of the time when Indira Gandhi had attempted to subvert democracy and had been voted out of power. And the motley collection of parties and individuals, who had formed a government after that, they had been voted out as well, when it was clear they were totally unfit to govern. We felt good about ourselves. What made us feel even better was that we were not like our neighbours across the border. In fact, it gave us great pleasure to define ourselves as not-Pakistan.

Then, recently, I read an interview with Mohammed Hanif, the Pakistani writer, who writes so critically and courageously about the sad state of affairs in his country. During the course of the interview, the Indian journalist interviewing him referred to a poem written by a Pakistani poet, Fahmida Riaz, who sadly passed away a few days back. The journalist quoted a line from her poem, '*Tum bilkul hum jaise nikle* (You turned out to be exactly like us)'.

Mohammed Hanif's response was, 'How different could we be? We drink the same water, eat pretty much the same food, we breathe the same air ...' And finally, he added, 'It's horrendous here, it's horrendous there'.

It hurt to read this. It shocked me. However bad things were in our country, how could anyone say we had become another Pakistan? We had our courts, sentinels of our democracy. And a free and enormously alive press. But both Mohammad Hanif's words and Fahmida Riaz's poem were couched in tones of such regret, that I thought we needed to take a long and hard look at our country. What I saw was not very reassuring; in fact, it filled me with dismay.

When the 2014 elections gave the BJP a clear and strong mandate, many of us were thankful, because we were tired of corruption and coalitions. We hoped to settle down to a sensible governing, to the progress that had been promised. But we were sadly disillusioned. We entered the Era of Mobs. Mobs which came out of nowhere, it seemed, mobs who indulged in lynchings, in barbaric killings in the name of the holy cow. Mobs who turned into moral policemen in the name of 'our culture'. Mobs who attacked people in the name of patriotism and nationalism. Mobs who imposed a kind of unofficial censorship, so that they decided whether a book, a film, a play, a painting exhibition, or a musical performance was fit to enter the public domain. These mobs seemed to have some kind of patronage, for very rarely were they punished for their crimes.

On an official level there has been a clamping down on dissent and interference with institutions. There has also been a rewriting of history, an attempt to create a narrative of the past in tune with the ideology and desires of the ruling party. Now, with elections approaching, we are back to vote banks and voter appeasement, which have always been the name of the game of politics in India. But the promises being made now, of a quick resolution of the Ram Janmabhoomi issue, in favour of Hindus, of course, the construction of a Ram Mandir, of a great statue of Shri Ram in Ayodhya, making it a symbol for the entire country, makes it clear that Hindutva, which was toned down in the 2014 elections in favour of development and progress, is to be a major issue in the coming elections. Sadly, the Congress has jumped on the bandwagon, grasping for more Hindu votes, though one hopes that for the Congress it is just an election strategy. But for the ruling party, these slogans are in pursuance of their goal, which is the conversion of India into Bharat, a Hindu Rashtra. Something very hard to approve of for someone of my generation, we who accepted the mantra in which Pandit Nehru believed lay the magic of India: Unity in Diversity. This mantra, along with Pandit Nehru himself, has been consigned to the dustbin of history and the 2019 elections have become a crucial test for the country. Will India become a Hindu nation, and will non-Hindus become second-class citizens in their own country? Will Article 14 of the Constitution apply only to some Indian citizens, not to all? This will have consequences that will change the shape of this country, indeed of the subcontinent, forever. And, therefore, something that should concern all of us deeply.

In all fairness, I have to ask myself whether those of us who have such fears are being unduly alarmist. Possibly none of these things will happen. Hopefully, voters will reject the idea of an India of intolerance and hatred. I also think it will not be easy to convert India into a Hindu nation. Hinduism is, by its nature, not a religion which lends itself to becoming a monolithic dominating institution. And yet, when I see mobs inflamed by politicians demanding a Shri Ram temple, when I read of leaders exhorting the masses to agitate for the temple, I am frightened. One cannot but remember the post-Partition violence and carnage. What is more ominous is the polarisation that happened during the 2014 elections. Independent India has held many elections, but there has rarely or never been such open and ugly hatred between political parties and politicians. We have experienced the residue of the bitterness of the 2014 elections during the past four and a half years. We have seen it in the way social media is used to troll enemies, see it in the shouting and ranting on TV, in the way abuses are traded, wild personal charges which should never be part of a political debate are made and so on.

The polarisation that happened after 2014 meant that not only the country, not just politicians, but even families were divided by a sharp, clean line. I know for a fact how much bitterness developed between friends, within families. There never was a midway meeting ground; the general understanding was that 'if you are not with us you are against us'. This has left its mark on the country and I fear it will be worse after the coming elections. My great anxiety is: will we be able to come together again? Will we be able to live in harmony as we once did, each religion, each culture having its own place in society, none threatening the other? Once the elections are over, will we be able to forget the hatred, the seeds of which have been sown so generously? Or, will the nation continue to be divided by a most dangerous divide—a divide based on religion? Politicians in India have consistently followed a policy of dividing people, but for the first time the divide seems alarming and threatening as it never was before.

There has been another problem in very recent times which has forced us to look once again at the question of equality before the law. For me, as a writer and a person who has been keenly alive to the injustice women have had to suffer, almost, perhaps, since time began, this is another matter of great concern. I am referring to the issue of women's entry into the Sabarimala temple in Kerala. I have to wonder why at such a time, in the twenty-first century, when it should be impossible to deny women their constitutional rights, the entry of women between the ages of ten and fifty to the temple is being so fiercely resisted? Why, day after day, mobs surround the temple and chant, not with devotion, but with a kind of ferocious frenzy to keep women away. Why they behave as if the temple is under attack. I am mystified that women themselves are part of this opposition; in fact, at times they are more fierce than the men. And I have to ask myself whether they have been so conditioned by society that the idea of entering the temple fills them with a superstitious fear. I ask myself how they can regard menstruation as something unclean, not a normal physiological process. Simone de Beauvoir, in her book *The Second Sex,* speaks of menstruation as life constructing a cradle in the body every month. A beautiful concept and a truth. Yet, people are so determined to keep women out of the temple on the basis of the fact of menstruation, that they defy a Supreme Court judgement.

Talk of tradition, of a god who does not want women of reproductive age near him, rouses a suspicion that the men are imposing their own misogyny on God. So, is it merely anti-women? Or, is it what it has now undoubtedly become—a part of the political game politicians always play, both major parties brazenly disregarding the Supreme Court judgement and backing the traditional stand so as not to lose any votes?

Whatever it is, it seems both unbelievable and sad that at a time when women have been steadily making headway in their struggle to assert themselves as an equal half of the human race, they should be regarded as lesser human beings because of menstruation. A fecund woman is praised; but how can there be fecundity without menstruation? In fact, looking at the unrelenting opposition, a suspicion dogs me: is the anti-women campaign in Sabarimala connected to the #metoo movement, is it a backlash to that movement? I get a hint of how the #metoo movement is regarded in the words of a famous and popular actor in Kerala, a man who is obviously not constrained by political correctness. He calls the movement a fad, a fashion, which will soon die out. These words for a movement in which women are trying to reclaim their right to their own bodies! For a movement in which two women in the USA have taken on two of the most powerful men in their country. In which Indian women took on a minister in the Central Government. But trivialising anything associated with women is a response which I, as a woman who writes about women, know, sadly, only too well. Yet, even as I write this, I read of large demonstrations by women in Europe against sexual violence. No, Mr Actor, this agitation will not so easily go away. I think at the very least, women will no longer be complicit in the wrongs being done to them.

More than thirty years ago, I wrote a novel, *That Long Silence*, which was about the breaking of women's silences. To me, the breaking of silences is the beginning of a revolution. And now, here are women breaking their silence about something which had remained secret and unspoken for centuries—sexual assault. I am very pleased that this has happened, I am pleased that the world is listening to women's voices and taking them seriously. I am pleased that whatever the outcome, one thing is true: men will now be careful about forcing their attentions on a reluctant woman, even if the woman is in their power. Hopefully, no man will ever be able to exploit any woman and get away with it. Above all, I am pleased that, finally, shame has gone back to where it belongs—to the perpetrator of the wrong. The strangest thing about crimes against women was that, unlike all other crimes, shame was attached to the victim. And therefore the silence. No longer—I hope.

Yet, I have some anxieties. Will the movement percolate down to women in small jobs, women who face harassment almost daily in their working lives? Will it help women for whom their jobs are of such vital importance that to speak out would be to endanger that job and make life harder for them and their families? And, once again, my great fear is, will the #metoo movement make the two genders always suspicious and fearful of each other? Will there be another polarisation, and will we have to live in a world of men against women? Will men and women be able to live together in love and harmony after women have asserted their right to be equal under the law? I think that the answer to this can only come from men. The ball is in their court.

One of the questions asked of the women who named men who had sexually harassed them was: why were you silent all this time, all these years? In reply I give a quote from Caroline Norton, an Englishwoman who lived in the nineteenth century, at a time when married women had no rights at all. She fought a long and bitter legal battle with her abusive husband for the custody of her children. In 'A Letter to the Queen on Lord Cranworth's Marriage and Divorce Bill' (1855), she quoted these words: 'History teaches ... that in all cases of great injustice among men, there comes a culminating point, after which that injustice *is not borne ...*'

I believe that the culminating point for women has now come.

Behind these two issues looms a bigger one, a threat to the shining promise of equality before the law given to all citizens by the Constitution. The Sabarimala issue is an indicator that women still have to fight for that right. And the threat to all non-

Hindu citizens of becoming second-class citizens, looms before us as a dreadful possibility. A country in which some citizens live with fear is a failed state. I am hopeful that the gender divide will not become a big issue because, a cynical thought I admit, we need each other. But the divide caused by religion is more dangerous; we have only to look at the various bloody civil wars being fought in the world to see what can happen. All those who want a Hindu state must think of the consequences of establishing it. Perhaps we need to go back to Rabindranath Tagore's well-known poem and think of the 'heaven of freedom' which he prayed for, which we can enter only when all of us, whatever our religion or caste, our class, gender or language, are equal. Considering the human track record, this seems almost impossible. But the fact that so many of us continue to love, support and cherish the people in our lives should give us hope. All that we need to do is what Arjuna did on the eve of the battle of Kurukshetra—we only have to expand the range of the words 'my people' to embrace all Indians.

(2018)

A Balancing Act

To look back at the history of human society is to see a continuous process of change, sometimes a swift change, propelled, perhaps, by a war or a revolution, but at most times a gradual transformation. The slowest, the most reluctant changes, however, have been in the status of women. Yet, my mother, who died at the age of 91, once said to me, 'I think I have seen more changes in my life than most people see in centuries'. She was speaking of the changes in women's lives and I thought, yes, it was a time of change. She was born in the first decade of the last century, the youngest daughter of the oldest brother of a large joint family. Like in all Indian families of the time, there were several widows in it, far more visible in Brahmin families because of their shaven heads and coarse red saris. These women provided the labour force of the family and also a kind of emotional centre for all the motherless children, of whom there were many, because women died easily then—of TB, during pregnancy, childbirth and of unknown causes. This was true of most families of the time. But my mother's family was different in one way, because her father, the head of the family, was an unusual man for his times. (Of course, this was Pune, an enlightened city of social reform.) He believed in education for girls, a change which began with my mother. While her two older sisters were married off before puberty, she and all her younger cousins went to school. My mother even graduated;

she was the first female graduate in the family. Her father was so delighted that, the story goes, he garlanded her on the day of her results. But the women in the family were neither admiring of, nor enthusiastic about, her degree. Later, she often told us how they derided her, scorned her education and her degree and how humiliated she was because she was not married until she was in her twenties. She remembered this humiliation all her life, which is why, perhaps, to get married and have her own home, husband and children became the most important thing to her. (Though at the end of her life she was a frustrated and angry woman, repeatedly saying 'I have done nothing with my life!')

It was different with her daughters, my sister and I. Born two and a half decades after her, we were privileged like her in having a father who believed in educating daughters exactly the way sons were. He went a step further than my grandfather in believing that we should have our own careers (we were left free to choose what we wanted to do) so that we should be able to stand on our own feet. My sister found her goal in life very early; while yet in school, she decided she would be a doctor and worked steadily towards that end. I had no ambitions, none that I was sure about in the same way my sister was about hers. For me, it was enough to be free to go my own way. And to read. Small town though ours was, it was an educational centre and had a large public library. This, and the school library, constituted a treasure chest to me and I wallowed in these riches. Looking back now, I see that I was preparing myself for my future with my enormous reading. But at the time it was no more than a guilty passion to be pursued rather furtively, because my father, who placed great value on academic achievement, regarded my reading as a waste of time. And so I drifted, doing a BA with Economics, later studying Law. Marriage was the real catalyst. Suddenly I was a married woman and found myself in a place which was ready for me and which I slipped into, almost involuntarily. It was not hard to find out what I was supposed to do, because there were enough role models about me: mother and aunts and married friends who had assumed the role of a wife, and all that came along with it, easily and instantly. A letter written to me by my father's friend on my marriage remains to me the most visible and clear idea of what my role was supposed to be. This man, a doctor and a writer with an amazing intellect, told me that I now held the honour of two families in my hands, that the happiness of my new family was in my hands, that it was my duty never to forget these things and so on. I should have been crushed by the weight of my responsibilities, but I remember that I was, instead, vaguely flattered at the importance he gave me! (I later realised that this was how women had been conned into doing many of the unpleasant things they did!)

For a while I enjoyed the independence marriage gave me and was excited by the bustle of life in big-city Mumbai. I fell very comfortably into the rhythm of middle-class life in the city, though often, specially when I was among my in-laws and had to be a daughter-in-law or a sister-in-law, I had an uneasy sense of being a pretender, of wearing a mask which was sure to slip at some time. And then came motherhood. After which, life was too crowded even to think, leave alone trying to understand the doubts and discomforts. It was only when the children stopped being babies and no longer needed so much of my time and care that I realised that what I felt was a sense of incompleteness. I was now all that a woman was supposed to be: wife, mother, homemaker. It was a companionable marriage, I had two adorable boys; why then did the question '*Is this all?*' keep dinning in my mind?

Many years later, when I could look back and rationalise, when I had the words to express myself, I wrote about this time. And I said, with a clarity that amazes me today, that most of the turmoil within me was due to the fact that I was regarded only as a woman. That the roles I had to play as a woman seemed to deny my intellectual self, which had been a very important part of my self until then. *Roles, gender identity, finding the self:* it is almost embarrassing to write these words now, they seem so dated, so clichéd, so irrelevant. (Actually, their very irrelevance is heartening, for it says we have gone beyond the need for these words.) But earlier, it had been hard, almost impossible, to find words for the nebulous uneasiness that I felt. In fact, when I read Betty Friedan's *The Feminine Mystique*—very much later—the phrase, 'the problem without a name', struck an instant chord within me. In fact, I am now convinced that to get the words is the beginning of an understanding, well, at least a glimmer of an understanding. Unfortunately, at some time, many of these words became a joke; they were used to ridicule what was then called, a very revealingly pejorative term, 'women's lib'. I remember a movie of that time, a very popular one, in which a mother abandons her husband and son to 'find herself', while the man, the father, takes on the job of looking after the child. It made the idea of 'finding oneself' not merely a joke, but selfish and cruel. However, I was not trying to find myself; my feeling was of trying to get back the self which I seemed to have lost, an intelligent, rational, thinking person with a potential which would be recognised and fulfilled at some time.

The truth was that the girl I had been was totally unprepared for becoming the self-sacrificing, selfless, supporting-everyone person I was supposed to be as a wife, mother and homemaker. And I was not ready to accept the taken-for-granteds about women. I reacted violently against the silly jokes made about them, I was angered by the constant running down of their problems, their emotions and their ways of thinking. I could not understand the trivialisation of everything connected to their lives, the generalisations that put the entire sex into one category.

At some time, these feelings moved outside of my own self and embraced all women. Suddenly, as if my eyes had been opened, I saw the women who worked for me and my neighbours as domestic help, women who worked hard all their lives, struggling against drunken violent husbands, trying to educate their children. There were also little girls who came to me as live-in helps, girls who had either never been to school, or had had, perhaps, just a year or two of schooling, girls who would be married as soon as their parents found a man for them, which meant that they would move from one kind of bondage to another. This was the beginning of a realisation of how privileged I was. Unfortunately, it did not make me feel any better, nor did it solve the problem.

However, it was what I saw in my own home that brought everything to a point. My husband's was a rural, very orthodox family, something which had troubled my parents before my marriage. How would I, brought up as I was, fit into it? I was very nervous when my mother-in-law came to visit us. Justifiably, for it was a problem creating an environment in our urban home that suited her orthodox Brahmin widow's life. The rules of her life, which affected our entire routine and way of living, were irksome, more so because they seemed so pointless. (Not so pointless, I realised later, because they did make her life as difficult as possible.) But after three or four visits, it suddenly struck me that caste, or social status, made no difference to women's lives. She was a Brahmin woman, the head of a family with very large land holdings, the mother of four well-educated and well-placed sons. And yet, because she was a shaven widow, she had to live a life of terrible deprivations and innumerable taboos. I saw, too, that while the sons of the family had gone out and got themselves, very creditably, a good education, the daughters had to be satisfied with a few years of schooling, after which they were married off. The youngest was the only one to complete school, but she had to stop at that. There was no college in the village and how could a girl be sent out to live in a hostel, or anywhere outside her home? She came to live with us after our marriage so that her brother could find a groom for her. For the first time, I saw from very close 'the girl-seeing ceremony'. I saw the desperate need of the girl's family to get her married, I saw their humility, their willingness to accede to everything asked for. I saw the insulting attitude of the man and his family, the arrogant way in which they 'inspected' the girl. It is hard to believe it now (or perhaps it still happens), but the girl was made to walk so that they could see that she did not limp, she had to read out so that they knew she did not wear glasses! Something was stirring in me, a kind of rage. Pieces of the jigsaw puzzle were falling into place. There were still many gaps, there would always be a few blank spaces, but in spite of them I could see a pattern, a design emerging, in which the main motif was the powerlessness of women, their total lack of control over their own lives. And yet, though my eyes had been opened, I had also begun to realise that it was not easy to live my life according to the ideas I was beginning to have, when the family I was living in, indeed the entire society, was still steeped in the ideas I was rejecting. All these things came together and I began writing.

It was a very tentative beginning. I wrote small pieces at first, patterned on the 'ha, ha it's only silly little me' funny pieces written by women in women's magazines. The only one of my early writings I clearly remember is an article on the Suffragette movement in England. I cannot remember why I chose that topic and where it was published, or whether, in fact, it was published at all. But I remember, very vividly, my sense of amazement when I read of the huge resistance to women's demand for the vote—and this in England, the democracy we had been brought up to admire above all others! However, I soon realised that my métier was fiction. I began writing short stories, most of which were published in women's magazines, because they were 'women's' stories. After some years I stopped writing for these magazines, because I felt that they stamped me as a 'women's magazine' writer, which would not let my work be taken seriously. Though now I think that these magazines played their role in what was happening, because they provided, between the recipes and the beauty tips, the space for a certain class of women to express themselves. At that time, however, it was important for me to get out of them. More than this, I was beginning to be dissatisfied with the short story form as well; I wanted more space, I wanted more room for exploring people, ideas, emotions. And so the novel, which still remains my favourite genre of writing. According to Doris Lessing, fiction is better at the truth than a factual record. I agree with her. Fiction is to me the best means of trying to understand complexities and ambiguities, to bring in the various shades and colours that make up people and life. I also know that fiction cannot be used for propagating an ideology or for conveying a message. *I am a feminist but not a feminist writer:* I have said this often and it is amazing how often I am misunderstood. I don't see any contradiction between the two statements. The woman may be a feminist, but the writer cannot proclaim an 'ism' in her work, because to do so would be to mar the work. And for a writer, the aesthetics is as important as what is being said.

With the birth of the writer, the paralyzing confusion in the woman ended. The woman and the writer have traveled together since then. The woman watched the country, despite much covert and some overt opposition, get used to discussing women's issues and women's problems. She saw the slowly increasing awareness of some of these issues, saw them being taken more seriously. Invited, because she was a writer, to seminars, to film festivals focusing on women's issues, to protests and procession, the woman got a glimpse of the activism that made this possible. She saw too how society regarded any change in the status of women as threatening the family, in fact, society itself. And yet, slowly, laws were being changed, new laws were coming into being, judicial decisions were making an impact and family courts came into existence. But it was always a one-step forward, two-steps backwards movement. Always full of contradictions. While reservations for women in the village panchayats were introduced, the bill to reserve 33 per cent of seats in Parliament for women kept being pushed out year after year, by government after government. And if the media highlighted issues like female foeticide, dowry deaths, and rape, the same media was the vehicle for using women's bodies for advertising products, or selling them.

As a writer I seemed to move on a parallel path. I found my voice in a short story, 'The Intrusion', and then moved on to two novels which laid the foundation for all my work henceforth. Through these years, I moved on from the early angry intense novels with troubled women, who were deeply mired in their confusion, to questioning but more-sure-of-themselves and mellower women like Sumi, Savitribai, Leela, Jiji. And now men too, men like Gopal, Joe, Tony, Badri Narayan, Raja. Through my novels I explored women's minds, their emotions, their lives, their struggle to cope with relationships, with a world that too often refused to see them apart from their gender. They were women who introspected, rationalised, and questioned, but they rarely found clear answers: only possibilities. I don't know if these women impacted on my life, or whether my life helped to bring these women into existence, but I too rarely look for answers. Only for choices. And possibilities.

Today, both as woman and writer, I am convinced that the women's movement was one of the great movements of our times, a greater success in a way than the other big movement, communism. A greater success because, while communism, so much more acceptable in theory, failed in practice, feminism, to give it back its old label, while derided in theory, has been more successful in practice. I know that when I look around me. Like my mother, I too have seen many changes in my lifetime, changes which have been swifter and more radical. When I look at the same family in which girls had to forego education because they could not be sent outside the home, I see not only teachers, doctors and engineers, but also businesswomen, surgeons, counselors, scientists. They went out of their homes to study, some went abroad. Married and with children, they continue with their careers, though a couple of them have remained unmarried, insisting that they will choose for themselves when they feel the need to get married. They may never know it, but this change has been possible because of the work of a great number of women and men. At times, when I want to feel good, I tell myself that writing has been my form of activism and that, in a small way, I have been part of this movement as well. I like to think that, in finding my own voice, I gave a voice to other women as well. But the truth is that I do not believe that writing can change lives, and I know that writing in English, specially, can never have much impact on the lives of most Indians. I have to admit that writing was primarily *my* way of coping with the confusion, the turmoil within me and it became through the course of the years, a passion and a way of living.

'*To achieve anything you have to be ruthless*': this was the first line of my novel *That Long Silence*. Years later, without meaning to and making the connection only now as I write, I created Savitribai in my novel *Small Remedies,* a great musician, who ruthlessly sacrificed everything that came in the way of her music. In *Moving On,* there was the feisty girl, Jiji, who rebelled against her mother, the woman who wrote romances for women's magazines, but refused to let her daughter have her love life. Jiji was not reconciled with her mother until the very end. I know I have not been able to achieve such ruthlessness myself. I have always tried to harmonise my writing with my personal life, with my relationships. It has always been a kind of tightrope walking, a precarious balancing. This is the way I have chosen and I could never have done anything else. I believe that human relationships are the most important things in our lives; love is what all of us, men and women, need most, both to give and to receive, love is what we most hope for all our lives. But we fail, we fail ourselves and others, over and over again we fail. These hopes, these failures, are what I write about, this is what I want to understand in my own life.

(2009)

Section III

WRITERS, READERS, CRITICS AND REVIEWERS

A Missed Opportunity

In an account of his time in a German internment camp during World War II, P.G. Wodehouse has a story of how a fellow internee, bored with the constant talk of food in the camp, once followed Wodehouse and a Roman Catholic priest, hoping to hear some conversation that would give him some 'mental and spiritual uplift'. What he got instead was a discussion of the respective merits of two kinds of sausages! I was reminded of this on the second day in Neemrana when Prof. U.R. Ananthamurthy greeted me at the lunch table with a beaming 'Good food today', his plate raised in a kind of salute. Looking back, I wonder whether this was the one most genuine and meaningful statement I heard in all the days of this festival in Delhi and Neemrana.

And yet, one went to this festival with great expectations. In spite of the adverse publicity it was already attracting, with complaints from the writers who were not invited, it promised to be unique, a first-time occasion, with writers in all the languages *and* in English, both from within India and abroad, being part of it. And so there they were—writers from Nirmal Verma to Paul Zacharia, from Sitanshu Yashaschandra to Imtiaz Dharker, from Bhalchandra Nemade to Amitav Ghosh. However, if one imagined that this bringing us together was the real purpose of the festival, one was quickly disillusioned; whatever the initial purpose may have been, the award of the Nobel Prize to Sir Vidia Naipaul changed things. Both the title of the festival ('At

Home in the World') and the inaugural session, the centre piece of which was Naipaul, a writer whose home *was* the world, made it abundantly clear what the festival was really about: it was a celebration of a Nobel Laureate, of a Nobel Prize being awarded to a writer whom India, hopefully, even sycophantically, considered an Indian. When one looked at the titles given to the sessions, it became even clearer that this festival was also a kind of toast raised to the success of English writing in the world. For example, some of the titles of the sessions were: *A Way in the World, Midnight's Children, In an Antique Land, The Circle of Reason* and so on—all these the titles of successful novels of English writers.

The issues to be discussed in these sessions were equally significant pointers to the perspective of the festival: *Who is an Indian writer? Ideas of Home, Versions of India, Translating India, Exile, The Diaspora, Exoticizing,* etc., etc. All these are issues more relevant, or, perhaps, *only* relevant to writers who live abroad; or, more correctly, relevant to academicians and critics who are dealing with the writing of such writers. Writers rarely, almost never, concern themselves with such abstract issues, something which became evident in the first session itself, which was to discuss the solemn issue of 'the politics of identity'. The august panel, consisting of stalwarts like Nirmal Verma, Nabaneeta Dev Sen, Amitav Ghosh, Vikram Seth, etc., reminded one of students at an oral examination, giving stilted halting answers, despite the prodding of the genial examiner/ moderator U.R. Ananthamurthy.

The session on 'Who is an Indian writer?' fared no better. The very word 'Indian' proved to be a stumbling block to most writers. The consensus seemed to be that one never thought of oneself as an Indian, that this mattered only when one went abroad. (And, as Nayantara Sahgal reminded everyone, in times of national crises.) So why were we discussing this in India, where this was one of the taken-for-granteds of our lives? And when clearly one's identity was more linked to other factors like gender, religion, language, region, caste, etc.? Again, during the next session on *Partial* (?) *Exiles*, though most of the panel consisted of writers who lived abroad, 'exile' was a word they seemed to reject. As Amitav Ghosh said, he lived abroad because he had a job there and came to India whenever he wanted to. Which did not prevent Khushwant Singh from caustically calling the writers living abroad 'five-star' and 'champagne' exiles, and claiming the title of exile rightfully for himself, as one who had lost his homeland during Partition! To a writer, more interesting than these issues of labels was Ved Mehta's statement that exile meant a crystallising of the memory of an earlier home, something that was invaluable to a writer. This remark could have been followed by questions like: Does memory get crystallised or fossilised? And how does one continue to write about a life and society without being an intrinsic part of its daily living, its dynamism? How does one cope with the language which keeps changing? And what about writers at home like C.S. Lakshmi or Saniya, who write in one language (Tamil and Marathi, respectively), but live outside the region of its use? But the way the sessions were structured and, of course, the time factor, gave the discussions no chance to move outside the strictly academic format that had been imposed on them. Ajeet Cour's comments, for example, on the arrest of a university teacher after 13 December on the Narmada movement, were brushed aside by the moderator Farrukh Dhondy as being, mystifyingly, 'too serious'! When the truth was that Ajeet was speaking of something very relevant and significant—the role of writers in society. Was it because the moderator did not live in India that he was unable to grasp this? Or was it true that we were not there to discuss 'anything too serious'—which obviously meant political? Was this why there was no attempt to discuss something that should have been most important to writers, the terminology used in the festival, because this too would be political? Writers were constantly stubbing their toes on words that they felt awkward about. Like 'regional writing', for example. The fact is that the writing in any one language in our country usually stands on its own and is spoken of in that manner—like 'Marathi writing', or 'Bengali writing', for example. But when one needed to speak of them collectively—and always, it seemed, to distinguish the group from English writing—was the term 'regional writing' the right one? Lakshmi Holmström, the translator, said in a private conversation that the word 'regional' carried nuances of provincial, hence made it seem smaller and less significant. Whereas, to me 'regional' implies that there is a national against which it is set; and what is the national literature? English? Nothing could be more ridiculous than this idea, yet in this festival, which was carried on in English (obviously, because it was the only common language) and in which most of the issues discussed were those relevant to English writing, this point of view seemed to make its presence felt. There was a distinct sense of the elevation of this writing above the others, of its being the standard against which the others were judged.

There was also some confusion about the term 'Indian writing' itself; at times it seemed to mean the writing in all the languages except English, at times it seemed to mean only English writing. It was never used inclusively, which left many of us who believed that English writing was a part of the whole with a sense of chagrin. This whole issue of language—not in the sense of the *use* of language, which is what writers should be really interested in, but *which* language (we even had a session to discuss a dead-as-the-dodo subject: *Is English a foreign language?*) created a kind of polarisation—with the language writers in one group, the English writers in another. And those of us who lived in the country and wrote in English had an uncomfortable sense of being Trishankus, not finding a place in either of these groups. One could understand that the issues we were to discuss, as also the language in which we had to discuss them in, alienated the language writers. Nevertheless, the hostility towards English writing, in which the usual arguments were trotted out, was inexplicable—specially with the presence of so many English writers at the table who wrote, published and had readers within the country. Naipaul's comment on the inaugural day that language writers did not have a large readership and his gratuitous advice that they should write better to get more readers, seemed to cast a shadow on the entire conference, leaving these writers on the defensive. And Khushwant Singh's provocative statement that Indian writing lacked humour and that most of our languages had a poor vocabulary didn't help the atmosphere, either. The most sensible reply came from Sitanshu Yashaschandra who said that we all lack the information. We most certainly did: we lacked information about one another, about one another's language, about one another's literature. The only shared information seemed to be about the writers, the books and the literature that the media highlighted. And instead of facts, one got emotional and exaggerated statements, as also angry words, like 'traitors to their languages', which were used by Prof. Nemade against those who write in English. Shrilal Shukla's explanation of the dwindling readership in Hindi as being connected to the poor teaching of Hindi in universities ('The universities were our constituencies', he said) was a rare example of an honest analysis of a situation. So too Paul Zacharia's admission of the problems of writing in a small and close society, of the pressure this puts on a writer. These unusual forays into honesty came out of a self-confidence that was not afraid to face facts. This was the tone we wanted; this was the kind of understanding we needed. Equally interesting were the facts about two different language readerships that came from Khushwant Singh and M.T. Vasudevan Nair—Khushwant saying that 500 copies were the maximum that a book could sell in Punjabi and Vasudevan Nair telling us about how even a poetry book sold over 2000 copies in Malayalam. And there were the two opposing points of view—David Davidar, a publisher, saying he would do anything to sell a book and a language writer saying he didn't care about quantity (of sales), only the quality mattered—which revealed something interesting that could have been explored. On the whole, however, there was too little self-introspection, too little shared information or shared concerns, too much of the abstract and the irrelevant, too much emphasis on English writing, specially on its success and its celebrities.

A session on literary criticism was symbolic of all that was wrong with this conference. This should have been of much interest to all writers and should have given us a perspective writers badly need to take note of. But the absence of any important critic from India on the panel, and indeed in the festival itself (and though the omissions were too many to be referred to, I have to speak of the glaring absence of Meenakshi Mukherjee) distanced the whole session from most of the writers there. The moderator, David Pryce-Jones, who, obviously, had no knowledge of India or Indian writing, except what any writer/critic in the West would know, rambled on for an inordinately long time about Europe, Bosnia, universality, etc. And referred to Indian writing as 'news from the village'—something Amit Chaudhuri sharply responded to. In the little time left for the other panellists, we heard about the *Times Literary Supplement*, the *London Review of Books*, the Canadian scene, etc. After which the moderator was prepared to wind up the session, until reminded that there was one panellist yet to speak—Malashri Lal, the only Indian literary critic there. 'Do you want to speak?' she was asked in a tone that said, 'I'm sure you don't'. But Malashri, with admirable aplomb, said, 'Yes, I do' and spoke in the two or three minutes she had about women's writing and the criticism that dealt with it—subjects that had been left severely alone until then. And which, we were told in the next session, should continue to be unmentionables.

This was a media session in which Sir Vidia was to take part, the title of which was 'Midnight's Children', one of the themes to be discussed being 'the weight of history'. What one saw, or rather, what two of us (Nayantara Sahgal and I) felt, was the weight of a Nobel Laureate, who turned on us for having the temerity to speak about subjects *he* considered 'banal'—these two being colonialism and gender oppression. This incident has been much written about in the press, but what did not figure in any report was the tone of Sir Vidia's comments in which he spoke of how those who spoke of these things didn't write and of how HE did nothing but write and how every penny HE earned had been through writing. All these statements were a slap in the face to the writers there—for they seemed to imply that we were not serious about our writing. It seems unfortunate to me that he had no idea of how little most writers earned in this country through writing, of the fact that this meant most had to have another profession, and that, if you were a woman, you had the family as well, and possibly, a job too—all this for much smaller rewards than what a writer like Naipaul got. Not only did he wholly ignore the fact that we belonged to two different cultures of writing, unknowingly, Sir Vidia had also proclaimed that both the issues he had condemned as banal were still very much alive. If the colonial spirit was no longer around, why did we have to listen to such comments, to our writing being called 'news from the village' and the Rajasthani dances we witnessed one evening being called 'tribal dances'? Why did we take these in meek silence? And would a conference in any other country have writers/critics, wholly ignorant of the writing in that country, dominate a panel? As for gender oppression, what else was it but an affirmation of it when the whole issue was so brusquely brushed aside as being boring and banal? And how could anyone say that the insensitivity to women's issues no longer existed when we had a writer, Roberto Calasso, pooh pooh the idea that women had a sense of alienation from the myths or traditional stories, these being written by men? Calasso also scorned the idea of women rewriting the stories, or retelling them from their own point of view, since, according to him, we had no right to be critical of our 'glorious past'. (Iravati Karve's *Yuganta* was obviously a big mistake!) In fact, Calasso's grievance, voiced in earlier sessions too, was that we Indian writers failed dismally in not speaking of, or writing about, this glorious past. This time, however, it provoked the normally even-tempered Amitav Ghosh into an outburst, in which he raged against the 'astonishing impertinence' of someone telling us what we should be talking about, or what we should be writing.

Perhaps, in the context of globalisation, the title 'At Home in the World' was both timely and important. We do need to think of what is happening to our languages in the light of the increasing dominance of English (but not make it a war against those who write in English!), to ponder over how our languages are going to stand up against the onslaught of English—something, the anti-English brigade should have felt good to hear—which is a matter of worldwide concern. We do need to think of the increasing commercialisation of literature, of the book becoming another commodity to sell. But these issues were, if spoken of, only very lightly touched. The main problem was that the focus of the festival was wrong. Nevertheless, let me put the blame squarely where it belongs—on our own shoulders. Why did we never talk about what should really concern all Indian writers today (specially in the context of what is happening in Gujarat and elsewhere)—like the role of the writer and our inability to speak up, or our total insignificance in shaping opinions, for example? Did we too feel that these topics were 'too serious' to be touched upon, or irrelevant to the star of the festival? Why did we so wholly ignore translations, the importance of which became glaringly clear as we went on speaking with such ignorance of one another's writing? It makes me wonder whether we really deserve a Sahitya Akademi kind of seminar after all, with writers presenting one boring paper after another, the speakers coming on in an alphabetical order of Assamese, Bengali, etc.

In the session on history, three of us panellists spoke of our attempts to explore the silences, the gaps and the omissions in history. This festival itself seems to be one of silences, omissions and absences. As also one of unexplained presences. Like those who seemed to be there for no other reason but to form a group round Naipaul. In spite of good intentions, these things made the festival what I can only call A Missed Opportunity.

(2002)

On Writers, Reviewers and Critics

In *The Life of Charlotte Brontë*, the biographer, Elizabeth Gaskell, narrates the story of Charlotte telling her father about her novel. 'Papa', she said, 'I have written a book', and then she gave him a copy of *Jane Eyre*. But, before leaving him with the book, Charlotte read out some reviews of the book to him. At teatime, the father said to his other two daughters, 'Girls, do you know Charlotte has written a book and it is much better than likely?'

This story spells out to me the importance of reviews. It bolsters the author's confidence (when the reviews are favourable, as the reviews of *Jane Eyre* obviously were) and gives the reader a glimpse of the book she/he will be reading. For writers, a review is the one way of knowing how their work is being received by the world. Practitioners of the performing arts have an audience that gives them an idea of the reception to their work. But books are written in a solipsistic solitude by the writer and read by the reader in solitude as well. The only way the author can get an idea of response to the book is from reviews. Barbara Epstein, founding-editor of *The New York Review of Books,* says that she started it as a separate publication because of a strike at *The New York Times*. No reviews coming, she says, meant that an author's work of years was invisible to everyone but the author herself. Writers are clueless, anyway; after months, years of being locked in with their work, they are unable to see it clearly, unable to assess its quality. How is it?

Good? Bad? Indifferent? A masterpiece? Or a dud? A writer's mind veers between all these.

I must admit that I had absolutely no idea of the importance of reviews when I started writing. When the publisher of my first novel said they would bring it out in hardcover, I was not too happy. Naive and ignorant that I was, I thought that a hardcover, being more expensive, would sell less. But, no, said my editor. 'A book in hardcover gets more reviews'. He was right: this novel by a new writer garnered a great many reviews. I learnt that reviews mattered and, with my next novel, like all authors, I found myself waiting for reviews as soon as the book was out. I was impatient, hoping for good reviews, apprehensive, fearing bad reviews, happily ignorant of the fact that the very worst thing that could happen was that there would be no reviews at all. Not to have any reviews is to be ignored, snubbed, to be given a lowly place in the literary world. It means you don't matter. In fact, you don't exist. Even a small notice makes a difference, depending, of course, on who takes notice. A good example is of what happened to Barbara Pym, an English writer. When the *Times Literary Supplement* invited writers to give their opinions on who were the most underrated, and who the most overrated writers, Barbara Pym, a novelist, got two mentions as the most underrated writer. One of the two who mentioned her was Philip Larkin. The result was that a publisher accepted Pym's next novel, *Quartet in Autumn*, which was later shortlisted for the Booker. Not just that, all her books were reissued; it was a glorious revival for Barbara Pym.

Not to get any reviews is something that puzzles writers. The publishers have assured you that they have sent your book to all reputed magazines, journals, Sunday newspaper supplements. Why then this thundering silence? It took me some time to understand that there is a literary hierarchy which decides not only which books will be reviewed, but also how quickly they appear. Veteran writers, of course, get priority. So does a book by a celebrity, or by an Important Person, not necessarily someone in the literary world. Books that are controversial or sensational are next in the queue. India, with its unceasing 'Westward look', gives a book published in the West priority, specially one reviewed favourably by reviewers there. There are other signifiers of the importance of a book. A review of one of my novels appeared on the last page of a Sunday newspaper supplement. It was just three hundred words, if that, and tucked away between matter continued from the first page. The reviewer was someone I had never heard of before, nor since. I was no novice: this was my seventh or eighth novel. Until then I had had fairly substantial reviews, which were prominently placed, at times accompanied by an interview. So what had happened to make me slide so rapidly down the literary slope in such an undignified manner? 'Well, you see, I'm a failure as a writer. I'm out of fashion: old: shan't do better: ... my book out (prematurely) and nipped; a damp firework'.

This is not me; these are Virginia Woolf's words (*A Writer's Diary*). And why was she in such despair? Because her new book sent to the *Times* for review had only a 'short notice ... put in an obscure place'.

I had to laugh. Nothing like laughter to drive out the demons, specially the demon of self-pity.

Why do writers depend so much on the opinion of one person? Why do they take a bad review so hard? Because it is in print, which makes it permanent. Because it is there for anyone and everyone to read. Because it is humiliating to be criticised in public. Rarely do writers ask themselves the question: who is this reviewer? If you are a writer of eminence, you may get a good reviewer. Otherwise it could be anyone; there are no qualifications needed for a person to review. Doris Lessing, in her introduction to a later edition of *The Golden Notebook,* speaks of how 'a young man or woman, reviewer or critic, who has not read more of a writer's work but the book in front of him, will write patronisingly ... as if considering how many marks to give an essay ...' Often this patronising borders on presumptuousness. There are lazy reviewers who will not take the trouble to read the book carefully and form their own opinions but accept what has been already said about authors and their work. Doris Lessing's main complaint about the reviews of *The Golden Notebook* was that it was seen as a feminist book and therefore either acclaimed, or criticised, as being part of the gender war. Which meant that various themes in it were totally missed. Margaret Atwood calls this the 'put-down syndrome'. A reviewer spoke of the 'domestic images' in her poetry; seeing her poetry as women's poetry, the review focussed only on such images which could be categorised as 'domestic images' and ignored the rest. Eudora Welty, stamped as a 'regional writer', said, 'I just think of myself as writing about human beings and I happen to live in a region ...'

Whatever they think of the reviewer, writers are unduly elated by praise, or drowned in misery after a bad review. Even a writer of the stature of Virginia Woolf, who, one would have thought, would be above being affected by reviews, shows her extreme sensitivity to reviews in her diaries. Entries in the diary show her agonising even over possible reviews of yet-to-come books. She was apprehensive about the reviews of *A Room of One's Own*, now a classic. She thought it ominous that Morgan (E.M. Forster) would not review it. She was sure she would be 'attacked for a feminist'. She even prepared her defence against criticism. 'It is a trifle ... but I wrote it with ardour and conviction.' All this even before the book was out. When it came out, she writes baldly, briefly, 'it does well', adding, 'and it sells'. (Ten thousand copies! My mouth fell open with amazement.)

Yes, readers and sales are the best response to a nasty critic. My novel, *A Matter of Time*, got one of the nastiest reviews I've ever had to put up with. I was crushed. That it was a first-time reviewer who had reviewed the book made it a bigger insult. In the event, the book was later published by Feminist Press, translated into French, Italian and Marathi (for which it got the Sahitya Akademi translation award). It is still selling. In driblets, of course, but this is a book which came out twenty-five years back; it's a cheerful thought that it still sells at all.

One of the most galling things for a writer is that you cannot respond to a review. Even when the reviewer's pen has been dipped in malice and spite, as it sometimes is, the writer has to remain silent. What can the author say? It is an unfair and unequal battle. The reviewer is well-armed, the writer is weaponless, defenceless. No, writers can't respond. Fiction writers specially can't respond. An author of a book of non-fiction may, perhaps, argue with scholarly arguments about debatable facts. But how do you respond to a review of a work of fiction? Could I respond to a reviewer who scoffed at the use of the word 'cute' in a novel, a word which had been used by a teenaged daughter teasingly and fondly for her father? What could I say to a person who set out to review a book, ignorant of the fact that there is a difference between the authorial voice and the words spoken by a character, which are in tune with the character's age, gender, background, nature, etc. There is only one thing to do—make a wax doll and stick pins into it! To respond is to expose your hurt, your scars. Silence is the most dignified response. A literary brawl gives great pleasure to all the world, except to the writer, who will find that the spat keeps the focus on the objectionable review.

But there is one way of looking at nasty criticism. Virginia Woolf stumbled upon it after her fearful certainty that Wyndham Lewis had 'attacked' her in his book. She read Keats' famous lines about praise or blame having 'but a momentary effect on the man whose love of beauty in the abstract makes him a severe critic of his own works'. Keats goes on to say that 'the attempt to crush me in the Quarterly has only brought me more into notice'. And then comes the gloriously confident statement, 'I think I shall be among the English poets after my death'. An amazing statement from a young man who should have been demolished by a review as nasty as could be in a prestigious literary journal. But even wiser are these words: 'This is a mere matter of the moment.' Such maturity in so young a man! Where did it come from? From an intimation of his own mortality? Bravado? A desire not to show his hurt? Or a genuine understanding of the fact that a review was truly only a 'mere matter of the moment'? And this the man who, Byron said in a poem, was 'kill'd off by one critique ... snuff'd out by an article'. No, John Keats was made of much sterner stuff.

A few years back, moving from a large house to an apartment, I set myself the task of going through the huge accumulation of papers in my study. Among them was a plastic bag of crumbling, yellowing pages. Reviews of my books collected through the years. I sat in the midst of this mountain of judgements on my work and asked myself: Why had I kept these? What do they mean to me now? Do I still want to keep them? I know they will be trashed after I am gone. Why not trash them right now? Which is what I did, saving, though, a few 'good' reviews. 'Good' not meaning praise of my work, but those that were well-written. Oh, all right, let me admit it, those that were well-written *and* appreciative. But what did any of the reviews really mean to me thirty years later? Yes, reviews are a 'matter of the moment'.

Writers can, of course, cross over to the other side and review books themselves. There have been very eminent writers who did book reviews, T.S. Eliot and Virginia Woolf among them. But I have always been wary of taking on reviews, specially of Indian English writers, of my contemporaries. Could I be fair to them? Would I not be biased? To be unprejudiced is hard. Virginia Woolf, for example, spoke of James Joyce's *Ulysses* as a 'mis-fire. Genius ... but of the inferior water ... diffuse ... brackish ... pretentious'. This was in her diary. In her review she was even more condemning. She called it 'a memorable catastrophe—immense in daring, terrific in disaster'. Was it because he was a contemporary that she could not see *Ulysses* with greater generosity? In fact, is it possible to be generous and large-hearted to someone who is breathing down your neck, threatening to push you aside and go ahead?

I have changed my mind since then. I think that writers should review books. For, who else but a writer herself will know what the writing of a book means? Who else will know that it is the work of months, of years, when one is cut off from everything but the book one is working on? Who else knows how the machinery works? Knowing these things, a writer may be critical, but will never be dismissive of another writer's work, will never be harsh to a first novel, for she knows how fragile a writer's ego is. My view of authors being good critics has been bolstered by some excellent reviews. Martin Amis on John Updike's final story collection, *My Father's Tears and Other Stories,* for example, Joyce Carol Oates on Anne Tyler's *The Amateur Marriage,* or Colm Tóibín on Alan Hollinghurst's *The Line of Beauty.* The first two reviews, despite expressing some disappointment in the book being reviewed, spoke with great admiration and respect of the writers' entire oeuvre. Colm Tóibín's review of Alan Hollinghurst was totally admiring. This, in spite of the fact that Hollinghurst and Tóibín had both been on the Booker shortlist and Hollinghurst had won. John Updike himself reviewed Anne Tyler's early novels, appreciatory reviews recognising her talent. Notice from an established writer does a fledgling writer a great service.

One of the things that troubles me about reviewing in India is the importance we give to reviews that appear in the West. For all that we set so much store by these reviews, I must confess that I often find them a little inadequate. There is a sense of the reviewer seeing only the larger picture, missing the smaller details, the nuances, the unsaid, the gaps in a picture. A first novel, *A Burning,* by an Indian writer Megha Majumdar, had a very appreciative review by Ron Charles in *The Washington Post*; but I was flummoxed by the last line: 'Fortunately, all this [the events in the novel] takes place on the other side of the world and has nothing at all to do with us.'

Well ...! Does this mean that all the books we read which came from other lands had 'nothing at all to do with us'? Why, then, did we read them and absorb them so that they became part of us? Why did we agonise over a helpless Jane Eyre, over the sufferings of David Copperfield? This remark of the reviewer Ron Charles is unfortunate, but it unknowingly tells us the truth about how a reviewer from outside India looks at an Indian novel. An Indian reviewer in the *Indian Express* speaks of the author Majumdar having ticked off 'all the boxes that make the India story familiar'. A cynical remark, it seems to me, but one which recognises the need to give the West an 'India story'. When the truth is that there is no 'India story'; there are millions of stories of people living in India, of mundane lives lived on an even keel, lived perhaps against the background of social and political upheavals which touch their lives only obliquely. However, the fact remains that a favourable review written by a Western reviewer, however inadequate some may consider it, takes the book into a very different league.

While most writers are much aware of and responsive to reviews, they are indifferent to the other face of reviews, which is literary criticism. Literary criticism rarely touches writers; and yet, it is literary criticism which is responsible for a writer's eventual reputation and place in literature. Reviews are soon forgotten, but criticism remains for a much longer time. Enthusiastic and idiosyncratic reader that I was, literary criticism was an unknown factor to me, until I read F.R. Leavis' *The Great Tradition*. I was fascinated by the way he begins the book, announcing, almost regally, 'The great English novelists are Jane Austen, George Eliot, Henry James, and Joseph Conrad'. The tone of authority, the certainty, impressed me. In time I came to an understanding of the importance of literary criticism. Not only is it more lasting, its pronouncements have more weight, depending, of course on the reputation and the scholarship of the critic.

Yet, criticism remained a subject that did not interest me until I stumbled upon feminist criticism. It was being a woman who wrote which gave me an entry into the subject. I had realised by then that my work was judged only as the writing of a woman: it was allowed no entry into the general category of novels, or literature. I had read in Virginia Woolf's *A Room of One's Own* (does this qualify as a book of literary criticism?) of the prevalence of male values which spilled over from life into fiction. Therefore a woman's writing, according to male values, would always be judged as a woman's novel, and consequently of minor importance. When I read *The New Feminist Criticism,* I realised the importance and power of literary criticism. I found two truths in this book: One, that criticism could keep a book alive by holding it up as a classic or by including it in the canon. And two, that women had been systematically eliminated from both—being a classic or part of the canon. Elaine Showalter, editor of *The New Feminist Criticism* claimed in her introduction, that: '[W]hat we are demanding is a new universal literary history and criticism that combines the literary experiences of both women and men.' A very simple and reasonable demand.

And yet, feminist criticism was ignored, dismissed, or opposed, often its very existence denied. Ursula le Guin, an American writer, in her essay 'Disappearing Grandmothers', speaks of how women writers 'are disappeared', making it an act of commission rather than one of omission. She gives examples of Elizabeth Gaskell and Margaret Oliphant and speaks of how James Joyce was immediately and enthusiastically 'canonised' whereas Virginia Woolf had to wait long before being allowed a grudging entry into the canon. There is also an example in India of a talented writer almost wiped off the map—Attia Hosain. I read her novel *Sunlight on a Broken Column* (first published in 1961) as a young woman. It excited me. I had read no other book by an Indian writer which had given me this excitement. But Attia Hosain, it seemed, fell off the literary map, because she was never mentioned, while the male pioneers, R.K. Narayan, Raja Rao, Mulk Raj Anand and others were read, studied and celebrated. Thankfully, Virago, who had first published her, brought out her novel and short stories as part of their programme of reviving classics. In India, a feminist publisher, Women Unlimited, brought out, during her centenary years, a collection, *Distant Traveller*, with her stories, both published and unpublished, and the fragment of an unfinished novel. All this with an Afterword by critic and writer Aamer Hussain to illuminate both the author and her work. I single out feminist criticism not only to show the power of criticism, but also to emphasise how feminist scholars and critics have had support from feminist publishers. Virago resurrected writers like Rosamond Lehmann, Winifred Holtby, Antonia White, Molly Keane, Margaret Kennedy, Radclyffe Hall, Kate O'Brien and many others. I remember with pleasure the beautiful productions of my two novels, *A Matter of Time* and *The Binding Vine*, by the Feminist Press, with enlightening Afterwords by Ritu Menon and Sonita Sarker, which introduced me to a new readership.

One serious lack in Indian English writing is the lack of critics who can speak with both authority and knowledge. An academic, after her return from an international seminar, said, 'Our voices are not heard'. True. There is no critic's voice in India that is taken seriously. Now, more than ever, we need such voices. This is a time when English writing in India is exploding with young talent, when there are books in many genres, which was not the case earlier, there is literary fiction as well as popular fiction and non-fiction is making rapid strides. We need critics who can see this picture as a whole, separate the chaff from the grain and give this literature what it needs—a discerning and inside view. Critics who will see in this literature not 'India stories', but a literature which, like all other literatures, tries to grapple with the world around it.

(2020)

Measuring Novels

I first met Meenakshi Mukherjee at a seminar in the early 1980s. It was my first seminar and I was nervous at being among a crowd of scholars and veteran writers. Meenakshi sought me out—I was unknown and had only two novels published at that time—to tell me she had read my The Dark Holds No Terrors. *I could see she was enthusiastic about the book, about coming across a new writer. She then told me she had also read my* Come Up and Be Dead. *In response to my 'Oh I was just trying to write a mystery', she said, 'Why are you embarrassed about it? I enjoyed the book'. Twenty years later, when she was launching my* Moving On, *she said, 'Here is the good mystery she has always wanted to write'. It was there, in the bookshop, where the launch took place, that she bought two books of Orhan Pamuk. When she returned to Hyderabad, she wrote to tell me how much she had liked his books—again very pleased, I could see, by the discovery of a new writer. Pamuk was unknown at the time, undiscovered by the world; he had not yet received the Nobel.*

This piece is my tribute to Meenakshi. Wonderful reader and good human being. And the best kind of critic—one who loved and was excited by good writing.

In *A Room of One's Own,* Virginia Woolf argues, 'Where books are concerned, it is notoriously difficult to fix labels of merit in such a way that they do not come off'. 'Measuring', she adds a little later, 'is the most futile of occupations'.

And yet, academics, critics, publishers, booksellers never cease from playing the labelling, the slotting, categorising and measuring game—all for their own different purposes. Ultimately, they create a hierarchy in literature, which means that by the time books get to the reader they have already been given a certain value.

But is it not a good thing for readers to have markers and signposts to help them find their way through the large expanse of literature? Do not these markers help them to choose, specially today when there is such a bewildering variety and number of books? Would not a reader like to have some idea of the book? I have no idea what other readers want. I can only narrate my own experience.

When I began, I read anything and everything I could get my hands on. (I speak throughout of novels, my first and lasting love.) My reading was, of course, limited by what was available in the three libraries I had access to—my school and later my college library and the town's public library—and whatever I could borrow from the few people who had books at home. I now call it the Age of Innocence. Books came to the reader pristine and unmediated. There were no reviews, no media information about the book, or its author. No one guided or advised me, either. And so I read the Angela Brazil schoolgirls' books, the *What Katy Did* and the *Little Women* series, *Treasure Island*, *Black Beauty* and so on. And it was somehow possible to move almost simultaneously and without a jerk into Walter Scott, Jane Austen, the Brontë's, Mrs Gaskell, and George Eliot. I read *East Lynn*, and *The Rosary*, forgotten now, but great favourites with schoolgirls then. Then, of course, Dickens and Thackeray and, much later, Trollope. In time, with greater access to books, I read Daphne du Maurier, A.J. Cronin, Nevil Shute, Rumer Godden, Somerset Maugham and many others. P.G. Wodehouse became a great and a lasting favourite. So did Graham Greene. And there were the crime novels—Agatha Christie, Margery

Allingham, Erle Stanley Gardner, Dorothy Sayers. Much later came Ngaio Marsh, P.D. James, Ruth Rendell. At a certain point of time, I came across American writers—from Mark Twain to Hemingway to John Steinbeck. The Russians, from Chekov and Tolstoy to Pasternak and Solzhenitsyn. Many of these books stayed with me, phrases and sentences lingered in my mind, the characters became part of my life. And if there were some books which I read at a stretch, there were many I laboured over, a few I gave up on, many I longed to possess so that I could read them over and over again.

I list these names not to impress anyone, but to show the kind of reading it was possible to do at the time, when buying books was an impossibility and libraries scarce. It was from reading that I began to learn through the years what I wanted from a novel. A good, well-constructed credible story. Characters I could believe in. At least one character with whom I could sympathise and identify with; in fact, with whom I would travel in the novel. Language that let me enter the novel with ease and pleasure. Simplicity and originality. Knowing that the author was saying something of her own in her own way. No stereotypes. I also learnt what I did not like in a novel. The author intruding between me and the novel. Showing off. Affectation and pretentiousness. Clichés and banality. I was learning to make a difference between books which were one-of-a-kind, like *Wuthering Heights* or *Crime and Punishment* or Forster's *Howards End* and others which were not the same, yet made for very good reading—like du Maurier's *Rebecca*. Or Dorothy Sayers's *Gaudy Night*. Even the light-hearted, very enjoyable books of Georgette Heyer. And so I categorised books and authors according to my own taste.

It was some time after I began writing that I realised with surprise that the books I had begun with were the 'Classics'. Spoken of with awe. It was even later that I came to know a kind of an equivalent in contemporary fiction which was called Literary Fiction—something no one has been able to define satisfactorily.

It seems it can be best defined by a process of ruling out books which are not literary fiction. Crime fiction, for example. Or romantic fiction. Humorous novels. Adventure. These are today categorised as 'genre fiction'. 'Literature', says Ursula le Guin, herself a genre writer, who writes science fiction, 'is the serious stuff you have to read in college, and genre is what you read for pleasure'. And, she adds, 'guilty pleasure'. Writers, too, do not want the label of 'genre novel' attached to their work. Le Guin speaks of Margaret Atwood, who does not want her books to be called science fiction, because, she says, 'She doesn't want the literary bigots to shove her into the literary ghetto'.

Literary ghetto. Pretty strong words these. But I have to agree that Ursula le Guin has a right to her indignation, when I think of the fact that I had never heard of her until, very recently, a friend recommended her to me. Was it the fact that she wrote science fiction that made her less visible? Of course, I was not a science fiction lover; but surely, I thought, when I read her essays, wonderful essays, I should have at least heard her name somewhere. But no, I hadn't. Yes, there is a problem of being slotted into the genre novel space. Le Guin says that genre is only for classification in libraries, but I see problems there as well. Writers like John le Carré, P.D. James—obviously, they would go into espionage and crime fiction. But their books are excellent, as good as any so-called 'literary fiction'. And would *Wuthering Heights* go into the romance slot? Would George Eliot's *Middlemarch* be pushed into the 'provincial novels' category? Graham Greene has himself classified his novel *The Ministry of Fear* as an 'entertainment'. Strange, because a thread of intense desperation runs through the entire novel and stays with it even at the end. In more recent times, how would one classify Julian Barnes' *Levels of Living,* a novel described as 'genre-bending'? It is divided into three parts, the first factual, the second imaginary, and the third purely personal, being about his grief at his wife's death. What genre does this book belong to? Whatever it is, a book once categorised as literary fiction gets a sticker affixed to it saying: '*This is an important book.*'

I have come to the conclusion that all the books which can be submitted for a literary prize are literary fiction. The Nobel Prize is, of course, the Holy Grail of all literary fiction; it is the final accolade and gives the stamp of 'great' to the book and the writer who has received the prize. But like all prizes, the Nobel too has its own requirements of what makes a book Nobel-worthy. One seems to be that the writer and the books should be fairly unknown, obscure, rather than popular and much read. (Graham Greene, for instance, could never fit in.) Politics plays a big role in 'enNobeling' a writer—the politics of the Western world at that time. Which accounts for Pasternak and Solzhenitsyn. For, perhaps, Orhan Pamuk. (Kipling, that staunch supporter of Imperialism, could never have got the prize in today's world.) Which is not to say most Nobel-winners are not excellent writers (yet Pearl S. Buck got the prize!), but it was the political factor that finally weighed in their favour. Ultimately, these books set the standard of excellence, perhaps even of greatness.

The same is true of other major prizes as well, like the Booker, or the Pulitzer. Even those on the shortlist get the tag of 'among the best'. The books selected for the shortlist and, even more, the winner, become the yardstick against which others are measured. The books become hugely visible, because, in today's world the media reach is enormous, its influence huge. The books are talked about, they are widely reviewed, the reviews given more space. Unlike the Nobel, most other prizes are linked to the market—not just the winning book, but even books on the shortlist sell in great numbers. There are often controversies about the books chosen, and like with the Nobel, some duds. Many unreadable novels. Novels which if one reads years later one wonders—*how did this get a prize?*

The problem with prizes is that they are chosen through a process of 'negotiation and compromise'—the words of Hilary

Mantel, herself a Booker Prize winner. 'Prizes are not', she says, 'necessarily a judgement on the literary merit of a book'. Nevertheless, they come to the reader with the tag of 'the best'. Which makes a reader, who cannot like the book, doubt her/his own judgement. 'Is there something wrong with me that I cannot like this book?' she/he is bound to ask herself. Which also makes other books, which may be just as good and, but for some accidental circumstances (a different jury, for example, or in another year), could easily have got the prize instead, completely invisible.

This is a special problem for Indian Writing in English (IWE). IWE is a strange phenomenon. It must be the only literature in the world whose values are set outside the country. Books which get a literary prize abroad, books which are chosen by agents and published abroad, come to India with a ready stamp of approval. Books published abroad and praised by important Western critics or reviewers have a status which can never be attained by books published within India. Even if a particular book finds many critics in India, like Adiga's Booker Prize winner *The White Tiger* did, the excitement generated by the prize itself, by the debates, by the conflicting reviews, ensures that a great many readers read the book. The fact that there is often a conflict between opinions outside and inside the country about the book only adds to the interest in the book.

In IWE, apart from the 'coming from abroad' category, we have discovered another category—and this is the bestseller. Bestsellers have always been part of any literature; they have their place. But IWE, excited perhaps by this phenomenon, which was unknown till recently, overwhelmed by the figures which had never been dreamt of, have given bestsellers the kind of attention which makes these into 'books which must be read'. For readers, the thought is, perhaps, if so many people have liked this book, it must be good. And with the kind of marketing and promotion done, both of the author and of a book which publishers think promises to be a best seller, a reader stands no chance of forming her own opinion. We have left it to the marketing people to decide for us which books are important and which are not. Critics who have such a big role to play as mediators between readers and books are sadly absent from IWE. Critics in IWE have not been able to form their own critical standards and have not been influential in giving Indian books a place in the literary world; it is the critics outside India who have done that.

A visit to a bookshop is a depressing revelation; it gives one an idea of what is happening to our literature. You will find international bestsellers (Paulo Coelho, Alexander McCall Smith, Dan Brown, etc.), prize-winning books, books written by celebrities and the latest Indian bestsellers. The books visibly displayed are those which have had a great deal of media attention. I felt sad to notice during a recent visit to a bookshop that winners of Indian prizes (even of a prize instituted by the chain of bookshops this one belonged to) were pushed into a corner on the lowest shelf, whereas the Indian Booker Prize winners (and other books by these authors) were proudly displayed. Even worse, where were the kind of books which had formed the bulk of my reading as a girl—the middle ground books like those of Daphne du Maurier, Nevil Shute or Graham Greene? Where was the choice for a reader with her or his own taste in books? It seems that publishers, in the interests of mass selling, have learnt to dumb down readers' tastes and bookshops have no choice but to display only these mass-selling books. The reader can no longer have such an eclectic choice of reading as I had, can no longer experience the pleasure, like I did, of suddenly coming across an unknown author who delighted me. I remember 'discovering' Mrs Gaskell in this way, coming upon Trollope with a surprised pleasure, thinking, 'But, he's good!' And in later life too I have found some excellent books among the unknowns. *Disturbances in the Field*, for example, or

Bel Canto or *The Bird Artist*. If bookshops stock only what they consider safe and saleable, if critics follow the market and have lost their voice, what happens to the reader? And to literature? This matters even more today for IWE since we are seeing many new and interesting novels published in India and written, therefore, primarily for Indian readers. We need to find our own standards, which must come from the context of the place where these novels are located.

How do novels survive? By being read, by being talked about, by entering the canon. Above all, by being in print. Time, it is often said, is the best judge. But even time is powerless when books go out of print—and for reasons that have little to do with the merit of the book. Sara Paretsky, in an introduction to an anthology of crime stories written by women (*Sisters on the Case*), refers to a woman writer, Anna Katherine Green who, a century ago, created detective Ebenezer Gryce (a decade before Sherlock Holmes was born). And in 1915, Anna Katherine Green created an amateur woman detective, Violet Strange, long before Sara Paretsky herself and other women created such a character. But this author, her books and her characters are forgotten, they remain unknown, whereas Sherlock Holmes became a cult—this, because Conan Doyle's books remained in print and hers didn't.

Prizes notwithstanding, judging books is always a difficult task. How do we stamp one book as good, another as great? In Somerset Maugham's *The Moon and Sixpence*, an art critic brashly says that the only way of recognising merit is by success.[1] What is successful must be good. We seem to have come to that understanding today. Whereas, the truth is, in Margaret Atwood's words, 'We don't judge good stories by the application

---

[1] Somerset Maugham himself, who was never taken seriously by the critics, said, 'The critic I am waiting for is the one who will explain why, with all my faults, I have been read for so many years by so many people'.

of some set of external measurements ... We judge them by the way they strike us'.

Which states the truth: that the valuation of books can finally be done only by the reader. It is the reader who can and must judge for herself. How many readers are able to do this today and, even if they want to, what chance do they have of coming across books which may be the right book for them?

How to Read, or Rather, How Not to Read, the Writing of Women

This long title, more suited to a scientific paper, is also, I realise, flawed, because I am using the very category (i.e. the writing of women), which I strongly dispute; but it is the only way I can encapsulate what I am trying to say. The basic problem is that a woman author's text is still almost invariably read, not merely as a text, but as one written by a woman. Which means that many ideas about and stereotypes of women are inflicted on the writing, and, worse, the pejorative nuances which accompany the word 'woman' are foisted upon the writing as well. However, I will not get tangled in these issues which have been questioned and debated far too often. I would like to focus on one particular aspect of such a misreading of the text of a woman author, something I have become familiar with, because it continues to crop up in a very large number of academic responses to my work, and, I should imagine, to the responses to most women's work. This problem lies in subjecting women's writing to a 'tradition and modernity' test, so that the reading is one that perceives a conflict between tradition and modernity in the female protagonist. Subjecting every novel written by a woman to such a test is a vast oversimplification of both women's lives and the very concepts of tradition and modernity. And there are so many assumptions made in the course of such a reading that it is impossible to speak of all of them. I will bring up only a few points.

The first question I would ask is: are modernity and tradition two polarities, two distinct positions, opposed to one another? If this is how we regard them, then certainly it would seem that they can never coexist, and that a very positive effort needs to be made to bring them together. But this disregards the truth that these two are almost always operating simultaneously and continuously within all of us. We are inevitably caught up in both of these. Tradition, in the sense of a belief, a custom or a practice handed down to posterity (the dictionary meaning), is a natural and inevitable part of human life. Much of our lives—the way we live, the things we do, the ideas we believe in—comes to us from our immediate past, from our parents, and we in turn hand these down to our children. None of us starts with a blank sheet of paper—no, not even a child without parents or family, because even that child would imbibe much from the place she/he is nurtured in. The way we live our individual and social lives, our religious practices and even our social and political institutions are to a large extent shaped by tradition.

Nevertheless, it is equally true of human life that nothing remains unchanged, that nothing is fixed forever—except perhaps human nature. Change is a part of life itself, movement and flux the concomitants of it. Yet, the human desire for the safety and security of the known makes us conjure up an illusion of an unchanging world. Certain things, we like to think, never change. At the same time, it is also the nature of humans to be restless, to crave for movement, which is what propels humans into wanting change. Adventure and risks are a part of human history, as important as tradition, perhaps even more important, because the people we admire, the people we salute, are the innovators, those who brought about change. We are constantly searching for new worlds, both outside and inside us. The discovery of fire, the invention of the wheel, the tilling of soil and growing of food, keeping cattle, taming horses—all these emerged from human restlessness and questing, from the need to push the frontiers of living.

Life, therefore, is a continuous play of a desire for change, as well as the need for the known and the familiar. These two do not war against each other, but work together, creating a seamless and meaningful pattern of human life. Tradition is our link to the past. Yet, we don't want to get bogged down in the past because practical living becomes impossible otherwise: this is a human concern and is not confined to one sex. When this is how it is, to say that women are different, that they are more faithful to tradition and averse to change, is to set them apart from these human traits, from the story of humanity itself, it is to deny them their humanness and emphasise their 'femaleness'. To say that women are more wary of change is a generalisation that refuses to take into account this factor of the humanness of women. Undoubtedly, women, as bearers of children and nurturers of the young, look for security and safety for their young. But this does not wholly obliterate the human need for change, or the restlessness that craves for something more than the known. The human quest for knowledge, a very innate urge, has not bypassed women. Acquiring knowledge means questioning, thinking for yourself, it means turning your back on the unquestioning acceptance of any custom or practice that clashes with this knowledge, however hallowed the custom or practice is. It is possible that the status of women and their subordination to men has made it difficult, if not impossible for them to challenge any practice or custom openly. Which, however, does not mean that all traditions were wholeheartedly accepted and willingly practiced.

There's this too: to look back at human history is to see a continuous process of change, sometimes a swift change, at other times a gradual transformation. The old is constantly being replaced by the new. Ways of living, dress, practices, institutions—all these have changed through the ages. So, what are these traditions which we regard as sacrosanct and which women are supposed to be so loyal to? It is the family, the home consisting of parents, children, grandchildren, siblings, which we hold on to even today as the one safe unchanging place in a changing world. It is the tradition of the family itself, as well as the traditions within the family, that we cherish, it is these that women are supposed to uphold and be steadfast to—an important and a much-lauded role which has been given to them and which they, so we are told, are performing with great sincerity.

There is no doubt that the family is of enormous importance, perhaps more so today because it seems to be threatened; we are realising that it is not something we can take for granted. It is regarded, at least in theory, as a sacred place, something a man has to defend and a woman to nurture. At the same time, it is also the less important place; the outside world is where things happen, it is the place where important events take place. This is like the idea of women itself, which swerves between an abstract ideal of their enormous importance and the actuality of their total insignificance. But the reality of the family was, I think, correctly spelt out in Engel's statement that in a family the man is the bourgeois, the woman the proletariat. The fact is that the family, as it is, has been shaped by men for their purposes: to have children they can be sure are their own, to ensure that their property is passed on to their legitimate male heirs. Ironically, or maybe cheekily, women were put in charge of ensuring that the family survived in this form, they were made the upholders of the tradition of the family itself, as well as of traditions within the family. To hear a person speak of the importance of an heir, of the fears of the family line being extinct, to listen to talk of family traditions and honour, is to understand how much we have made ourselves believe in these illusions about the family. And most of these illusions are linked to women accepting their given roles. The family rests so strongly on this foundation that every small change in the status of women has seemed to threaten the existence of the family itself. It is the family which, more than any other institution, has perpetuated the subjection of women and fixed their roles and places in it so firmly and definitely that these have become almost sacred and untouchable. And, therefore, to challenge these traditional roles and duties required more courage than most ordinary women would have. Yet, to say that women are willing upholders of tradition, that they wholeheartedly support existing traditions, is to close our eyes to some of these truths. It also means ignoring the dissenting minority, a silent minority, perhaps, but one that is part of all human groups. This minority is of great importance in human history, because it is with the dissenting, thinking minority that every change begins. We also need to remember that silence does not always mean acquiescence; human beings are ingenious: they can always contrive to step beyond the permissible. Women, because of the restrictions they have always had to contend with, are even more clever in this. They have used the little space allowed to them, worked out strategies that subverted the rules and masked protest, as well as rebellion.

This apart, the family has changed over the centuries, as well. The concepts of democracy and individuality, urbanisation, greater possibilities of movement, easier communication, contraception, literacy, women going out to work, the increasing number of nuclear families—all these have changed the family structure greatly from what it was. Many of these factors have also weakened the power that the family wielded over its members. Consequently, women's lives have changed enormously. Most women have welcomed the change; they are receptive to the change partly because it has often meant an improvement in their lives, partly because of pragmatism. It is important, as I said earlier, to make life possible. To be part of the world, to play one's role in the world as well as inside the home, not to have one's entire life dictated by others—why would women not want these things? To believe that they uphold traditions—which are almost always restrictive and confining of women—is to imply that they accept these restrictions that have been imposed upon them by males in their own interests.

Moving on from the reality in the world to writing, the next question that I need to ask is: What is meant by women writers synthesising tradition and modernity? Are women writers supposed to be following the same path in their writing as women are presumed to be treading in their lives? Are women writers specially desirous of and specially equipped to do this synthesising because of their gender? Do men have no desire to do this? Or are the men incapable of it because of their gender? And is this synthesising a virtue only in women, but not in men, like brashness, which is frowned upon in women, but not in men? But, mainly, can we continue to regard women writers as a separate species? Yes, we do carry our gender differences into our writing, but so do we carry the other differences as well. Each of us is unique, with experiences and an imaginary world none else can have; in fact, we carry our baggage of differences with us whatever we do. Gender difference is but one of these. And yet, the basic truth is that when a writer is writing, she is purely a writer, converting these experiences, ideas and all else into writing in almost exactly the same manner a man would. Just as important is the fact that writers write of individuals, not of a generic group. The singular, the particular, the one-human—this is what the writer is concerned with. So, when I am writing, I am not writing of a generic class called 'women'; I am writing of one individual. It could be a woman called Jaya analysing herself, her life and her relationships at a critical moment in her life, looking at the man-woman relationship with special care because of her understanding that her gender has shaped her life and relationships to a great extent. At the end of this frightfully honest self-analysis, Jaya has changed. The idea that after this she goes back to the point she started off from is laughable, because, what then does it make of this intelligent, thinking woman's self-introspection? And her decision does not come, at least not wholly, out of her being a woman; it comes out of her human intelligence and human understanding. This decision is not imposed upon her by the writer, either. To imagine that I as a writer, having certain thoughts about how women should live their lives, impose these ideas on the characters I create, is to deny the entire wonderful process of creativity and how it works. If Jaya decides to continue with her marriage, it is not because she is accepting the traditional role of a wife; on the contrary, she has rejected all the traditional ideas of roles in the course of her thinking. As she says, she has begun to see the world differently. And, therefore, she goes back into the marriage a changed person, knowing her life can never be the same again.

The problem of imagining that women writers lean towards the traditional comes from what I can only call the disease of reading a book as one written by a writer who is a woman and who is, therefore, presumed to have a certain mindset. Both the writer and her characters trapped, apparently, in the image of upholders of tradition. Why is it, I was once asked by an academic, that your women who are troubled by patriarchy, who suffer under it, don't rebel? I had to wonder what he meant by rebel. Loud gestures, apparently, angry sounds, perhaps, like the banging of a door. To expect this is to imagine that a writer sets out a situation with problems and issues and that these are finally resolved clearly and decisively. To think that the characters in my novel should rebel against patriarchy also presumes that I have set out to give a clear and loud message against some social wrongs. That the novel is written to work out this manifesto. To go on from this to thinking that, because there is no such loud and clear message in the novel, the writer is advocating a status quo, a return to the earlier position, with nothing changed, or, at the least, only a carefully and cautiously worked out compromise that allows for the injection of a little of the new, is to miss the point entirely. I, as a person, would like women to be decisive and firm, to stand out against injustice. Like Aru in *A Matter of Time*, I am impatient with those who put up, or seem to put up with wrongs, who don't fight it. But at the end of the novel Aru realises that her mother and grandmother, the two women who she felt were refusing to fight, were coping in their own ways. She understands that an active resistance is not the only way of warring. She herself will always be an active fighter, but she understands that there are other equally valid ways of fighting. So do I, as a writer, know that humans differ, that they will respond to situations in different ways.

The idea that a woman writer accepts the status quo also ignores a very important truth about writing: that writers write because they are troubled with the way things are in the world, they are angry about any form of injustice. It is this dissatisfaction, this anger, that is the driving force of all serious writing, whether by men or by women. Charlotte Brontë's *Jane Eyre* is a classic example of a woman's suppressed anger against the confines of her life. Jane's restlessness, her agitation lead her to think: '... restlessness was in my nature; it agitated me to pain sometimes.' Naturally, Charlotte Brontë was very critical of Jane Austen. *Pride and Prejudice*, she said, is 'a carefully-fenced, highly cultivated garden'. 'The Passions are perfectly unknown to her', she said about Jane Austen at another time. In other words, no restlessness, no agitation in Jane Austen's novels. Jane Austen has also been criticised for having ignored the world in her novels, unlike the writers who came after her. The novels of Charlotte herself, of George Eliot and Mrs Gaskell contended with unpleasant social realities. It took a much later writer, Julia Kavanagh, to judge Jane Austen differently. 'If we look under the shrewdness and quiet satire of her stories', she said, 'we shall find a much keener sense of disappointment than of joy fulfilled'. The subtext of her novels reveals her awareness of a woman's sad lack of financial independence. Something which she and her sister Cassandra, spinsters both, had to cope with. After their father's death, they (and their mother) had to depend on their brothers' generosity, specially Edward, who was better off than the others. And in return they had to be available to Edward's family whenever needed. 'Single women have a dreadful propensity for being poor', Jane wrote to a niece. Obviously, when she began earning money from her novels, it meant much to her. The money 'signified not only success, however modest, but freedom. She could give presents and plan travels'—Claire Tomalin's words in her biography of Jane Austen.

Yes, Jane knew that money mattered. In a letter to Cassandra, she pleads with her to accept a gift. 'Don't deny me', she writes, 'I am very rich'. Jane's novels tell us, if in a very nuanced way, that a woman's financial dependence on a man was galling, that the lives of women without their own money meant humiliation and acceptance of servility. No, Jane Austen was in no way upholding the status quo. Through her pictures of bad marriages, of Mr and Mrs Bennet in *Pride and Prejudice*, of the Palmers in *Sense and Sensibility*, she criticises marriages which resulted from a passing physical attraction and led to unmatched couples and unsuitable marriages. And behind the façade of Mrs Bennet's foolish habit of chasing husbands for her daughters, there was the entail. The lack of a son meant that the widow and her daughters would lose the estate, which would go instead to the nearest male heir. Mrs Bennet's desperation to have Elizabeth marry Mr Collins has much to do with keeping the estate and family home within the family. And Charlotte Lucas accepting Collins was a practical decision, made purely to attain the status of a married woman; his foolishness meant nothing as against her freedom from dependence. In fact, Jane Austen's novels are replete with her subtle criticism of the society of her times.

The problem of reading a woman writer through the narrow focus of her gender is compounded by the fact that the text is now also subjected to a feminist reading. This demands a conclusion in conformity with the generally accepted ideas of feminism. The question asked of the text is: do you adhere to the feminist ideology? But the truth is that women, like all humans, have many forces working on them, often at the same time. There's history, culture, religious and political faiths and beliefs, the class and family you are born in, family beliefs, the people with whom you live, relationships and mutual expectations. Feminism is but one of these forces working on women's lives and feminism is something each woman will see differently. And therefore, decisions differ; all women cannot take the same path. Nor are the alternatives confined to rebelling or conforming, walking out or remaining as a victim. There are many contradictions in the choices made, much confusion before a choice is made, if at all. Which, according to the critic looking for feminism in a woman's writing, is not acceptable. But it is this rather complex situation that the writer portrays. It seems to me that women writers today are very honestly presenting the dilemmas and the ambiguities of women's life, often with great subtlety, sometimes brilliantly. For example, K.R. Usha's English story 'Sepia Tones', which looks at the Annapurna image thrust on women with amazing clarity, Pratibha Ray's Oriya story *The Curse* which deals with women's hungers, including sexual hunger in an almost tongue-in-cheek way, C.S. Lakshmi's Tamil story 'A Kitchen in the Corner of the House', which uses a small space in a kitchen to say many significant things about women's lives, Maitreyi Pushpa's Hindi story 'Faisla' which conveys with touching honesty a woman's problem of choosing between being true to herself or to a relationship. My own story 'A Wall Is Safer' has as its protagonist a woman who has opted to give up her career in the interests of family life. She is not happy with the purely domestic life she is leading, but she does not regret the choice she has made; she knows she could have done nothing else. Nor does she look upon herself as the victim; it is her choice and she is willing to live with it, to live with the regrets as well. Is this woman accepting traditions and rejecting modernity? I don't think so. I see this as a pragmatic decision, which is as feminist as a decision to go on with her career at the cost of dividing a family. The point is that the greatest revolutions can take place in the mind; all revolutions begin there. How this thinking is translated into action is another thing; it is not necessary to walk out, to commit adultery, to divorce, to show defiance or a rejection of tradition. None of these are modern, anyway. Adultery is as old as the hills and so is ending a marriage. But each person takes a decision depending on the circumstances of her/his life. The point is having knowledge, the point is being able to act on that knowledge, the point is taking responsibility for one's decision.

Another way of misinterpreting is by putting what has been said in the text within the framework of women's roles in society, of trying to fit the text within these confines. My novel, *The Dark Holds No Terrors*, has an open ending, yet it is most often read as ending in a way that is sympathetic to what society expects of a woman (that she goes back to her marriage); I find this very revealing and infuriating. There is this too, that the title of rebel often comes at the cost of fresh stereotypes, different from the old ones certainly, but doing nothing to set the picture right. But this is the only way it seems that the woman's voice can be heard.

Truly, human lives are fascinating, the choices people make myriad, based on factors which perhaps they are unable to wholly grasp themselves. Most human lives are also incredibly confused, and it is exactly out of this confusion that a writer writes. To read a novel only as a novel written by a woman is to miss out much, indeed most of it. To read it as a feminist text, or see it through the lenses of feminism, is to dismiss everything in it that does not resonate with feminist tones. In other words, it is a gross misreading, not a reading. Readers, specially academic readers, need to go into the text without the baggage of expectations that they carry with them, expectations that come from seeing the writer as a woman, a woman of these times who ought to write in a certain way about women. To look for an infusion of feminism in the book and when it is not there, at least in the way it is expected to be, to conclude that the character—and the writer as well—is opting for tradition, is to presume that women are less writers and more social activists. We need to learn to read women's text without these blinkers. To understand that when a woman writes, she is first a writer and then a woman. It is absolutely necessary to get out of the bog of seeing any writing shaped *only* by the gender of the writer.

Above all, we need to remember that in writing, in expressing themselves and in giving in to the urge for self-expression, women are doing what they were not supposed to be doing. When a woman writes, she is in fact flouting tradition; she is proclaiming herself and saying, 'I will speak, I will say what I want to say'. The very process of writing is a loud declaration of the self—something that tradition barred her from.

Macaulay's People

Writers rarely trouble themselves with abstract questions about writing. However, very early on in my writing career I found myself confronted by the question of where my writing belonged. A question that perhaps came out of the absolute isolation in which I wrote: I did not know any writers who wrote in English, I had not read any books like the ones I wrote/was writing, I had no response from readers to my writing. In fact, I did not know whether I had any readers at all. My writing seemed to fall into an abyss so deep that I did not get back even the faintest whisper of an echo. I had seen my father, a writer in Kannada, living in the midst of his literary world, enjoying discussions with friends, writer-colleagues, admirers, having a play reading each time after writing a new play. I remember him reading, a crowd sitting around him in rapt silence, I remember the lively discussions that often followed. When, years later, a friend asked me why I didn't read out from my writing to a group, I was taken aback until I realised that he came from a tradition of reading/reciting poetry aloud to the accompaniments of 'Wah Wahs' from the listeners. A tradition that belonged to writing in the Indian languages (bhashas), not to English. (This was way before literary events and festivals.) I smiled at my friend's ignorance, blissfully unaware that I had mentally separated English writing from bhasha writing.

However, when I read a review of Zadie Smith's essays *Changing My Mind*, the reviewer's reference to Smith's congenial attitude to her literary past, which made the writing of her novel *On Beauty* possible, made me understand that this novel was her tribute to E.M. Forster's *Howards End*. And that it was possible for her to connect herself to Forster and *Howards End* because she belonged to the same tradition. Was there any writer to whom I could connect myself in the same way? I remembered with some embarrassment that I had once, when asked during an interview about my influences, connected myself to the English writers Jane Austen, the Brontës, Mrs Gaskell, George Eliot. I did realise in time that this was not wholly true, because my writing was deeply rooted in my society. And in any case, after reading F.R. Leavis' book *The Great Tradition*, I no longer dared to put myself in the company of the English writers. Leavis, in his book, traces a clear line of tradition of the Great English Novel, beginning with Jane Austen, going on to George Eliot, James Conrad, Henry James and D.H. Lawrence. With this, Leavis firmly—and rightly—shut the door in my face.

In any case, I had become aware by then that my place was in the midst of the great sprawl of Indian literature in multiple languages. Surely there was room for English among the many languages that made up Indian Literature? But it was not that simple. If this meant that I belonged to the class of Indian writers who wrote in English, something in me protested. The extreme simplicity of R.K. Narayan's world, the self-conscious spiritualism of Raja Rao, the earthiness of Mulk Raj Anand, as well as his language, and the slight contempt for India that lay under all Ruth Praver Jhabvala's writing—how could I put my writing among these? The language alone could not link me to them. At the same time, the bhasha writers made it clear that English writing had no place in Indian literature. That it could not belong, not only because the language, English, was the language of the colonisers, but also because it was impossible to convey Indian culture in this foreign language. And, an even greater sin, Indian English writers wrote for a Western readership, they wrote to make money. Mercenaries, in other words.

So where, then, did I belong? And more importantly, did it matter? Was it necessary to belong somewhere? It did matter. Looking back now, I can trace the struggle I had in writing my two early novels, *The Dark Holds No Terrors* and *That Long Silence* to this very fact of my being so isolated. An isolation enhanced by the fact that at the time I began writing (the late sixties and the early seventies), there was a hiatus in Indian English writing; it was as if someone had hit the pause button. The older writers were flagging and there were few new names emerging. Since I had no role models, I had to write entirely out of myself, so to say, to find my own language. Language is always a problem when writing in English about people living in India, most of whom do not speak English. Many of the early writers had found their own way of coping with this problem, but I knew that I did not want to write like any of them. I would go my own way. Jane Austen, when she wrote *Northanger Abbey,* was revolting against the tradition of the Gothic novel, so popular at that time. Whereas I, when I began writing, never consciously thought that I was writing in English; how then could I revolt against something which I never took into account? To add to my problems, one of the novels I was writing (*The Dark Holds No Terrors*) was about rape and sadism in marriage, about a woman's success emasculating a man. And the one I was to write after this (*That Long Silence*) was almost a long monologue by a woman sitting within the four walls of her home, trying to understand herself and her life, thinking of her relationships and her roles—all these defined by her gender. They were not easy novels to write. But what was most difficult, even more than the language, was to find my own voice. Which I ultimately did. And with the voice came the language.

In the course of time, in spite of my misgivings about Indian English writing, I found myself becoming, to my own surprise, a supporter of the writing. I was not an enthusiastic champion of Indian English writing like Prof. P. Lal. I was aware of many drawbacks, a number of flaws in the writing; there was much that made me uneasy. But I fervently believed that writers had the right to write in the language they wanted to, and I could never agree that language barred a writer from excellence. However, I disagreed with Prof. Lal when he called the Indian writer in English an 'Alien Insider'. Alien? Did he too think, like the bhasha writers, that writing in English was rootless? Didn't this writing have its roots in India? Everyone, that is, everyone who is even slightly knowledgeable, knows that it was Thomas Babington Macaulay's *Minute on Education*, arguing strongly for English education for Indians, which was the beginning of the use of the English language in India. This was in 1835. Speaking in the British Parliament, Macaulay made a demand for 'creating a class [of Indians] who may be interpreters between us and the millions we govern'. Surprisingly, there was great enthusiasm, even among some Indians about English education. Ram Mohan Roy, the revered reformer and writer, sang songs of praise to the English language, as did the poet Michael Madhusudan Dutt. For many Indians, English was the symbol of modernisation and Westernisation, which our own culture, tired and flawed, badly needed.

The irony was that English, which was to be used to make Indians better servitors of the British, became a link language for Indians during the freedom struggle. And, what was not expected either, the language was also adopted by Indians for creative writing. Michael Madhusudan Dutt, Henry L.V. Derozio, and later, Toru Dutt—all of them wrote poetry in English. Ram Mohan Roy's prose writings and Bankim Chandra's first novel *Rajmohan's Wife* were in English. Bankim Chandra later moved on to his own language, Bengali, and was in his time so popular that his novels were translated into almost all Indian languages. An intriguing fact that I got from the massive work on Indian Literature brought out by the Sahitya Akademi (*A History of Indian Literature, 1800–1910: Western Impact, Indian Response. Volume VIII*) was that Bankim Chandra's historical novels were influenced by Walter Scott's novels and that even Wilkie Collins had some influence—something which may surprise English haters and baiters, who look at bhasha literatures as being pristine, wholly uncorrupted by foreign influence. And what would, perhaps, be equally surprising to them is the fact that some new literary genres came to India with the English language: the novel, the short story, the essay, genres which were taken to great heights by writers like Bankim Chandra, Sarat Chandra Chatterjee, Premchand, Rabindranath Tagore, and many more. Shakespeare was immensely popular and was translated into almost all the Indian languages. Gandhiji's journal *Harijan* was trilingual, in Hindi, Gujarati and English. Certainly, English language writing in India had a respectable, even an honourable beginning.

Yet, compared to the literatures in the bhashas, English writing was a poor plant. Taking the example of Kannada literature, there were, in the middle of the last century, two intellectual centres in the Kannada-speaking areas—Mysore and Dharwad. It was a lively scene and Kannada literature grew in vigour and strength. Novels, poetry, drama, essays—all the genres flourished, and readers responded to the writing with enthusiasm. English, however, had few writers, not many readers, and a widely dispersed readership at that. It did have a recognition outside the country, though, which made it almost parasitically dependent on the appreciation of Western critics, on endorsements from the West. Which, in turn, led to Indian English writers suffering from what Meenakshi Mukherjee, the critic, calls the 'anxiety of Indianness', this Indianness being a quality their books needed to travel abroad. In fact, English writing allowed critics and writers outside the country to establish a standard of excellence for itself. Unlike American literature, where, according to a theory by feminist critic Nina Baym (in *The New Feminist Criticism*), early American critics felt that, having liberated themselves from England, they could not have English literature as the standard of excellence for American writing. They therefore decided on 'Americanness' as a standard, which became part of the American tradition, like 'Indianness' was of Indian English.

Indian English writing was later called postcolonial, or even more unfortunate, Commonwealth writing, misnomers both these terms. It meant wrenching a literature out of its place, trying to plant it where it did not belong—and this only because of the language. 'The Empire strikes back' theory, an offshoot of this, was an even more skewed way of looking at the writing from India. To connect English writing to a short-lived foreign power seemed to me to be illogical and ridiculous. I had no doubt that English writing was part of the literature of India, a literature whose beginnings went back to very ancient times.

Meenakshi Mukherjee speaks of Indian writing having a discontinuous tradition. Which was proven when *Midnight's Children* by Salman Rushdie entered the scene. This novel made a complete break from the earlier tradition. Nothing like it had been seen before in Indian English writing. An epic novel with a large canvas, the nation as the backdrop, it was flamboyant, did away with glossaries and explanations and brought the Indian English novel firmly mainstream and centre stage. It won the Booker Prize, and many talented writers followed Rushdie, a number of them taking to Rushdie's magic realism. This was a generation born after Independence and far removed from British influence. It was also a time when India moved out of its protective cover and opened the country to the world. It was simultaneously the era of globalisation as well as of economic liberalisation. Paradoxically, even as English writing in India found a place for itself in the country of its birth—the Sahitya Akademi included it in the list of languages under its umbrella, its annual award given to books in English as well—the writing became more international than before. Indians became known names on the international scene: Vikram Seth, Amitav Ghosh, Rohinton Mistry, Kiran Desai, later Jhumpa Lahiri and many more. Expatriate writers dominated the scene. (Arundhati Roy was an exception, as was Aravind Adiga, later.) These English writers were a talented group. Born after Independence, they were not conscious of the fact that they were writing in English as the earlier writers had been. Self-confident and assured, they wrote literary fiction which found appreciative readers the world over. It certainly helped that at this time there were Indian academicians and critics in the Western, mainly American universities, critics who brought Indian writing, both in English and in translation, to the notice of the Western world. Countries, specially in Europe, held literary festivals which celebrated Indian English writing. Even I, who was not one of the internationally known writers, went during this time to festivals in France, Germany, Australia, South Africa, Spain.

Material circumstances matter to writers and writing. As Virginia Woolf pithily put it, 'Dogs will bark; people will interrupt; money must be made; health will break down'. Economic liberalisation meant that suddenly there were more publishers in India. Which in turn meant that writers in English were now primarily writing for a readership within the country. A readership which had now grown to a respectable number, mainly because of the lure of English education. An Indian readership also meant that nothing had to be explained, nothing contextualised. English writing got a boost like never before. We no longer had to keep banging on the closed doors of Western agents/publishers. But as against this, there were two not very happy consequences of the success of English writing abroad. Indian writers who were not, for various reasons, published abroad, found themselves being ignored even at home. And bhasha writing and English writing, which had earlier been linked, however precariously, by nationalism, now seemed cut off from each other. The success of English writing also made the bhasha writers take up an adversarial position as never before. If nationalism had linked the two, the success of English writing split them wide apart. Meenakshi Mukherjee's statement of English writing having a 'discontinuous tradition' seemed justified, because Rushdie and the writers who came after him, took no note at all of the earlier English writing—of Raja Rao, R. K. Narayan, and Mulk Raj Anand and their contemporaries.

This disjuncture was proven yet again in the new century when a fresh breed of young writers emerged. A young writer, Chetan Bhagat, wrote a novel which spoke directly to a generation of global Indians, young people who travelled easily between India and the West. His novels *Five Point Someone* and *One Night @ the Call Centre* became wildly popular and gave him a whole lot of readers, beneficiaries of the global world like the writer himself. Chetan Bhagat's writing, like Rushdie's, also spawned a whole lot of new writers, who seemed to have no connection to the writers just before them. There was a complete break from the earlier tradition. But this time, the writers did not ignore their predecessors, they spoke openly against the writers who had come after Rushdie, they spoke with disdain of literary fiction, of the language used by these writers. Our readers can understand our language better, they claimed. There was no doubt that they were a success and their books sold like books in India had rarely done. Their success gave these writers the confidence to ignore the Western market, which had been the hallmark of success for earlier writers.

There is an interesting twist to the tale, because some of the new breed of writers ventured into mythology, to retelling stories from the Puranas and the epics. This genre has become extremely popular among readers who had perhaps lost touch with their past, eagerly wanting a taste of old stories. This is something totally unexpected. Or perhaps not, for one of the factors that influences a literary tradition is zeitgeist, the spirit of the age. The reignited interest in the epics and puranas may be connected to the political ideology that is now dominating India, the policy of Hindutva, of glorifying our past. Which only goes to show how many things influence a tradition. Purity and corruption are words which cannot really applied to a tradition. Society, people's lives and ideas and literature are twisted together into one skein.

When, recently, I saw an English book on the Mahabharata translated into Kannada, I thought it unusual. Kannada books were often translated into English, but English books, specially works of contemporary writers, were rarely translated into Kannada. But perhaps it is the great hostility towards English writing and writers that should seem strange, for our history, our tradition, is one of multilingualism. I was fascinated to read in Stewart Gordon's book, *The Marathas (1600–1818)*, of the confluence of languages in South India in the seventeenth century. I quote him: 'The language of the Dakkanis (Muslims who had been living in the South for generations) was a mixture of the Arabic and Persian of their origins, the North Indian Urdu of their past, the Sanskrit of Brahmins, and the Marathi, Telugu and Kannada of their subjects.'

Today when I hear or read writers and critics in the bhashas being critical of 'Western influence', condemning those who follow the 'Western model', I think of the easy mixing of languages in India earlier. And I think of the poet A.K. Ramanujan who said, 'I am the hyphen in Indian-American', the man who wrote poetry both in Kannada and English, who translated classical poetry from Tamil and devotional poetry from both Kannada and Tamil. He rejected nothing but absorbed everything into himself. It was not just Ramanujan, a number of Indian poets wrote poetry in English, poetry which was wholly Indian in spirit. Arun Kolatkar's long poem *Jejuri* is a splendid example of a poem which is very much in the Indian tradition, if in English. This is the tradition I would claim if I were asked to speak of influences. Literature rarely comes out of negation. It is not, no, never *Neti, Neti, Neti*. (Not this, not this, not this.) It is always *It is this, it is this, it is this.*

(2020)

Section IV

TEXTS AND GENRES

On Poetry

There are fashions and changing trends in literature just as there are in clothes; different genres come to the forefront at different times, rule for a while and then, slowly, imperceptibly, God knows for what reason, move away to give place to another genre. It has been the time of the novel for quite some time now in the field of English writing in India. I am told that publishers when approached with short stories suggest, 'Why don't you write a novel? We might look at that'. And so, even an excellent short story writer will put the stories aside and embark on a novel. In the last few years, the trend is changing slightly and non-fiction seems to be gaining ground with readers and publishers. Amartya Sen's book, *The Argumentative Indian*, is said to have sold more copies than any recent novel, Suketu Mehta's *Maximum City* has been a bestseller, Ramchandra Guha's books on recent Indian history and on Mahatma Gandhi are much-read and William Dalrymple's latest book seems to be on the way to success as well. Will this trend change too and, if it does, what genre will take over? One thing we can be sure of: it won't be poetry. At this moment, poetry is a complete non-starter. This, though the country looks like it is teeming with poets. The problem about poetry is that it seems to be dreadfully easy to write. Which accounts, perhaps, for the large number of amateur poets. But where are the readers for poetry today? I find that even the novices (*specially* the novices!) read no poetry other than their own. And the remorseless logic of business dictates that if there are not enough readers, publishers are not interested—not even, unfortunately, in good poetry.

And yet, human creative expression began with poetry. To watch a child's delight in rhymes is to get a glimpse of our past. Besides, oral texts needed to be memorised, which is why most early texts are in verse, which is easier to memorise. In our country, from the Vedas and the epics to the *Bhagwad Gita*, everything was in verse. Drama, later the only competitor, also had shlokas interspersed in the dialogue and dramatists like Kalidasa were excellent poets as well. When they called drama 'drishya kavya' (visible poetry), they were paying it the highest compliment, for poetry was considered the highest form of literature, the best form of creative expression. In fact, the writer was a poet and a poet the writer. And while most of the writing was religious, there were also romantic poets, the same as there are now. There's some incredibly romantic—and erotic—love poetry in Sanskrit. Here's a poem, supposedly written by a woman: 'All I remember is / I was in his arms, / but who he was, and who I was, / and what we did—/ well ...' (From *Sanskrit Love Lyrics*, transcreated by P. Lal). The poetry of Bilhana (an eleventh-century poet), even in translation, can bring on goosebumps. Equally remarkable is the early classical Tamil poetry, which has been so beautifully translated by A.K. Ramanujan. Truly, we have a great tradition of poetry. Bhakti poetry (devotional poetry) flourished in all the languages at one time. It was a movement in which the most dispossessed, including lower-caste men (and women, who, whatever their class or caste, were not allowed to read and write), spoke to God in their own language, bypassing Sanskrit, which was in any case barred to them. The language used was simple, something most would understand. The Bhakti movement, as it is now termed, was a democratic movement, those who had been given a low place in the caste hierarchy asserting themselves and moving away from the pervasive Brahmin influence. The songs are sung even today and are hugely popular. All classical music sessions end with devotional poetry. Each one of the saint-poets, as they came to be called, has a wonderful story of how they left the world and devoted themselves to God. There's a story of an illiterate woman, Bahinabai, living in a village in Maharashtra, who sang while she worked in her home, songs which she created herself. She could not write and, if not for her son who wrote them down, they would have been lost. Then there are the ghazals, poetry of love and loss, written mainly in Urdu and yes, the always-loved lyrics written for films. At one time, poets who wrote lyrics for films gave us wonderful unforgettable songs, in which the words and the music came together in a remarkable harmony. Even its use as a jingle for an advertisement cannot destroy the magic of '*musafir hoon yaaron, na ghar hai na thikana* ...' (I am a traveller, friends, I have neither home nor a place of my own). There's a wonderful song sung by Mohammed Rafi, who was one of the most popular of playback singers: '*Sukh me sab saathi, dukh me na koi*' (In happiness everyone is with you, in grief there is no one). And there's Mukesh with his incomparable voice singing '*Sajan re jhooth mat bolo, khuda ke paas jaana hai, na hathi hai na ghoda hai, wahan paidal hi jaana hai*' (Dear love, don't tell me lies, you have to face God one day. There are no horses or elephants there, you have to walk). Wah! I think it's fairly clear now that I loved film music.

Sadly, the poetry taught to us in school seemed to be devoid of any magic. It was merely stuff to be learnt and memorised. We grumbled, we read the poems reluctantly; and yet, I am surprised that so much has stayed with me over the years. There's 'If I should die, think only this of me' from Rupert Brooke's 'The Soldier', lines we read tearfully, in choked voices. And 'In Xanadu did Kubla Khan a stately pleasure dome decree ...' from Coleridge's 'Kubla Khan'. 'She left the web, she left the loom ...' from Tennyson's 'The Lady of Shalott'. And Keats's 'Now more than ever seems it rich to die / To cease upon the midnight with no pain'. I thought Wordsworth boring, his love of Nature pretentious and exaggerated, but who can forget 'I wandered lonely as a cloud' from 'Daffodils'? Or Yeats' 'I will arise and go now and go to Innisfree'? A poem, we were told, conceived when the poet was standing in the midst of the busy traffic at Charing Cross.

Daffodils? Charing Cross?

The point was that the English poetry we studied had no context. There we were in a small school in small-town India reading poems written by men (yes, I realise now, mostly by men) who lived in times and countries we knew little about. I learnt much later that English poetry was at its peak from about the middle of the eighteenth to the end of the nineteenth century when remarkable poets wrote remarkable poetry and led remarkable lives. Romance still surrounds their names, and their lives as well as their poetry have become legend. Keats is famous as the genius who died tragically young. Shelley, the man who lived and loved passionately and whose drowned body was found with a volume of poetry in his pocket. Byron, another great lover, who loved many women, including his sister, but not his wife. And there's the story of Robert Browning's love affair and elopement with another poet, Elizabeth Barrett—one of the great love stories of literature. Talking of Browning, a friend of mine once quoted to me, entire, his poem 'My Last Duchess', which gave me gooseflesh when she reached the lines: 'Then all smiles stopped together. There she stands / As if alive'. This poem was no favourite of mine, until my friend recited it. Truly, poetry must be recited. Specially a poem like 'My Last Duchess', which is extremely dramatic.

When my two teenaged sons were in their crucial years of college, I decided to do my MA. There were times when it seemed a terrible mistake, an exercise in futility. What did I want an MA degree for? Yet, looking back now, I have no regrets. How can there be any when it made me read John Donne's poetry (which was like a clap of thunder and a flash of lightning), Shakespeare's sonnets, Emily Dickinson, T.S. Eliot. Would I have read this poetry otherwise?

Well, this is a surprise! How is it that I, no poetry lover, am speaking of poetry with such fervour? It's because of the memorable lines that the poets offer us. Lines that can stun you. 'Busy old fool, unruly sun': this, the first line of a love poem by Donne, written over 400 years ago! And Shakespeare's 'The expense of spirit in a waste of shame / Is lust in action ...' Prose, said Coleridge, is words in their best order, while poetry is the best words in the best order. True. You can't get away with sloppiness in poetry. Flaws cannot be concealed under tons of words. Each word stands on its own, each word counts. Look at this: 'The sword of morning came down to cut me off from my lover' (From A.K. Ramanujan's translation of a classical Tamil poem). I can almost see a sword flashing down, light glinting off it, as I read this line.

A number of aspiring poets come to me with their poems. I'm not a good judge of poetry; nevertheless, I know that much of the poetry is simply dreadful. How can anyone believe that a sprinkling of 'thee' and 'thou' can convert bad writing into poetry? Don't they read the Indian poets and see how the language can be used? Though our poets are eclipsed by the novelists today, it was the poets in India who, according to me, were more successful in using English as a creative language. I think poets broke free of their colonial past earlier, they found their voices when the novelists were still struggling to find their own. We've had poets like Nissim Ezekiel, Kamala Das, Jayanta Mahapatra, A.K. Ramanujan, Arun Kolatkar, Dom Moraes, A.K. Mehrotra, Keki Daruwala—it's a long list of accomplished poets.

In recent times, poetry is finding its place in English writing: there are even festivals dedicated only to poetry. Something that was always part of the bhasha literatures, Kavi Sammelans (poets' meets) frequently took place and were very popular. What a pity that publishers are reluctant to publish poetry. It may not be financially viable, perhaps, but isn't it a crime to let a whole genre die of neglect? Why can't we have anthologies like *The Golden Treasury*? Why don't we have more tiny collections which you can keep in your purse or pocket and read when waiting for your bus, train, or flight, in the bank, or in the doctor's consulting room? Why don't magazines and newspapers give at least some space to poetry? I was excited when I found lines of poetry inscribed in the carriages in the Tube in London. Why can't we do that?

Is poetry then dying in India? Not if one sees how the internet has quickened interest in poetry. There are journals and magazines, such as *Muse India* and *Kavya Bharati*, where poets get published and find readers. And it is certainly not dying if one sees what is happening in the languages. I'm thinking of an event that happened in Bangalore recently. It was the reading of the poetry of a famous Kannada poet, D.R. Bendre. Some twenty enthusiasts, including eminent writers, journalists, actors and bureaucrats, read the poems, while an equally distinguished audience listened with rapt attention. The hall was overflowing; people sat on the floor, in aisles, stood outside in the corridor and on the staircase. In that room the dead poet came alive, his poetry came back, resonating in the listeners. I saw this in another event which celebrated the Marathi poet G.D. Madgulkar. The response of the crowd to the poetry was amazing. The poetry was not just read, or recited, it was sung. This is how it is in Kannada as well, the poetry of major poets being sung, the music composed by known composers. These songs become almost as popular as film songs. A friend told me (this was years back) that in Kerala, cab drivers played cassettes of poems by known poets, which had been converted into song, as they drove around.

I admit I was wrong. Yes, poetry is very much alive. And true, people need poetry because a single line or a stanza of poetry can encapsulate an entire human experience. As, for example, these lines of T.S. Eliot:

> As we grow older
> The world becomes stranger, the pattern more complicated
> Of dead and living.

It does, indeed!

(2006)

The Dreaded Denouement

'Emma', says Fay Weldon in her *Letters to Alice* (a must-read for every Jane Austen aficionado), 'opens with a paragraph which sends shivers of pleasure down my spine: it glitters with sheer competence: with the animation of the writer who has discovered power ...'

In fact, there are a great many books which open with confidence and competence, but many of them trail away (*Emma* does not) as if the writer is unable to keep up the level of energy with which she/he began. Actually, though the beginning is also, as every writer will confess, difficult, and going on, though a little easier, has many moments of stumbling and faltering, for some reason, the end is the most punishing. Going through an old notebook recently, I came across a record of my struggle to end a novel. It was my second novel and had moved without too many hiccups until I got near the end. It was when I was floundering about that I woke up one night with a few lines running in my mind. They were so clear that when I began to write them down, the lines almost wrote themselves. The sense of 'I got it!' unfortunately vanished in the morning, because these lines were, I realised, the beginning of the novel, not its end.

'In my beginning is my end', says T.S. Eliot. I could say about a novel: 'in my end is my beginning', because the end of a novel, the way I see it, seems, much rather, like a new beginning. The end of the novel I mentioned earlier (*The Dark Holds No Terrors*) was a new beginning for Saru. From that point on she would be setting her feet on a new path. But whichever way I see it, as a novelist I have to choose an arbitrary beginning and an end. At what point do I begin the story? Because the characters are already living their lives when I get to them. And at what point do I conclude? What happens afterwards?

A clear-cut ending is the easiest. To begin with 'once upon a time' and end with 'and they lived happily ever after'. To give the good their rewards and the wicked their punishment. 'Reader, I married him', Jane Eyre tells her readers, and we sigh in satisfaction. Marriage, in fact, was the staple ending of a great many novels. There's also the final parting, an ending like Nora's banging the door. And there's death, the greatest finale of all. Shakespeare, we have to admit, did endings superlatively well, on a grand scale, both in his comedies and tragedies. This kind of certainty no longer seems possible today, not for me anyway, who believes that there is no point of absolute certainty in any human life. No point which is the beginning or the end; life is a continuous flow.

I recognised with my first novel that finding a way to end the novel which was satisfactory, plausible and inevitable was never going to be easy. My problems are compounded by the fact that my novels rarely have a plot and because I never begin with a story. For the first novel I wrote, I had a plot and a number of neatly listed characters. That novel was never written; instead, I wrote quite another novel, *Roots and Shadows*. I never tried plotting a novel ever again. For me a novel begins with people who gradually take on a life of their own. As I come to know them better, I hear snatches of dialogue, I see them in certain situations. And there is what I call a central image, a picture that keeps me company through the writing of the novel. (In *The Binding Vine*, for example, it was the picture of a group of women and children sitting in a dimly lit room around an old steel trunk.) This is all. I know that there are writers who have a story line, even chapter summaries, when they begin. I don't, perhaps because I believe that people make things happen, that events happen because of the interaction among people. My characters, in other words, bring their stories along with them. I have to discover their stories as I write. Inevitably, the ending is unknown, shrouded in the dark.

What makes my job harder is that in my novels most things happen in the character's mind. In *That Long Silence,* for example, the ending had to come through Jaya's introspection, through a chaotic mass of memories. Nothing dramatic happens. Often, it is a change of vision, an understanding the character gets about herself/himself. I reach the point through a gradual unfolding, much like the opening of that wondrous flower, the Brahma Kamal, which Jiji and Raja watch together at the end of *Moving On*. A slow opening, petal by petal, finally revealing the flower. In *Small Remedies* there was a slowing down as I neared the end, a cessation of noise, a silence after all the turmoil and agony of Madhu's grief. This was the mood which surrounded me while I wrote. And the two scenes, that of the child's upanayanam, and of Hasina singing in the temple, were the slow steps leading to Madhu's recovery. It was a quiet reflective ending, a gradual winding down.

The point is each story carries its own ending within it. I cannot impose my own idea of how their story should end on the people I create. 'Why did Sumi die?' is the question often asked by readers who read *A Matter of Time*. 'It hurts', they say. It hurt me too. I did not want her to die. I wrote a version in which she lived. But somehow the truth of the story could not take this. I had to rewrite it the way it is now. I have to admit, though, that I enjoy the thought of getting to an unknown end. What excitement can there be, I often think, if I knew at the beginning what the end was going to be? Yes, it's true I have a vague picture of what might happen. But very often things take a different course, the unexpected steps in, as it does in life as well. When coming to the end of *Moving On,* I kept seeing a picture of Jiji and Raja jogging together companionably in an early misty morning. But, somehow, words never accompanied this picture. So I had to let it go and the end became what it is now, with Jiji trying to find the words for her relationship to Raja.

In any case, my novels never end with a bang, with a dramatic happening. Most often the characters reach some kind of an internal understanding. To frame something so insubstantial and nebulous in words is hard. It becomes enormously important to find the right words, words that have power, words that will remain in the reader's mind. I have to work hard for them, but sometimes they come to me unexpectedly, like a gift. As did the beautiful lines from the Upanishad in *Small Remedies,* for example: 'May this life enter into the immortal breath, may this body end in ashes. Remember, O Intelligence, remember'. Yes, to remember was what mattered—this was Madhu's revelation, this was what was going to help her to accept what had happened to her in the past, to enable her to live her life in the future. And there was the last line of *The Binding Vine,* which too came to me suddenly, surprising me as much as the revelation surprised Urmila, whose thought it was.

What is the person going to do with this new understanding, this knowledge? I don't know. I share the reader's curiosity about what happens later. I enjoy the sense of completion I get when I read the earlier novelists who take us into their characters' future. But generally, I sense a point beyond which I cannot follow my characters. Will Raja and Jiji in *Moving On* get married? Will Jiji's daughter, Sachi, accept their marriage? I don't know. The only way to find out is to write another novel about them, because it is only in the process of writing that I get to know what my characters are going to do. The one thing that seems certain to me is that they will not go back to the point from where they started. Which is why I am intensely irritated by the number of readers who think that, because she has not slammed a door, Saru in *The Dark Holds No Terrors* goes back to her husband. Even if I cannot follow her into the future, I know that being what she is, having learnt what she has, she will not go back to her bad marriage. Only in *A Matter of Time* did I make a leap into the future, giving glimpses of what would happen to my characters later. Strangely, this was not at the end, but tucked away somewhere in the body of the story.

For me, the novel is not over when I have written the last word. As Charles Dickens says in his Preface to *David Copperfield*, at the end of writing a novel, there is both pleasure and regret. Pleasure in the achievement, regret 'in the separation from many companions'. Truly, the characters become companions, they cling to me, they refuse to let me go. Until new people begin to creep into my mind, clamouring for their story to be told. But twice these new people have been characters from earlier novels, characters who kept haunting me, until I gave in and brought them back into my writing world. *Shadow Play* came out of *A Matter of Time* and *In the Country of Deceit* from my very early crime novel, *Come Up and Be Dead*.

Once all the characters make a graceful exit from my writing life, it is the real end of the novel for me; it is truly 'The End'.

(2007)

Locating the Novel

There is no better way of beginning my talk than by quoting Eudora Welty, who says: 'Time and space make the framework that any story's built on'. I agree with this. For many reasons, I am more troubled by locating a novel in time than locating it in space. It's not just the niggling little details of dates, actual moment of time and tenses that are troubling, but the bigger problem of what memory presents us with. Memory is an absolutely amazing human faculty and it makes us what we are. Without it, we would lose grasp over our lives individually. And, collectively, if we lose our collective memory. At the same time, it is also what can cause a huge amount of confusion, and paradoxically, clarity as well. Memory ignores the concept of time, making a chronological sequence of events impossible; in fact, writing a novel is a little like traveling through different time zones.

Locating a novel in space is a not only a little easier, but an intrinsic part of the story the writer wants to tell. This is because every human desires to find a place of her/his own. To look at the way animals mark out their territories is to realise that finding a place of your own on earth is an atavistic instinct. The need to belong, the need to find your own space, is part of every human story. For me, locating the novel is extremely important, it's not just one of the details I have to get right. Without their locale, my characters are flat. Single-dimensional. Where people live is not only a great part of their lives, it also influences what they are and what they do. Sometimes, rarely, the story springs out of the location, something that has happened to me, not with novels, but with short stories. A seaside place, a beach enclosed between cliffs and a house on top of the cliff—this brought about one of my early stories, 'The Intrusion'. Another one came to me with the picture of a man partly submerged in a lake; this was 'The Last Enemy', Duryodhana's story. It is as if when the story finds a home, it begins to live and grow.

Many of my novels are set in a small town, if not entirely, at least partly. These towns may have different names and different features, but essentially, they are the same town in various avatars—the town I was born and grew up in. The Rajnur I created for my novel *In the Country of Deceit*, the town in which Devayani lives, played a greater role in the novel than my locations generally do. When I went back to my town sometime after I had completed *In the Country of Deceit*, I was both confused and bewildered. I had recreated Rajnur out of my memories of this town, out of the requirements of my novel and my vision of Devayani's town. My creation was quite different from the town I was seeing.

It is a strange feeling looking for your past in the town you think you knew so well. Is this the road we used to go to school on? Where's our house, for God's sake? And what happened to the maidan with the cenotaph—the centerpiece of the town? Memories of the town, dreams in which it returned, and the fiction in which I'd recreated it, clashed; they were so enmeshed it was hard to disentangle them. The distant muted whistle of the train, the chirping of sparrows in the morning, the cheerful sound of the police band from the police headquarters miles away—were these memories? Dreams? Or imagined, like much else? The one thing that remained clear was the fascinating history of the town which I had read for *In the Country of Deceit*. Part of a region which kept changing hands, the town was finally ceded in the beginning of the nineteenth century by the Peshwas to the

British—to Sir Thomas Munro. The man who brought peace to the area, as the chronicles say, and was commended in the House of Commons as 'an accomplished statesman, a skilful soldier who won not just a territory but people's hearts'. High praise, indeed. Though it's more possible that people were tired of constant invasions and changing rulers, of paying of taxes to anyone who made himself a ruler, even for a short time. In any case, the British established themselves in the town and made it their headquarters. Soon there were schools, churches, a golf course, and a club, of course. Vestiges of this colonial past remain: a cenotaph for a British officer, ruined churches and large government bungalows, with gardens of gerberas, cannas and zinnias, the inevitable bougainvillea trailing down the portico roof.

I had borrowed some of this history for my novel, kept its location, changed the internal geography, ignored many features and highlighted others to give Devayani her home town. All the time I was writing the novel, I was living and moving about in Devayani's Rajnur. I walked the streets, I knew my way around the place, I entered many homes—Devayani's, of course, also Rani's, Iqbal's and even Sindhu's home, which entered the novel only once and that briefly. This familiarity with Rajnur made the town I was seeing strange to me. My memories had been overlaid by my creation and the town I had known as a child seemed to have slipped out of my memory.

It seems to me that cities do not allow you this liberty of recreation, specially those that are too well known, since many of their features are an indelible part of them. But to see what a writer like Dickens does with London is to realise that such a presumption is wrong. In each of what one may call his 'London novels', he offers us a slightly different London. In *Bleak House*, it is a city of fog and the Chancery Courts. 'And hard by Temple Bar, in Lincoln's Inn Hall, at the very heart of the fog, sits the Lord High Chancellor in his High Court of Chancery': words in the very first chapter. In *Our Mutual Friend*, it is the river which dominates, the river which runs through the narrative like a refrain. But it is a menacing and deadly river, where 'fishermen' fish out dead bodies and in which men are savagely attacked and left to die. And the chapters where the detective Bucket and Esther Summerson go in pursuit of Lady Dedlock are absolutely brilliant; they not only give us, almost palpably, a sense of great haste and Esther's fright and confusion, we are taken through London at night and get to know Bucket's intimate knowledge of the city, of every little street in it. Then there is *Little Dorrit*, which is the London of the prison Marshalsea and the streets on which Little Dorrit walks to and fro from the Marshalsea. Yes, Dickens is a genius at evoking an atmosphere; with the atmosphere he recreates the city each time, making it the right locale for the characters in that novel.

The point about recreation is that the author has to possess the territory, to make it her own. The location can never be a replica of any actual place, but subtly altered, so that it fits the story and becomes the right locale for it. The need of the novel is paramount, even greater than the need for authenticity. Mark Twain is supposed to have said that he moved cities, counties and even states if his writing needed it. P.D. James takes actual cities—London, Oxford—but often adds a disclaimer at the beginning of her novel, warning us that she has taken some liberties with the topography and with buildings, some of which come from her imagination. Whatever it is, the locale created is one that the writer becomes totally familiar with. And the writer hopes to make the reader see it as vividly as she does. Not through too much detailing, because it is not through endless details that the reader 'sees' the place, but through one or two markers which immediately light up the stage, so to say. Anita Desai in an essay titled '*Feng Sui*, or Spirit of Place',[1] puts it beautifully:

---

[1] Anita Desai. '*Feng Sui* or Spirit of Place'. *A Sense of Place: Essays in Post-Colonial Literatures*. Ed. Britta Olinder. Gothenburg UP, 1984.

'What we [she means writers] are doing is essentially the same. We are plucking the reader by the sleeve and saying come with me, follow me, I have something to show you'. The reader, she goes on to say, has to believe in the reality of what he is seeing, to be persuaded that what he is seeing is a vision and not a delusion.

Strange contradiction indeed, to make the unreal real, to make the reader believe that fiction is the reality. In fact, it is because of this need that writers often give fictional names to places where their characters live, even if, like me, it happens to be a real town you are creating it out of. This is because the reader needs to enter the place without carrying the baggage of her knowledge of the actual town or city. Narayan's Malgudi may be a recreation of Mysore, but would the town have been so magical, so vivid, if it had been called Mysore? It is not just towns or cities which are recreated, entire regions sometimes are, which become real to the reader, specially when used in a series, in novel after novel, like Thomas Hardy's Wessex. And there's Anthony Trollope's Barsetshire. It is impossible not to believe in the reality of that fascinating world of chaplains, Deans and Bishops, of Slopes, Mrs Proudies and Dr Grantlys with his 'Good Heavens! Good Heavens!' These imaginary areas are no less real than an actual existing region. The point is not whether it is a real town or a fictional one, but whether the reader is able to believe in its reality.

When Amitav Ghosh, very strangely, considering the kind of novels he has been writing recently, calls the novel 'parochial', in the sense, he says, of belonging to a parish, he seems to be echoing Jane Austen's oft-quoted statement in a letter to her nephew that '3 or 4 Families in a Country Village is the very thing to work on'. This is exactly what she did. 'Country Village' may seem a strange phrase, but one has only to read her novels to know exactly what she means. And I think few novelists have achieved such an intimate and felicitous connection between her characters and the places they live in. One can scarcely think of the Bennets living anywhere except in Longbourne, or of Meryton without the fat and comfortable Mrs Philips entertaining red-coated soldiers or imagine Darcy living anywhere else than Pemberley. And there's Emma and Hartfield, and, of course, Fanny and Edwin and their beloved Mansfield Park. They belong. In Jane Austen's novels, her characters finally find not only their partners, but their homes as well, in what I think is a beautifully satisfactory way.

Without meaning in any way to put myself in the same bracket as Jane Austen, I have to add that in the course of my writing career I have very often met the charge, or the criticism, of being very limited or restricted as a writer. Of not moving outside the home, of locating my novels within the closed space of a family. It has always seemed to me very ironic that while the family and the home have, in the abstract, a huge importance in human life, literature connected to the family or to the home becomes minor. Trying to look for a reason for this, I have concluded—this is only my opinion—that one of the reasons is the fatal conjunction with women. Anything connected to women becomes minor. Personally, I consider the family an important place, not for the sentimental and emotional reasons to which its importance is often ascribed, but because it is the place where we learn about life, about living with others, it is where we learn about love and jealousy and hostility, about how humans can support one another and how they can destroy one another. The family is the place where emotions are open, more honestly expressed and at times exaggerated. It is the place which anchors us when we are still strangers to the world. And, for me, the family and home are so closely connected that it is hard to disentangle them. Recently, asked to write a piece about the family, I decided to write about my mother's family and found myself writing about their family home instead. For me, the two were so enmeshed I could not write about one without bringing in the other. Perhaps it is for this reason that the home plays such a big role in most of my novels. The family home is at the centre of *Roots and Shadows*, whereas, in *A Matter of Time*, it is almost another character in the story. And in *Moving On*, Jiji, when she finds her home threatened by criminals, resists, because she suddenly discovers that for her the house is imbued with the goodness of her uncle, aunt and her father, the people who built it. *In the Country of Deceit* begins with a demolition and a rebuilding and the rebuilt house is where Deyavani gets her moment of 'touching the sky'.

'Most crimes are committed for women, land and gold', the lawyer Iqbal tells Devayani in *In the Country of Deceit*, quoting a Kannada adage. I saw this when I worked briefly with a criminal lawyer. He had a large number of clients accused of committing murder and almost all these murders were the result of a dispute over land. In today's world, a home is the equivalent of what land was earlier. I got an idea of what a home means when we were building our own house and saw the rituals that accompanied each stage. The construction workers did all the rituals with enormous faith. And there's the way the old resist leaving their home until the very last, the way the young, wherever they go, keep coming back home; these give a glimpse of what the home means to us. In fact, in *Emma*, when Mr Knightley decides that, after marrying Emma he will leave his home, Donwell Abbey, and live with Emma and her father in their home, the reader, at least the astute reader, realises that he is making a great sacrifice for Emma. Unromantic lover he may seem to be, but this sacrifice tells us, more than words can, of his great love for Emma.

Another reason why a novel set within a home or a family is regarded as minor is possibly because of the recent trend of novels which sprawl across the globe. I remember when I was writing *In the Country of Deceit*, there was a moment when I asked myself what I was doing writing about a woman who had lived in a small town and was likely to live there all her life. And this at a time when people are constantly moving throughout the world and novels move across countries and continents. When novels about people who belong nowhere and yet belong everywhere are highly rated. I knew the answer, of course: this was what I wanted to write, this was what I would write. Nevertheless, this game of major and minor which is played in literature makes me wonder whether we need to have a hierarchy of novels, depending on where they are located—starting with rural novels (though political correctness, at least in India, would make us elevate this to a much higher place), small town novels (would we call these 'provincial novels'?), novels set in cities, in metropolitan cities and at the top, novels which use the entire globe as their locale. I learnt more about this hierarchy when I called a certain place a village and I was sternly corrected and told that it was a taluka town. After this comes the district town. As for villages, I learnt that there is something which ranks even below the village. In Kannada it is called a *ku-grama*. I was curious, having heard the word often and looked it up in the dictionary. I learnt that it meant a 'godforsaken place where nothing is available'! If we are to seriously play the game of major and minor, why not give novels their places according to this hierarchy?

In India in the last century, we had novels which dealt with the movement of people upwards, that is, from a village to a town and from a town to a city. Movement stopped there, though, rarely, there were young men who went outside the country. To England, mostly. Now the journey continues—to another country, to another continent and so on. A natural progression which finds its way into literature from real life. Novels, after all, give us a picture of life. Therefore, in a way, these novels are following the same path earlier novels did. And, actually, there is nothing new in the idea of the constant movement of people. Humans have always been travellers; to look at human history is to understand the fascination travelling has always held for humans. Nayan Chanda, in his book, *Bound Together*, speaks of globalisation stemming, 'among other things, from a basic human urge to seek a better and more fulfilling life'. And, he adds, 'it has been driven by many actors who can be classified, for the sake of simplicity, as traders, preachers, adventurers, and warriors'. A very interesting thought indeed. It opened up a large number of ideas for me. However, the fascination of traveling has never denied the great importance of home. In fact, if some people went out to escape, many often went out to seek better homes and a better life—something that still continues. And even Ulysses, the indefatigable traveller, journeyed only in order to get back home. In our own mythology, we have the story of Ashwatthama, whose horrendous deed of killing Draupadi's sons in their sleep made Krishna curse him. The curse was: May you live forever, may you always travel, always travel alone, hated by all who see you. And, lastly, may you be homeless. A horrifying curse.

The truth is that much, no, almost everything in writing depends on the skill of the writer. For example, the novel *Gilead* by Marilynne Robinson is set in a very small town in the US, giving us the story of an old man who has lived there all his life. Nevertheless, the novel contains the expanse of the world, because it contains a world of love and hate, of forgiveness and reconciliation. This is the world all humans inhabit, the world which unites all human beings, unlike the physical world which has many differences which separate us.

Some time back I read a review written by Pankaj Mishra of Rushdie's novel *Shalimar the Clown*. In the review he made two statements which puzzled me. He said that the writers who wrote provincial novels, like Gustave Flaubert and George Eliot, could not have written about the world because they did not know the world. And then he goes on to say that Rushdie's novel is full of generalisations and superficialities, because of his inadequate knowledge of the world. I was a little puzzled by something in these two statements and later realised that they contradicted one another. And, even more importantly, there was a basic flaw in the premises on which he based his statement. I do not think that either Flaubert or George Eliot wrote 'provincial' novels because they did not know the world. No one person can know all the worlds. Apart from physical worlds, there's a man's world, a woman's world, the world children inhabit and so on and on. Each one of us inhabits a different world, so to say. If more women write about women and more men write about men, it's only because they know their own world best.

I was recently asked the question why I write only about the 'elite' and why I never write about Dalit women. My answer was that I would have to be foolhardy to set my novel in a world of which I know nothing. Whether I have the right to write about them is another matter. I have been recently hearing the term 'cultural appropriation', which means writing of the experiences of a minority group to which you do not belong. Lionel Shriver, the novelist, raised a furore during a literary festival in Australia when she criticised this idea. Does this mean she asked, that she could only write of smart-alecky 59-year-old 5-foot-2-inch writer women from North Carolina? She defended the right of a writer 'to write about any situation if it served her artistic purpose'. Artistic purpose—that's another complicated matter. A friend and I once discussed the question whether it is right to subject the writing of Dalit women to the test of 'artistic value', or do we value them only as social documents? Writers like Bama (Tamil) or Urmila Pawar (Marathi) have written of their own experiences as Dalit women. Women who are thrice discriminated against—because of caste, poverty, and gender. Their writings give us glimpses of a world of pain and humiliation, one that no upper-caste person would have intimate knowledge of. Do we then say that the upper-caste writer should never write of Dalits? Or even if they write, can upper-caste women write the way Bama, or Urmila Pawar do? Without having personally endured the experience of being Dalit women, is it possible to write about their suffering? Hard questions to answer. I myself believe, like Lionel Shriver does, that a writer cannot be barred from writing about anything or anyone. Yet, there is no doubt that without complete knowledge of the world and the people you are writing about, it is possible that the work may be flawed.

I recently came across a prize-winning short story in which, as a reader, I could not get past the lack of knowledge about the communities the author was writing about, well-written though it was. The mistakes jarred. The fact that the author had located her story in a locale of which she had only a superficial knowledge was very clear. A recent bestseller in the United States, written by a white American woman, in which the protagonist is a Mexican woman, has been much criticised for the inaccuracies about Mexican life that the book contains. As far as I am concerned, I need to know everything about my main characters, every small detail of their lives. I may be a little vague about the supporting actors, but with the main characters I can't afford to falter over any detail. I have to write from the inside, I need the intensity, I need to go deep into my characters, which means that I need to have absolute clarity about where and how they live.

Writers grasp the knowledge that is part of their territory. When I first went to Mumbai as a young girl, I was both fascinated and put off by the unbroken rows of uniformly drab ugly buildings. But what caught my imagination more were the homes I saw in these buildings when I was sitting on the top deck of a double-decker bus. The little tulsi plant growing outside the window, the clothes hanging from the balconies, the brief glimpse of lives being lived within those four walls—these fascinated me. I watched them with the avidity of a voyeur, even though the people were just going about their usual innocent household chores. But the fact that the various activities I was watching are normally not seen by outsiders gripped my imagination much more than the far more exciting life that I saw on the streets of Bombay. The private, the hidden, rather than what is public and open. Yes, writers have their own different territories and whether it is a large territory, or just a 'little bit (not two inches wide) of ivory' (from *Letters of Jane Austen*), a novel cannot, or should not, be judged as significant or insignificant only on the basis of this.

I think that more important than knowing the world well, or even understanding it, is for the writer to enter the world she/he is creating, and not just see it, but to feel it, and experience it, and then invite the reader to share this world. Yes, like Anita Desai says, the writer has to pluck the reader's sleeve and say come with me, I will show you something. It is only when the reader is able to share the experience of the world with the writer that the novel will work for the reader.

(2009)

Thoughts on Translation

There is always a special, an indescribable feeling about going back to the place one has grown up in. I spent only fifteen years in Dharwad, but they were the first fifteen years of my life and the place has left an indelible mark on me. Harish Trivedi, when he first wrote to me, said 'you can show us around'. I don't think I could do that. Not only will the landscape of the town have changed immensely in all these years, the Dharwad I remember may have no relationship even to the town I lived in. I have a map of Dharwad within me, a map which I have carried around and which is, I am sure, quite different from the map of the actual place. All fiction writers take actual places and then change them around, often adding disclaimers at the beginning of the book. I have never used the name Dharwad, but the unnamed town in *The Dark Holds No Terrors*, Saptagiri in *That Long Silence,* Ranidurg in *The Binding Vine* and, above all, Rajnur in *In the Country of Deceit* have all been fictional recreations of Dharwad.

Dharwad now has a reputation as a place which breeds musicians and writers and it has become self-consciously aware of this reputation in the last few years. But to me the remarkable thing about this town is something quite different. My class in school consisted, I think, of twenty-two girls. Of these—I once made the tally—seven became doctors, one a mathematician who became a banker, one a college teacher and I became a writer—this makes nearly half the class. Which, when you think of the time and the place, is quite remarkable. Equally remarkable is the enormous reading I did in my years in this town. It's not my reading that's remarkable, but that I was able to get all these books to read, considering the fact that there was no bookshop for English books in the town and very few people had English books at home. I got all these books from my school and college libraries and the public library that was established when I was growing up. Once again something remarkable, when we look at the paucity and the kind of libraries even in a city like Bangalore today.

But I am not here to talk of Dharwad, least of all about myself. I am supposed to give the keynote address of your conference, the theme of which is 'Translation and Postcolonialities'. However, I am going to do a surgical amputation of your theme and speak only of translation.

Translation has been very much on my mind since very recently I spent a few days with three friends, one of whom is a publisher of translations, and a translator herself, and the two others are professional translators from English (mostly of Indian writing) into European languages. As for myself, I realised many years back that as a writer in English I was in effect a translator—because we are not only translating our lives here into English, we are also translating the words of those characters who would not be speaking English. I am also, in a very tiny way, a translator myself, having done some translation from both Kannada and Marathi into English

For three days my friends and I talked about translation and the various issues involved, generating much excitement and a host of new ideas in the process. Our talk was only about the actual process of translation and we agreed that the most important part of translating, the primary act so to say, is choosing the text to be translated. The two translators were very vocal about the need for them to feel a sympathy with the text, to love the text. From my own little experience, I too know that the urge to translate comes from a need to share what you are enjoying with other readers. It was the publisher who brought us down to earth asking—what about commissioned work then? The question was easily bypassed, because the two translators confessed that they were now valued enough to refuse the work they do not want to do. But most translators do not have that luxury. Translators may recommend a book, but ultimately it is the publisher who decides what book is to be translated. And publishers' choices are both determined and limited by economic considerations and by what is more likely to sell.

Even otherwise, the desire to translate a book can be thwarted by other factors. Let me give an example from my own experience: I had decided that, for my father's centenary, I would translate his autobiography. Eventually I gave up the idea because (a) it was too long and (b) most of it dealt with events and people in Karnataka and would therefore, I thought, not interest readers outside the State. I then discovered a section in the book in which he wrote of his experiences in the theatre world—as a spectator, as a writer, a director, the founder of an amateur group and so on. Reading one passage in which he wrote of his response to two actors of the Marathi theatre, I was suddenly elated. And I thought, I must translate this, I want to do this. There was also a practical consideration—something which can never be ignored—that this portion of the book would interest readers from all over India, specially those interested in the theatre. Which made me understand that though a writer does not think of readers before, or when actually writing, the translator has to take the readership into consideration.

There are other reasons for rejecting a text. I knew a writer who had undertaken to translate *King Lear* for the Sahitya Akademi, but the very first lines of the play made him give up the idea. The play begins with a conversation between the Earls of Kent and Gloster about Edmund, Gloster's illegitimate son. I have to quote these lines.

> Kent: Is not this your son, my Lord?
> Gloster: His breeding, sir, hath been at my charge ...
> Kent: I cannot conceive you.
> Gloster: Sir, this young fellow's mother could: whereupon she grew round-wombed and had indeed, sir, a son for her cradle ere she had a husband for her bed.

It was the word 'conceive' that defeated the writer. Puns are always the bugbear of translators.

I myself once rejected a text for a very different reason. This was a play too, for which the epigraph was a verse by an old Kannada poet. Since the title was taken from this verse, I thought it necessary to translate it as well. It was a simple verse which speaks of the futility of asking God for anything by referring to various persons who did ask and ended with disastrous results—like Dhritirashtra asking for sons and so on. But there was one name in it (Dyunamaka) which was not familiar to me. I asked a great many people whether they knew who Dyunamaka was; surprisingly, no one seemed to know the story. By the time the answer came from a friend's mother, I had realised I did not want to translate this poem. It was not hard to translate the words, but what would the entire thing mean to a reader who did not know the mythology? And if Kannada scholars were baffled by this story, what hope was there that English readers would understand? There was much here which was embedded in an intensely personal and deeply felt mythology. The significance would be lost unless the reader was familiar with the myths. And so ultimately, I did not translate the verse and I changed the title.

These examples say much about what translation means and raise many questions. A.K. Ramanujan says that everything can be translated, though he adds a caveat that it should meet the right translator. (Which is almost as good as saying it should remain untranslated.) But some texts are so deeply embedded in their own culture that, translated, they could become a travesty of their original selves. Is it right then for the translator to omit those parts which cannot be happily conveyed in English? How many liberties can a translator take? And how much control does the author (if alive) have over the translation? (Tagore, it is said, carefully chose those verses from his *Gitanjali* for translation which translated well into English.) If the author is the translator, another question arises, since most confess to doing a rewriting during the process of translating: does this qualify as a translation? Clearly no translator can inject her/his ideology into the work. But is it permissible to subtly bring in changes more in tune with the translator's own ideology and contemporary ideas? (Like using 'her/his' for 'his', 'human' for 'man', etc.?) There are, of course, besides these, many problems about language—like what kind of language do you use when it comes to dialect, slang, etc.? Even the simplest words can be huge stumbling blocks because they are used in a language in a particular way. And what about style? And how much does one gloss, or footnote? And can one incorporate a word or two in the text itself to explain something? One of the things I discovered during the process of translation is that Indian languages use the passive voice much more. Is it okay to convert it into the active voice? Or will that be a violation of the style of the language? And can you contemporise writing of an earlier age? Film-makers have done it—but can translators take such liberties with a text?

A great many of these questions become relevant when the translation is from an Indian language into English—which is what translation most often seems to imply today. The days when books were translated from one Indian language to another in a happy and copious flow seem to be over and the kind of bilingualism which once existed seems to be a thing of the past. I would not be surprised if one Indian language is translated into another through a translated English text. Today, bilingualism generally means an Indian language plus English. Obviously, the importance of English in a global world has made translations into the language hugely important—both for economic and political reasons. To be part of the world literatures we have to move into English. Even those who decry Indians writing in English regard translation into English as a necessity for this purpose. Unfortunately, these translations don't often work; the books chosen, many of which are regarded as the best in the language, often fail. Many of us have asked ourselves the question: When we have read so many translations from different languages into English and enjoyed them, scarcely realising that they are translations, why do our translations fall so woefully short of those standards? Is it a lack of good translators? And is this due to a lack of professionalism and poor payment? Is it because of too many languages? A culture indecipherable to the outside world? The complexity of our society? Or (and these are John Updike's words, used however in an entirely different context) is trying to convert our languages into English like '*dancing with a partner who hears a distinctly different music*'?

There is also the factor of political correctness, which dictates that certain texts demand translation, and a piece of writing is chosen because it is an important social document. This kind of reasoning is almost lethal when it comes to creative writing, because too often literary considerations are looked upon as superfluous and are jettisoned. Shama Futehally, in her wonderful piece on A.K. Ramanujan's translation, speaks of first-rate scholars whose translations do not quite succeed. Their motto is 'handle with care' and the translations, she says, in very evocative words, leave readers 'honourably reading away' instead of leaving them 'astounded and joyful'. I think it is a shame we don't have more translations from one Indian language to another and from English to other Indian languages.

Ultimately, all questions have to be answered by the translator. It is for the translator to make the choices, to take decisions, to deal with problems as they arise, to devise strategies for each one. To me, translation is a personal and individual act. I see translation as a kind of private and intimate conversation between the original author and the translator. I have often felt a kind of communication between myself and the writer when I am in the process of translating. Which is why translation can be as little contained in theories as creative writing can be, and theories can be as stifling for the creativity of translation as theories are for literature. Theories are necessary—but only as a kind of framework, which may be ignored. The gut feeling of the translator sometimes has the last word and often rightly so.

No translation is perfect. Though we scarcely think of it, most religious texts come to us in the form of translations. We accept them as sacrosanct, but no translation is final and forever. Ramanujan speaks of making the translation relevant to contemporary readers, something which he has done with great skill. P. Lal, another translator, also says one is translating for one's contemporaries; creative writing may be done for a hundred years, not translations. And therefore the need felt to retranslate a work by each generation.

It is no longer possible to look upon translation as a worthy and uplifting cause—and damn the money. Governmental institutions did their bit when there were no private publishers willing to take the risk of publishing translations. But governmental institutions have their own problems and handicaps. And experience has shown that they are not really equipped to deal with work which embraces both creativity and economics. We have to accept the fact that it is to private publishers we have to look if we want books to reach a large number of readers. Publishing is closely connected to the market; no publisher will publish a text without having the confidence that the book will sell. Which means we need quality translations; if not excellent, they at least need to be competent. We need editors who will know both the languages and vet the translations. We need better payments for translators so that the best people will get into it. Teachers, doctors and writers have always been supposed to be above money. Teachers and doctors have proven that this can be disputed. And some

English writers have become rich through their writing and earned much disapproval because for some reason we Indians want our writers to be noble and poor. But writers will write, however small the rewards. Translators, however, have a choice. And therefore, unless it becomes more worthwhile, we will continue to have amateurs who have great enthusiasm, but not much else.

I have learnt much from the very little translation I have done. I have learnt to respect the work of another author. I have learnt that books belong to a certain time and place and that they cannot be wrenched out of their context. I have learnt to respect words, learnt about how exquisitely precise they can be when you search for an equivalent in another language. Often, you have to roam through an entire forest of nuanced meanings before getting a word even close to the original one. I have learnt about the democratic relationship between languages. There is, one realises, no major or minor among languages; they all stand on an equal footing. To translate is to learn about the futility of the politics of language, to understand the stupidity of linguistic jingoism.

(2009)

The Short Story

It gives me great pleasure to be part of this Sahitya Akademi National Seminar on the short story in the Indian languages. I am sure the short story must be pleased about it as well. Or perhaps, it will be surprised, if not startled, at having so many scholars and writers talking about it for three whole days. For the truth is that the short story is not used to being the focus of attention; in fact, by now it has got used to being regarded as a minor form of literature and of secondary importance. There may be many reasons for this, though a reason that would immediately come to mind is that its length precludes the short story from being considered important. But this argument will not hold water, for poetry, however short it is, is greatly honoured and respected. Years back, Nadine Gordimer, speaking of the short story said, 'Why is it that the death of the novel is good for a post-mortem at least once a year, while the short story lives on unmolested?' This perhaps is the real problem: that the short story is looked upon as the younger sibling of the long story, and the novel, like every older sibling, gets all the attention, denying the short story its due.

If length is the defining factor, some of the questions that can be asked about the short story are: how short can the short story be? And when does a short story become a novella? Or, if length is not the only thing, what other factors need to be present in the short story? But I am not going to talk about these things. There are others much better qualified to do so. In fact, I have been only a reader and writer of short stories. The realisation that I needed to speak a few words here sent me scurrying for some material on the short story and I came across two strangely contradictory statements. The short story, according to S.K. Das (in the *History of Indian Literature*), is the youngest of literary forms. Whereas, in an introduction to a volume of 'Major American Short Stories', the editor, Walton Litz, informs readers that the short story is the most ancient and enduring form. As a matter of fact, both the statements are true. Stories are indeed as old as humanity. Some of the earliest stories have been found in Egyptian papyri. And all ancient religious books are full of stories which are used to drive home a point, to teach a moral lesson. Our own epics do so and the Mahabharata, specially, is a veritable compendium of stories. The Nahusha-Indra story, the Yayati-Sharmishta-Devayani story, the Nala-Damayanti story, the Shakuntala-Dushyanta story—all these come from the Mahabharata. The Puranas, too provide a feast of stories, as does the Bible, specially the Old Testament, which abounds in stories—the story of Solomon, of David, of Moses, of Ruth. Moreover, all civilisations and all cultures have a store of non-religious stories, of folk and fairy tales, like Aesop's fables, *Arabian Nights* and so on.

The truth is that humanity has always needed to tell its own stories to itself. It is through telling our stories that our lives become real, it is through our stories that we get some understanding of who we are. Stories are a kind of signpost, saying, 'I am here' or 'I was here', they are the footprints which show us the way we have travelled, telling us where we have stumbled and why. But while oral stories are an ancient form, written stories are a late arrival; the short story, as a literary genre, came much later—in fact, after the novel.

For three days, scholars and writers here will be talking about the short story in various languages, about its beginning, its development, about different writers and their contribution.

My own knowledge of Indian short stories is limited to one language, English. And therefore I will speak as a reader and writer in this language. However, I would like to say at the outset that reading in English has one great advantage: translations are available from a great number of languages, both Indian and foreign. Therefore, it was possible for me to read Guy de Maupassant as well as James Joyce, I could read Chekhov as well as Somerset Maugham, Tagore as well as O. Henry. In those early years, I scarcely realised that the stories of Maupassant and Chekhov were translations and that the writers I was reading came from different lands. Ibsen and Tolstoy were the same to me as Katherine Mansfield and E.M. Forster. Sadly, however, there were very few translations from the Indian languages then. The earliest Indian language stories I remember reading were in a volume called the *Nehru Abhinandan Granth* (brought out, I think, on Pandit Nehru's seventieth birthday) in which there was a section on fiction. Two stories I read in that volume are still fresh in my mind. One was a translation of a Marathi story and the other was translated from Bengali. Though I have forgotten the titles of the stories and the names of the authors (I think the Marathi story was by Na Si Phadke), I remember that one of the stories was of a young man preparing to go to a party to which he has been very casually invited. And the other was of a young boy selling boiled eggs to soldiers during the war in Kashmir immediately after Partition. In different ways, both were equally poignant. I have such a vivid memory of the stories that they must have seemed remarkable to me. Sometime after, I read a collection of Tagore's stories. There was an immediate sense of identification and intimacy. It was like entering a home one knew intimately, like meeting old friends. Later I read Premchand, who was, along with Tagore, one of the more translated Indian authors.

In time, things improved and there came anthologies of translated stories. The first anthology of translated stories that I read (I still have it) is a Sahitya Akademi publication brought out in 1959. In that I read stories by Masti Venkatesh Iyengar, Ismat Chugtai, Kartar Singh Duggal. Besides the Akademi, P. Lal and his Writers Workshop contributed greatly to a reader's access to more Indian short stories. Later still came the Katha series which continued this great service of giving readers stories in the bhashas. It is because of all these anthologies that I was able to read Malayalam stories by Madhavan and Paul Zacharia, Marathi stories by Gauri Deshpande and Asha Bage, a Kannada story by Ananthamurthy, a Hindi story by Maitreyi Pushpa, a Tamil story by Ashokamitran, an Oriya story by Pratibha Ray, and so on. Some of these stories were among the finest I had read. Among them I would include Bolwar Mahammed Kunhi's Kannada story, 'A Piece of the Wall', Asha Bage's Marathi story 'Wings', C.S. Lakshmi's Tamil story 'A Kitchen in the Corner of the House', another Tamil story, Sundara Ramaswamy's 'A Day with My Father', K.R. Usha's English 'Sepia Tones'—there is an endless list of stories which are worth critical acclaim. Madhavan's 'Mumbai', in fact, brings to mind Kafka's *Metamorphosis,* while Bolwar Mahammed Kunhi's 'A Piece of the Wall' is one of the best I have read on the Babri Masjid demolition. Maitreyi Pushpa's and Usha's are stories of inner conflict and quiet revolutions, and Jayant Bendre's 'May We Be the Way The Lord Meant Us to Be' gives us a chilling, but close-to-the-truth story of the entry of violence and terror into an ordinary citizen's home.

Both Humayun Kabir and S.K. Das speak of the short story in India as being a result of the impact of the West. But reading stories like these makes one feel that Indians have an innate genius for the short story. There is a free flow of narrative in many Indian stories, a seeming lack of artifice, a sense of intimacy, as if two people are sitting together, the author narrating the story and the reader listening. It seems to me that the short story in India is still closely linked to the oral tradition, with very happy results.

You will note that I have included a short story written in English among those mentioned above. Yes, though English is not included in the seminar, English writers have written stories the same way as writers in other languages have, stories that came out of their own selves, stories that came out of the society around them.

I myself began my writing career with short stories and wrote a great many of them in the early years. There is a theory that women take more to the short story, both because of their capacity for sharp observation and details, as well as because it is a form that is more possible for them, since women, specially those with young children, always have a much shorter space of free time available to them. As Sylvia Plath the poet said, the writing has to be done before the baby cries and the milk arrives. There is much truth in this. But there was another reason why I wrote so many stories, a reason that has little to do with the circumstances of my life and my convenience and much more to do with the form of the short story itself. This reason came to me when I read an epigraph to a collection of short stories by Katherine Mansfield. I quote: 'A little bird was asked: Why are your songs so short? He replied: I have many songs, and I should like to sing them all'.

These are Chekhov's words.

At that time my mind was thronging with so many characters, with such a variety of human experiences and predicaments, with so many catalytic moments that I needed many stories to write about all these things. I could not have written seventy novels; it would have required more than an entire lifetime. But I could write and did write more than seventy short stories. All the reading I did, mainly in English, undoubtedly influenced my writing, but the stories themselves came from deep within me, from the society I lived in. That the stories were written in English is an irrelevant detail. This is true about most Indian writers in English.

Writing short stories taught me much. It taught me about brevity and precision, about swift and yet marked character development. I learnt that, for me, focus and intensity had to be part of the narrative. Above all, the short story provided me with a laboratory for experimentation—of themes, narrative styles, techniques and language. Much of what I tried out in the short stories—and which I thought worked well—went into the novels. Yet, the novel is not, as is often regarded today, the ultimate goal; one is not moving *on* when one writes a novel. From the short story to the novel is a lateral movement, because the story is an end in itself.

There is often a debate about which is the better form, the short story or the novel. Edgar Allan Poe, one of the pioneers of the American short story, calling the story a prose tale, says that it 'fulfils the demand of high genius'. But he, of course, was biased because he was a short story writer himself. I have also heard it said that the short story belongs to the realm of elegance and perfection. These, I imagine, are defensive statements; but the short story needs defence as little as it needs criticism. There is really no need to compare, since these are two very distinct genres of literature; the short story was not born out of the need to do what the novel could not. But if I have to compare, I think of the short story as a hundred metres sprint and the novel as the marathon; the two forms require different skills. If one listens to D.V. Paluskar expounding a raga in three minutes, which was the length of the gramophone record in those days, one will realise what the short story does. And when one listens to Bade Ghulam Ali Khan or Bhimsen Joshi, expounding the same raga with the same perfection in over fifteen minutes, one realises that what matters is not the length, or the time, but the talent, the skill, and the genius of the artist. The short story needs the focus of an archer or a sharpshooter, the craftsmanship of a miniaturist, and the ruthlessness of a saint in shedding the unwanted. Extra words may be absorbed by a novel, they may be hidden in it; but one unnecessary word in a short story will stand out. The novel can carry extra weight, but in a short story the flab shows; no amount of loose clothing can cover it. Chekhov's famous statement about drama, that if you have hung a pistol on the wall in the first act, it should be fired, applies to the short story as well. And, just as there have been great novels, there have also been great short stories which have become classics. In India, Tagore's 'The Postmaster' and 'Kabuliwala', for example, or Ismat Chughtai's 'Lihaaf', which brought her much notoriety, remain classics. In the world, there are Washington Irving's 'Rip Van Winkle', O. Henry's 'The Gift of the Magi', Gogol's 'The Overcoat'. I consider James Joyce's 'The Dead' a masterpiece. In fact, this story clearly shows how the same writer takes on different avatars in the two forms. I could not and still cannot read Joyce's *Ulysses*, while this story remains an all-time favourite. In a short space it gives the reader a whole world of emotions, all the complexities of human relationships.

One more reason why I could write so many stories in those days was because there were magazines and Sunday supplements of newspapers which published short fiction. In the decades since then, space for fiction (I am speaking of fiction written in English) has dwindled enormously. In fact, fiction is almost never published by magazines or the Sunday paper supplements; it has been nudged out by political news, sensations, cricket and films. I consider this one of the reasons for the paucity of short story writers in English. That there is a strong link between the health and vitality of writing and publishing can be most clearly seen in the difference between the short story in the bhashas and in English. In the languages I know, and I am sure in the others as well, magazines and Sunday supplements not only have space for the short story, there is always an annual issue, whether for Diwali or Dasara, in which it is a matter of prestige to have the fiction—short stories or novellas—of well-known writers. I know that in Marathi, good writers are 'booked' months in advance and writers too make a point to have a short story ready for these special issues. I subscribe to an ideologically driven women's Marathi magazine, with a small circulation. This little magazine (they don't take ads which do not conform to their ideology) not only runs a short story competition every year (male writers are also welcome), they also have one story in each issue which is translated from another language into Marathi. It is not surprising, therefore, to find that writers in the bhashas have been able to build up a reputation on the basis of their short stories alone. G.A. Kulkarni, the Marathi writer, stands tall among readers and critics both, though he wrote only short stories. Saniya, a contemporary Marathi writer, has a reputation which rests mainly on her stories. In Kannada, Masti Venkatesh Iyengar, a Jnanpith winner, is admired mainly as an excellent short story writer; the simplicity of his stories has endeared him to readers. And today, there are writers like Vaidehi and Jayant Kaikini, who are widely known because of their short stories alone. But novelists also have reputations as short story writers. U.R. Ananthamurthy, the iconic Kannada writer, had numerous volumes of short stories to his credit as well as novels. And there is Saadat Hasan Manto, the brilliant Urdu writer, who lived in India until Partition and then moved to Pakistan. He was a film script writer, but it is his stories, specially his brilliant Partition stories, which have found new life decades after his death. He has now got all the recognition he was denied earlier.

In English, not only are there no magazines or journals which give short stories space (there are some online ones now), publishers will tell a young writer who comes to them with a collection of stories, 'Sorry, we don't do short stories. But if you have a novel, we might take a look'. The result is that a young writer is compelled to write a novel, though she may be best at stories, though her heart may be in writing stories. Which is a pity, because English is not bereft of good story writers. As a judge at short story competitions, I have occasionally come across stories of great promise. But will these writers be allowed to follow this talent of theirs? Earlier writers, like R.K. Narayan and Anita Desai, to give two examples, were also known for their stories; but today few writers concentrate on the short story. Jhumpa Lahiri began her career with short stories, some of which are brilliant. I find her stories superior to her novels, because she has that nuanced and delicate touch which can be best seen in the short story. Prof. Lal's Writers Workshop gave a great boost to the short story form by publishing innumerable collections of short stories, both English and translations from the bhashas. Prof. Lal must have encouraged a great number of aspiring writers, some of whom later moved away from him to mainstream publishers.

If there are any doubts about the connection between publishing openings and the growth of the short story form, one has only to look at the American scene. Undoubtedly the great strength and vitality of the American story comes from the large number of journals and magazines that published fiction. P.G. Wodehouse could make a good living in the US from selling both his short and long fiction. And it is in the US that many novelists are also known as great short story writers. The short story has been called a 'national art form' in the USA and the list of great American short story writers is most impressive—from Washington Irving, Edgar Allan Poe and O. Henry to Raymond Carver, Flannery O'Connor, Eudora Welty, Henry James, John Updike, Joyce Carol Oates—it is indeed an astonishingly long and distinguished list.

As far as India is concerned, the short story plays a role no other genre of literature can. It is the most translatable of all forms; novels are long, translation takes a great deal of time and it is hard to find a publisher unless the work is commissioned—something which discourages anyone wanting to translate a novel. Poetry is hard to translate and rarely translates well. The short story is the ideal form. I always think of Indian literature as an archipelago of islands. The translator is the boatman who can take us from one island to another. Readers are able to get a panoramic glimpse of Indian writing through an anthology that provides translations from different languages. I am sure that many of us are eager to know the other literatures in our country, to get an idea of the kind of literature being produced. We cannot possibly read novels from all the languages, but in one anthology we can get a glimpse of several literatures. The welcome news is that the short story is becoming popular, not only because our lifestyles make it easier for us to accept anything which is less time-consuming, but because we have learnt about the versatility of the short story. It can be made into a TV serial, into a play, into a movie. Satyajit Ray made a brilliant movie (*Shatranj ke Khiladi*) from a short story by the Hindi writer Premchand. Many of Manto's short stories have been turned into plays now and have been very successful. I myself had not heard of Manto until his stories were converted into plays. Perhaps, like Nadine Gordimer said, a continuation of her earlier quote, 'like a child suffering from healthy neglect it (the short story) survives'.

There are always trends and fashions in literature when one form of literature seems to dominate over the others. Like, for example, drama dominated Marathi literature in the early years of the last century. (In fact, the Marathi short story was said to have been influenced by drama!) The time of the short story is yet to come, for we have not really celebrated what Indians have done with this form of literature. I hope and am sure it will be done during the course of this seminar.

I congratulate the Sahitya Akademi on this initiative. Humayun Kabir, in the first anthology brought out by the Sahitya Akademi, promised that many more would come and that each anthology would be translated into all the major Indian languages. I have no idea whether this has happened. If it has not, I hope it eventually will, for I can think of no other institution but the Akademi which can take up work which may not be hugely profitable, but worthwhile in so many other ways.

(2012)

Section V

PLACES RECALLED AND WRITERS REMEMBERED

Elephant Walk

The Thunchan Festival in Kerala is an annual gathering of writers and scholars from all over India, held in honour of Thunchathu Ramanujan Ezhuthachan, a great sixteenth-century poet, who rendered the two great epics, the Ramayana and the Mahabharata, into Malayalam, which made them accessible to the common people. M.T. Vasudevan Nair, the Malayalam writer and Jnanpith winner, when he invites me to the festival, tells me that Tirur, where the Thunchan Memorial Centre is situated, is about four hours' drive from Cochin. My friend Gita Krishnankutty receives me at the airport, a spanking new building with impeccable aesthetics, and takes me to her ancestral home in Chengamanad. As always in Kerala, I'm amazed by the idea of this being a village; such a contrast to the villages I've seen in North Karnataka, poverty-stricken places with crumbling mud and stone houses. Gita's ancestral house is not my idea of a village home, either, and her mother, a translator like her daughter, is equally unusual. The lunch, however, is typical Kerala—jackfruit, banana, brown rice, avial. The jackfruit dish is delicious. I ask for the recipe. 'Pluck a jackfruit of just this size ...', Usha, my hostess, says, pointing to the tree outside. I give up the idea.

On our way to Tirur, Gita suggests we visit the Guruvayoor temple. We are lucky, the crowd is not too large today. We are told we can have a darshan in fifteen minutes. While we wait,

Gita tells me how, as children, they helped to light the oil lamps in the niches in the wall. It looks beautiful, she says, when they are all lit in the evenings. The idea of letting children participate seems equally wonderful to me. Soon the idol is brought out and the crowd, which has been exclaiming in delight over the richly caparisoned baby elephant, on which the idol will be mounted, immediately prostrates itself reverentially—with such unison, that it is like the wind passing over a field of wheat. The elephant, with a sedateness belying its youth, takes the idol round the inner sanctum thrice, unperturbed, it seems, by the cacophonous music that precedes it. Then we are let in—women first. The urge to stand before the idol has to be curbed, people behind are impatient. The priests keep urging us to move on, not harshly, but with a gentle 'you can always come back. He'll still be here'. It is Gita who translates this for me, giving me a sense of the courtesy in the language.

The next morning, we wake up in Tirur to the fanfare of pipes and the rhythm of drums. Music that quickens one's heartbeats. There is excitement in the air, people are gathering for the procession. This is not a religious procession; the *utsav murti* (festival idol) here is an iron stylus. The same one, it is said, which was used by the great poet for his writing. Only a legend, maybe, but the devotion and solemnity on faces spells out total belief. It's a picture postcard scene—women and girls in the typical Kerala gold and white, their freshly washed hair loose, trays of flowers and lamps in hands. An umbrella is held above the stylus, as if it truly is an idol. Writers and scholars join the procession, but the Tamil poet Kanimozhi runs about energetically trying to get pictures. When the procession returns, there is a ceremony in which various writers speak briefly in their own languages. I hear Marathi, Gujarati, Hindi, Kannada, Tamil, Konkani, Malayalam. This too is a tradition, I'm told; a newly evolved one, but attaining the same sanctity as the old ones.

After this is the National Seminar, in which writers speak of the nation and the writer. All seminars and conferences have a sameness about them; so too this one. What is remarkable here, however, is the audience—a large audience, everyone, young as well as old, listening with an untiring attentiveness. My admiration for the audience is reinforced when I see them, the next day, listening patiently to a seminar on education, even though it is well past lunch time. The speakers too go on with undiminished gusto, but a young man, sitting outside under the trees like us, grumbles, 'No one is speaking of the pay scales!' I am reminded that this is Communist country. The simplicity and austerity that proclaims itself everywhere tells me how and why Communism could get a foothold here. The meals, as simple as the people's clothes, are cooked and served by volunteers from the town, some of whom are eminent people. It is considered an honour to serve guests at this festival. The serving men stand about, chat, urge guests to eat and even bravely try out their Hindi on outsiders! It's vegetarian food, something, we are told, that's hard to get elsewhere in town since this is North Malabar, which has a large Muslim population. Tirur is next door to Calicut, the place where Vasco da Gama first landed and was astounded, both by the opulence of the place, as well as the number of Arab traders. Gita tells me that the word for bazaar here is 'souk', a word which comes from that past. Fascinating how language can evoke history.

We wake up the next morning to the sonorous chanting of the poet's Malayalam Ramayana in a male voice. I see the man later, sitting alone in the large hall, an oil lamp glowing in the semi-darkness; he is chanting from memory. We have time to go round the Centre today. There is a small temple under a tree, the same tree, legend goes, under which the poet sat. A Nux Vomica tree, but the leaves of this tree are, it is said, not bitter. Even more pleasing than this legend, however, is the information that no rituals are performed in this temple, for to do so would be to bar non-Hindus and lower castes from it. I'm equally impressed when I'm told that parents, of all castes and religions, flock with their children to this place on Vijayadasami (Dasara) day. Here, in the Saraswati *mandapam*, the children learn their first letters. What is just as amazing is that writers come from all over Kerala to guide children in writing their first letters. A remarkable knitting of literature into the lives of the people. And unique, surely?

All the days I'm there, crowds continue to stream into the Centre. It's a combination of a tourist place, a place of pilgrimage, as well as an educational outing. Hordes of children pour in and walk in an orderly single file through the place. Once they have done with the tour, the teachers relax and have coffee and snacks at the all-women managed canteen, while the children chat, giggle and stare at the visitors. Gita and I are the uneasy victims of this unrelenting curiosity. When Gita speaks to them in Malayalam, she is let off. I'm the stranger now; they turn to me and, laughing at their own daring at speaking in English, ask, 'What is your name? How do you do?' With this, their stock of English is exhausted. Conversation peters out. We enjoy their company, nevertheless. Headscarves, sandalwood and kumkum on foreheads and crosses round necks spell out the three different communities. Yet, essentially, they are all alike in their bright inquisitiveness, in their delight in speaking to strangers. The girls are bolder than the boys who hang back, until a group approaches, shamed, perhaps, by the girls' boldness.

If we attract curiosity, our host MT, as he is popularly known, attracts awe. I can see he is a legend to the people here. A crowd collects round him. He ignores them at first, then turns round and confronts them, almost, it seems in desperation. For a moment they stare at each other in silence. Finally, he begins to talk. The questions come thick and fast. 'They all want to know about Leela', he says, explaining that Leela is a character in a story of his. I'm again amazed by the way literature is a part of people's lives. I see this again in the writer-reader interaction, during which writers and questioners sit in a circle, an outer ring being formed by a large audience who listen raptly. The moderator translates questions and answers into Malayalam for them. He seems to be a skilful translator; the whole-hearted audience response spells this out. School children, too young to understand, listen in respectful silence. And when, after a while, the teacher beckons, they get up and walk away noiselessly, careful not to disturb the gathering.

In the evening we go to the Thirunavaya temple nearby. It's a Vishnu temple, the idol being called 'Nava Mukundan'. Why 'Nava' (new)? The priest has no answer. An older priest, relaxing after the morning's puja, legs stretched before him, his face as spotless and gleaming as the puja vessels, which have been scrubbed and placed to dry in the sun, shakes his head too. The idol is on a height, scarcely visible to worshippers. The Devi, however, is closer, at a lower level. I get echoes of past lives, of distant fathers and intimate accessible mothers. Across the river, which runs by the temple, are two more temples of Brahma and Shiva. 'Can you see them?' an old priest asks, adding mischievously, 'You need young eyes to see them'. It's peaceful, sitting on the steps leading to the river. Nearby a family goes on with its rituals. Funeral rituals I gather; the river carries away the offerings like it does everything else, and upturned pots bob on the surface. This, the Bharata, is the longest river in Kerala, Gita tells me; but now, due to relentless dredging of the sand, a shadow of its old self.

On my way back to the airport, my companion, a poet-bureaucrat, speaks of poets and poetry, of how poems are sung or recited, and the cassettes played by taxis on their long journeys. The river seems to be travelling along with us, disappearing at times, but invariably returning to give us company. The car often slows down, at times it stops; something is holding up the traffic. When we move on, we find that the hold-up was due to an elephant. We see a group of them marching with a majestic dignity by the roadside, a branch or a banana stem in their mouths—their snacks for the journey, obviously. This is festival time, I'm told, and the elephants are moving from temple to temple. In a while, I get used to them; there's no longer any surprise at seeing them. But my delight in their serenely majestic presence never fades.

Communists, temples, elephants, rivers, writers, poets and legends—all woven together into a complex fabric. And yet, the question I've not been able to ask anyone remains: why, for God's sake, do they call it 'God's own country'?

(2003)

Mapping Bangalore

When we first came to Bangalore, it was still part of Mysore State; Karnataka would be born a few months later. To us, Bangalore was part of a twinned entity called Bengluru-Mysuru, the duller sibling, the commoner, as opposed to royal Mysore. Though we came here ten years after Independence, it was still incredibly feudal and loyal to its portly Maharaja, and people said 'Namma Maharajaru' reverently, with folded hands. It was a time when more jhutkas plied on the roads than buses and autorickshaws, two-wheelers meant bicycles, girls wore long skirts (rudely called parachutes, because of their billowing capacity), and almost every woman wore flowers in her hair.

The year was 1956. My father had been appointed as Drama Producer in All India Radio, Bangalore. He had come here before us and perhaps my mother had hoped he would have a home ready for us when we arrived. Instead, we were whisked off to a hotel, the Modern Hindu Hotel at Ananda Rao Circle. We didn't know it then, but we had gone straight to the heart of the city; we were only a stone's throw away from the Railway station, from Gandhinagar, and, most important of all, from the area called Majestic—the hub of the city. In the hotel itself, we imbibed the essence of Bangalore—a mélange of aromas: of agarbatti and flowers, of coffee and sambar and sagu masalas. And there was the distinctive Kannada, peppered with Swamis, Sirs and Ammas. A strange Kannada, we thought it, studded with English words. What was galling was that they thought it was *our* Kannada that was strange and incomprehensible. In just a few months there would be an influx of government servants from other regions into Bangalore and the newly created suburb of Rajajinagar would soon be flooded with Joshis, Kattis, Kulkarnis and Patils speaking our Kannada. But, to our chagrin, we would remain outsiders until the city found other outsiders to contend with.

To go back to 1956—my father must have realised that a hotel was not the place for his family, for we quickly moved into a temporary home. A colleague of his offered us the use of some rooms on the first floor of a relative's house in nearby Nehrunagar. The road was parallel to the railway line and, sitting on the large balcony above the portico, we could wave to the passengers of the trains that clattered past. I remember the beautiful red polished floor of that house, so typical of Bangalore houses then, of how it shone, almost like a mirror, and how cool it was under our feet when it rained. It was an interesting household; our host had 'married' a second time to get a child and an astrologer had promised that a child would 'soon come'. Unfortunately, we were not to know if that happened, for in a fortnight or so we left the place and moved into our first real home in Bangalore. This house, in Kumara Park, was like the innumerable Housing Board houses scattered through the city, and it had, in the landlords' terminology, one 'hall-u', two 'rooms-u', a 'kitchen-u' and a 'bathroom-u'. The entrance was a small grilled space, from where you could see who your visitors were, as well as watch the world go by. It was also the place where family and visitors shed their footwear when they entered. I remember when my father once had a reading of his play, which took place in the 'hall-u', someone carried away all the footwear—ours, as well as the visitors'—while the reading was going on. A whole lot of theatre enthusiasts walked home on their bare feet that evening!

We lived here for nearly two years, but scarcely came to know any neighbours, except our landlord and the couple who lived behind us. People in Bangalore, we realised, didn't believe in neighbourliness; they preferred to stare out of their windows when you passed by, to give you a blank stare when you met. During festival times, however, unknown little girls in long skirts came with invitations. Accepting these invitations meant that we were now met by occasional smiles and my mother with the inevitable inane question, 'Oota aaytaa?' (Have you eaten?). Nevertheless, the houses were so close that we were often granted intimate glimpses of our neighbours' lives. Living in such close proximity to others was a strange new experience for me; before this, we had lived in Dharwad, where our closest neighbours were beyond shouting distance. It was here that I saw the repetitiveness of women's lives, heard their conversations in the afternoon when their morning chores were done, noting the cadences in their voices as they spoke. Here that I saw how different women were when no men were around. Sounds that came back to me years later when I began writing.

Opposite our home were the tall walls of a boys' hostel, a place which came to life in summer when it was rented out for weddings. Through the long summer months, we listened to film songs in Kannada and Tamil blaring on the loudspeaker. I soon got to know most of the popular film songs of the day—my introduction to the movie culture in the city. I had come from Bombay, *the* film city; nevertheless, I was overwhelmed by my first sight of Kempegowda Road (KG Road to the locals. Bangalore had a penchant for abbreviation—I soon learnt to say KR Circle, NR Circle, etc.). More amazing than the number of theatres on the road were the posters outside them. Huge outsize posters with lush garlands nailed round the heroes' faces on the first day, heroes with pudgy faces and luxuriant moustaches, some trying to look dashing in tights, cloaks, masks and swords in their hands. There was the same kind of fleshy opulence about the heroines, who had mounds of flowers in their sleek hair. This was before Kannada activism and fanaticism began; no one questioned the fact that Tamil movies predominated. Only a couple of theatres showed Hindi films. One of them was Majestic, the theatre which gave the entire locality its name. I remember seeing the film *C.I.D* there. Kempegowda theatre, which also showed Hindi films, was a dark and dingy theatre, but my memories of it are forever coloured by a carefree, debonair Dilip Kumar singing '*Suhaana safar ...*' in *Madhumati*.

This area, Majestic, soon became a part of my life when I joined the Government Law College at the Mysore Bank Circle. Classes were in the morning. In my memory it was always cool and fresh when I walked along Seshadripuram Park, past the school where a huge pandal would spring up during Ramanavami to hold the head-nodding, thighs-clapping music aficionados. Past the usual 'lodge' with men's underwear and wet towels hanging on the railing, on which the young men leaned, calling out comments as I walked past, head held high, trying to ignore them. Waiting for my bus, opposite the Swastik theatre, I could smell flowers from the market behind me, horse dung from the jhutka stand, I could hear the bells from the temple nearby. I'm sure it rained sometimes, it must have been cold and hot as well, but I don't remember ever carrying an umbrella or wearing a sweater. Life was peaceful and innocent and the people quaintly old-fashioned. Yet, incongruously, there were plenty of wine shops. People here drank—something that seemed to us, coming from Morarji Desai's Bombay where Prohibition prevailed, shocking.

By now I had settled into the rhythm of this city, its gentle pace more familiar, so that I learnt to amble rather than trot. I had begun to cope with the indolence of the people, the 'doesn't matter' attitude, to appreciate the leisurely pace of shopping in the city. When we went to a jeweller on Avenue Road just before my wedding to get some jewellery made, I remember that we sat there for two entire days, my mother and I, picking out the best rubies for a necklace, stones of the right shape, size and colour. And this in an open shop, with people on the road walking past, within touching distance of the precious stones! I think of that when I see the dazzling glass-fronted jewellery shops today, swarming with security and closed-circuit TVs. Sari-shopping in those days was mainly in Chickpet, with the added attraction of a stop in a Balepet eating place, where you got the best dosas in town. The famous writer, Shivaram Karanth, it was said, stayed here when he came to Bangalore. The Cantonment was another world altogether, foreign territory which we visited occasionally for English movies, for loafing on South Parade (M.G. Road to newcomers!) or Commercial Street, or for rare family treats in Koshys. Cubbon Park, with its spectacular flowering trees and its air of peace, was a slice of Heaven. I can remember a time when my father lost his way in Cubbon Park. It was dark, a fine mist-like rain was falling and there was not a person or vehicle around. We drove round and round in circles, until my father accidentally found his way out.

We moved house an amazing number of times in those early years. Looking back, all the moves seem painless and easy to me. Perhaps they were, for we had minimal possessions and my mother, very competently, and without any fuss, coped with every change. But when my father announced that we were to move to Malleswaram, my heart sank. Until then we had lived mostly in the area around Kumara Park; these were the newer and posher areas. Malleswaram seemed incredibly old-fashioned and dowdy. But, of course, we did move there; this was to be my father's last move.

Malleswaram was like a snooty old lady, stately houses in large compounds with stone walls looking as if they had been there forever. The names at the gates, to our awe, said 'Zemindar of this' or 'Raja of that'. We never saw any of them, though, nor did anyone take note of us; there were no curtain-whisking neighbours here. Our house was a doll's house among giants. But it was here that my father found his place in Bangalore, our house becoming a hub for theatre, as well as for literary people. I can remember the writer Masti Venkatesh Iyengar beaming kindly at me, V. Sitaramiah, another writer impeccably dressed in the old Mysore style, Dr Shivaram's booming voice and jokes. Dr Shivaram was a doctor with a large practice as well as a writer; to listen to the conversation between him and my father, both very intelligent men but with opposing views, was a treat. The Niranjans, then a young literary couple (she too was a doctor), visited us and I can remember an even younger Girish Kasaravalli (later to become one of the most famous film directors in Karnataka) when he came to invite my father to his wedding.

The Sixth Main Road, on which we lived, was a quiet shady street, just a few roads away from the market and temple area on one side and the railway station on the other. The sound of trains hooting when I went to sleep and when I woke up became familiar in a while. In fact, the quaint little station became part of our lives. When I came back with my children, we took them there to see the trains go by. And my parents, in their later years, regularly walked there every morning, timing themselves by the trains. My bus stop was on Margosa Road, a short distance from the market area. Going to college in the mornings, I walked under a canopy of the gulmohar, passed the ubiquitous old man plucking flowers with the crook of his walking stick from others' gardens, inhaled the aroma of freshly roasted and ground coffee from the one shop that was open at the time. On the rare occasions when I came home a little late in the evenings, the roads were almost deserted and I walked home at a rapid, almost running pace, nervously watching my own shadow growing longer and shorter between the few streetlights. Malleswaram was a place where one walked. My friends and I walked every evening to the 18th Cross and beyond, my parents walked to the city railway station, to Gandhinagar and Rajajinagar. We walked to the post office, to the banks, to the market, to the—well, one just walked everywhere.

When I left for Bombay after marriage, I little thought I would come back to Bangalore. But fourteen years later, when my husband was offered a job in NIMHANS (the National Institute of Mental Health and Neuro Sciences), we returned. Both Bangalore and I had changed; I was no longer a girl, but a woman with two children. And Bangalore had begun its march ahead, though it was still a steady decorous progress through planned suburbs. We were to live on the NIMHANS campus, a place which had been, as the cemeteries which we passed before we got to it indicated, outside the town. At first, I didn't realise the slight odium attached to living there. 'NIMHANS' I would say to the bus conductor, to be met by a blank stare and then a grinning 'Ucch aspatre-aa? Why didn't you say so?' Nobody, it seemed, was willing to call it NIMHANS; it continued to be 'ucch aspatre'—the Mental Hospital. Our houses on the campus were in the midst of nowhere. We tried to civilise our surroundings, we got rid of thorny weeds and parthenium, we grew papayas and bananas, planted a cassia, a sampige. But for long it remained a wilderness. Once, before our houses were fenced in, our neighbour, an early riser, found one morning that he could not get out of his house; it had been bolted from the outside. Looking out of a window, he saw a group of huddled sleepers in the portico. When he called out, one tousled head was raised and a sleepy voice said, '*So jao*' (Go to sleep). Our neighbour, a man who enjoyed the unusual, did just that. When he woke up, the door had been unbolted and the group of nomads had gone. We had an unbidden guest too, a recalcitrant snake in our backyard, which defied all our efforts to get rid of it and refused to leave. Even the snake-catcher went away defeated. Finally we left it alone, being careful not to go there at night. But we saw it once or twice when it came out to sun itself, a beautiful shining cobra.

We were surrounded by hospitals and localities with names I had never heard—Byrasandra, Lakkasandra, Hombegowda Nagar, Audogodi. I was fascinated by the dark, broody Christian cemeteries on the Audogodi road where branches of lush trees drooped heavily and protectively over the ancient graves and tombstones. A symbiotic relationship, for the trees grew so huge, they seemed to be enriched by the dead. I promised myself that I would go and wander among the graves one day, read the names etched on the tomb stones, find out who those dead were.

But it was not to be. My husband gave up his job in NIMHANS and once again we packed our belongings and set off for another house, this in a distant (it seemed so then) suburb, Banashankari, a place I had never seen. Those were the monsoon months and my memories of that year are of constant heavy rains, a very rare thing in Bangalore. Our house was damp, dismal and full of cockroaches; once again we were in a row of back to back houses, in a street of curtain-twitching neighbours. I took long walks in the evening during which I saw a new locality taking shape. Houses were coming up everywhere. But my own creativity seemed at a standstill; I could not write. The greatest solace of my life was to go up on the terrace and see the hills in the far distance, to watch the monsoon clouds and feel the breeze on my face. Far away, I could see a lone bus plying on a road that seemed to lead to nowhere; that way, I was told, lay Padmanabha Nagar, soon to become a new layout. The small street with its cheek-by-jowl houses was claustrophobic and I was glad when we moved out in just a few months, first to a house near Ashoka Pillar in Jayanagar, and then back to Malleswaram, to the apartment my father had built above his house. A totally changed Malleswaram. Unknown cars drove past with people from the new apartment blocks that had come up in the past few years in place of the old bungalows. Only the old bungalow opposite ours held steadfast, its large compound and all the trees in it intact. A new generation of children were throwing stones at the mangos on the trees along the stone wall. Not urchins now, but students of a school on the next road, who, having no playground, came here during their breaks to play cricket. All morning, while I sat at my table trying to write, I heard raucous cries of 'Out!', 'Not out!' or a triumphantly strident 'Four!' or 'Sixer!' In the evenings my father sat out, looking anxiously at the sky, waiting for rains, fanning himself with a piece of paper. Where were the clouds? Where had the rains gone? And what was happening to the traffic? It was becoming increasingly difficult for my husband to travel all the way to South End Circle and back, something that pushed us into taking a decision: the time had come to possess our own little bit of land in Bangalore.

We built a house and moved to Jayanagar. A suburb where every fifth house had a name plate that said 'Retd Chief Engineer' and where more people spoke Kannada than elsewhere. Like all householders in Bangalore, we planted trees. Frangipani and parijaat within our compound, a neem and gulmohar outside. And as they let down their roots, so did we. By the time the frangipani flowered, the gulmohar stretched across the road and the parijaat shed its flowers to create a white and red carpet every morning, we had learnt to say 'Kamplexu' for the Shopping Complex, to call the row of parks 'Rose Gardens'. We got to know the places for the best dosas, masala and chutney powders. I travelled every Sunday to Malleswaram to visit my mother. The drive through the quiet roads on Sunday mornings was like a journey to the past. The roads were so familiar I could have driven with my eyes closed. With my mother's death my links to Malleswaram snapped. Jayanagar was truly home. But like a spider's web, a fine tracery of lines began to connect us to the rest of the city, to family and friends—Defence Colony and Banashankari, Mathikere and Koramangala, Sanjaynagar and J.P. Nagar.

How much land does a man need? Tolstoy asked. A forty by sixty piece of land seemed enough to knit us into this city.

(2006)

The Unconquered Fort

Three hundred years of colonial rule have so cut us off from most of the world, except Britain, that the present wave of globalisation seems a new phenomenon. But our entire West Coast is dotted with reminders of earlier contacts with the world, mainly with those who came to trade—this, even before the Europeans arrived. One of the important relics of the maritime history of India is the island fort of Janjira. Its fascinating and little-known story, as well as its proximity to Mumbai (a mere five hours' drive), make us decide to visit the place.

Our destination is Murud in Raigad district. One can get there by boat as well, but we travel by car, taking the Goa highway, going past Wadkal Naka (the breakfast halt) where we get off the highway, and then past Alibag. After Alibag the road becomes more interesting as it winds round the hills. Now, there's a whiff of the sea and we get occasional glimpses of it. And then comes Murud. A fishing village at one time, perhaps, but now something a little more than that, though clearly not a madly popular tourist destination.

Our resort, we find with pleasure, is beautifully located. We have only to descend a few steps to get to the beach. It is high tide when we get there, and the distant purring of the incoming waves is a very pleasing sound. But we decide to explore the town first. Stepping outside the gate, we find we have to walk in single file on the few inches of space given to pedestrians, while buses and trucks thunder past us. We give up and go to the beach, which is quiet, almost like a private beach. And peaceful, something we do not expect in a place so close to Mumbai. Post-monsoon (the best time to be here), the sea is well-behaved, its monsoon unruliness a thing of the past. Nevertheless, there are no swimmers, not even the locals. And no hawkers, either. It is now low tide and we can see that the sea has ebbed a long distance, leaving stretches of glistening wet sand. There is a pony offering rides to kids and a horse-driven little open carriage which goes jingling up and down, the bells playing a gay tune as the pony trots from one end of the beach to another. We watch the sunset, always the most spectacular show on earth, and end the day looking forward to tomorrow and Janjira fort, the purpose of our visit.

Once again, we drive through winding roads as we make for Rajapuri jetty, from where we take the boat for Janjira. As we walk to the jetty through a narrow lane, we are only a few inches away from houses on either side; but though the doors are open, scarcely anyone turns to look at us as we go past. Obviously, they are used to tourists. But our co-passengers must be locals, for they get into the boat, a very basic sailing boat, with the ease of veterans, while we struggle to find our footing on the narrow, wet planks. Suddenly there is a buzz and we see the fort. We know it is an island fort, but we are not prepared for the astonishing sight of it, rising, like an offering, from the sea. That it is built on rock comes painfully home to us when we have to land. No soft landing, this. Because of the rock, the boat can't get too near and we have to leap off it on to the rock. There is a man waiting below to help the old and the faint-hearted. 'My bhai' the boatman says about the man; he is also to be our guide. 'Follow me', the 'bhai' says and obediently we follow him up the steep slope of the rock and into the fort.

Janjira fort has a long and strange history. There are contradictory reports about its origin; some say that it was built by the Kolis, others that it was built by Siddi Johar in the twelfth century. The Siddis are Abyssinian Muslims who came as traders, some of whom settled in India along the coast. The guide's story does not tell us why they stayed on, why they needed to fortify themselves and how they got enough money to build this astonishing fort. Whatever it is, in time they established their presence on the coast (there is even a Marathi word for Abyssinia—'Habshi') and became part of the tumultuous history of this part of India during the sixteenth and seventeenth centuries.

The fort is mostly in ruins now, but we are shown the rusty cannons, the look-out apertures which enabled the inhabitants to see anything approaching, and, the greatest miracle, a large fresh-water well, which made living possible here. It is tiring going up and down among the broken walls and slippery slopes, but when we get to the top, we have a wonderful view of the sea. While the guide tells us about the existence of a tunnel under the sea (which has never been found) and a concealed backdoor escape route, I think of the miracle of the monsoon winds which brought ships and people from various lands as traders, adventurers and colonisers, some of whom stayed on and became a part of this country. Like Malik Amber, the most famous Siddi of all, who strengthened the Janjira fort and rose from being a slave to becoming the regent of Ahmednagar. He had perfected the art of guerrilla warfare even before Shivaji and defeated both the mighty Mughals and the Bijapur king at the Battle of Bhatvadi in 1624.

The guide's patter seems to consist more of legend than of facts, but he is right in stressing the power of the Siddhis, who at one time were, a historian says, the strongest active power on the Konkan coast. The guide is right too when he says the fort was never conquered. The Dutch, the Portuguese, the British—all of them failed. Even Shivaji, that great taker of forts, could not conquer it. His son, Sambhaji, after successive failures, built another fort, Padmadurg, which the guide points out to us across the sea. The young and dynamic Bajirao Peshwa failed too, though he captured a great deal of Siddi lands in Raigad district. Strangely, while all the other powers have now vanished, the Nawab of Janjira (at some time, a Siddhi chief metamorphosed into the Nawab) still has his palace in Murud. (Out of bounds to tourists, unfortunately.)

Two hours are not enough to see the whole fort; you need two days, the guide says. But another boatload of tourists is coming in, it is time to leave. This is our last evening and we have promised ourselves a ride in the ghoda-gadi. It is a wonderful experience riding in the carriage to the accompaniment of the gay jingling bells, the tiny sound somehow making itself heard above the resonance of the waves.

We walk back to our resort, leaving the susurrating murmur of the waves behind us, softened and muted by the surrounding silence. In the resort, there are families everywhere, adults relaxing over drinks, children running about. Fairy lights strung along the paths have been switched on; the place looks enchanting, the people transformed. It is peaceful and relaxed. A great place, we agree, for a weekend stay, combining relaxation and a slice of not-much-known-history of the country in equal measure.

(2008)

The Globalisation of Bangalore

If the concept of globalisation includes, as I think it surely does, an idea of connections between events and places through the world, this facet of globalisation has always been with us. To me, a very interesting illustration of this phenomenon is what happened to a small town, Karwar, on the west coast of India. There was a move to develop this beautiful natural port during the time of the American Civil War, when the blockade made it difficult for the British manufacturers to get cotton from the United States. Karwar, being close to the cotton-growing areas, seemed an ideal solution. However, before this could be done, the war ended, the plan was dropped, Karwar went back to being a small town and Bombay, which could have been threatened by the new port, heaved a sigh of relief.

I see the same kind of connection between Bangalore entering the global world through software and the existence, in the early part of the last century, of a great engineer and visionary administrator in the State of Mysore—Sir M. Visvesvarayya. It was his influence and vision that made this area produce so many engineers—many of whom joined the government projects in the first phase of industrialisation after independence. This was followed, some decades later, by private engineering institutes which cashed in on the need for more engineers. This, in turn, produced a large pool of engineers, which, added to the scientific pool that was already existing in Bangalore, provided the foundation for the emerging software companies to build on, making the city the focus of the software revolution in India. And so, Bangalore, which in the fifties was just a largish town, changed rapidly and completely and shows today, more than any other city in India, the glittering façade of cosmopolitanism. The very young men and women in these software firms earn a salary that the earlier generation of engineers could never have dreamt of, money that this generation wants to spend. Which is converting Bangalore from a city of pensioners, of a sedate middle class which ate its dosas, drank its coffee and went to bed at nine o'clock, to a throbbing and lively city of young people. A city of pizza huts, pubs, bars, swanky restaurants, designer clothes and department stores the like of which we had not seen in India—all of these catering to the needs of the young to whom the good life is an American way of life. Or what they think is the American way of life. Which has created a new kind of division in the city.

There always were four worlds in Bangalore—the old Kannada world, the Christian Anglo-Indian world, the Muslim world and the Tamil world. Four separate and distinct worlds, yet all of them coexisting companionably together. Now we have two worlds: those who can participate in and get their share of the new prosperity and those who, for many reasons, can't. Physically too we have two cities. The old city is still there, but is being pushed steadily to the periphery, while this new young city takes over the centre. The middle class is gradually being eroded, clinging precariously to old values and old standards, while the ground under them is sinking under the weight of inflation and removal of subsidies. The houses they built for themselves, for their children and for their children's children are being sold and they are moving away to smaller places further away. In place of these houses, which are instantly demolished, we have opulent apartment blocks with swimming pools and 24-hour security service. More and more older people are living alone, left to fend for themselves, a phenomenon visible everywhere, but specially in Bangalore where the number of young people living abroad is vast. There is a disparity between an aging population, which is getting increasingly isolated because of the lack of public transport in the city, and the very mobile, moneyed young, a disparity which, if not as horrendous as what one sees in cities like Bombay or Calcutta, still hurts.

There are greater and more disturbing disparities in the area of medical care. In the last few years, following on the heels of Bangalore's new visibility and prosperity, a number of very large hospitals have come up in and around Bangalore, with very modern equipment and a highly qualified staff. Some are as good as any abroad and, in fact, are specially designed to attract people from abroad, offering package deals which give cheaper medical care than anything available in a developed country. In contrast to this, the local people, specially those with little money, and the destitute, have nothing but the government hospitals, which are a byword for neglect and corruption and lack everything that a hospital needs, including human caring and compassion.

The other area of great disparity is in education. International residential schools are a recent phenomenon in Bangalore. Children are driven directly from the airport to these schools, and, when they finish schooling, many of them move on to an American or a British University. These schools are islands of luxury—which is all right, because people who can pay have a right to the best. What is not so good is the fact that the students have no contact at all with the city, the people, the language, or the culture of Bangalore And what is really terrible is the contrast between these and other schools in Bangalore, which are of three kinds: good English schools for the well-to-do, bad English schools for the not-so-well-off and, at the bottom of the ladder, Kannada schools, most of which are in an appalling state, with crumbling buildings, bad teachers and, often, not even benches for the students, or blackboards for the teachers to write on. Since the children who go to these schools belong to the poorer and the powerless class, there is no chance of anything being done to improve matters, either. In any case, it sometimes seems these schools will be an extinct species since everyone, just everyone, wants to have an English education.

Which brings me to a very visible effect of globalisation—the increasing use and the power of the English language. The desire for more opportunities, the desire to move into another social class, are making English education almost a necessity for an ambitious parent or child. Most agree that this is reprehensible, for, as the intellectuals are crying out, it brings about an alienation from one's own culture. But just as bad is the backlash to this, which has come out of language being made a political issue by politicians for their own purposes. And, therefore, this doubt about alienation from our own culture has been converted into fear and translated into an aggressiveness and hostility which forgets the reality of the need of people for more opportunities. And yet the anger, like there is in the assertion of one's own ethnicity in these global times, is real. It is this anger that lies under the surface of this glittering city, this anger which is the thin sharp blade between the two Bangalores. And though Bangalore is a gentle city, and the people tolerant and civilised, I am afraid this anger will erupt sometime or the other.

Even if the disparities which globalisation brings on are very disturbing, we know that we cannot halt the progress of events or go against the tide. Nevertheless, we must take note of some things. We need a globalisation that does not mean only a free flow of capital and goods, but includes an opening of borders, a free flow of information, of knowledge and culture. And of people. Right now, countries choose who and how many outsiders they will allow in—a decision taken in accordance with *their* own needs—in which they blatantly exploit the fact that the need of those who go out for employment is much greater than the need of those who want labour; this, because there are enough nations in the world to provide cheap labour. And so, people from not-so-developed countries accept the terms dictated by employers. This is not being equal. And if you are not equal, you are not free. I think of these highly educated engineers and doctors as being almost the same as the bonded labourers who went out to Fiji, the West Indies, or Sri Lanka. I see this domination even in literature; what sells outside the country is what the West considers good Indian literature, what fits into their concept of good Indian writing. Many of us in India, writers and critics, are uneasy about the popularity of a certain kind of Indian writing abroad, about it's being more visible even in our own country. One has an uncomfortable feeling that it is the powerful and rich countries who make the decisions about what is good writing. I see a parallel to this in the beauty contests, in which young women shape themselves to fit into a certain idea of beauty—a conformity to a Western idea of beauty. Globalisation, in other words, has begun to mean a standardisation; and the standards are those of the rich and the powerful. Standardisation is always the enemy of excellence, of originality or genius since it means a cutting away of the edge of differences.

Globalisation has brought new people from all over the country and outside to Bangalore; it has taken away the old inertia and passivity, of waiting for the government to do things, to take charge. But it has also brought in a culture, which, backed by money and marketing, threatens to swamp the original face of the city. However, a capacity to absorb, to adapt, has always been a part of our civilisation. I see a symbol of this resilience in the new fast food joints in Bangalore which have sprung up all over the place and give cheap South Indian food. They are holding their own very successfully against other fast food joints (the burger and pizza places) which are an import from the West. In these Darshinis, as the South Indian fast food joints are called, I see the shape of the future of Bangalore, in fact of India itself. We accept what comes from outside, but we hold on to our own, nevertheless.

(2002)

A Review of *The Life of Harishchandra* by Raghavanka, translated by Vanamala Vishwanatha

The avowed intention of the Murty Classical Library (MCL) is 'To present the greatest literary works of India from the past two millennia to the largest readership in the world'. To which one could add that this library, as it emerges volume by volume, will also be a corrective to the generally accepted idea that classical Indian literature is only in Sanskrit. There have been translations from other languages, of course, but this is the first time that a concerted effort is being made to get texts translated from diverse languages and in different genres. A recent addition to this eclectic collection is a thirteenth-century Kannada text, Raghavanka's *Harishchandra Charitre*, translated by Vanamala Vishwanatha into English as *The Life of Harishchandra*. It is a poem of fourteen chapters, presented, except for the lament of Chandramati, in sextets (shatpadi). Though written in the style of classical Sanskrit poetry, it has been localised by the poet, who has brought in his native place Hampi (in North Karnataka), given the river Tungabhadra an almost Ganga-like status, and raised his local deity Virupaksha above all gods, making the story, as the translator says in her brief but illuminating introduction, 'a Kannada text'.

The story of King Harishchandra, a man who never swerved from the truth, even at the cost of great suffering, is known throughout India. A very old story, which exists in the Vedas, the Mahabharata and the Puranas, it has stayed alive for centuries through stories, poems, drama. Old stories continue to live, they never lose their charm, because they are reinterpreted in each retelling. Raghavanka has taken the bare bones of the Harishchandra story, fleshed it out and done a very creative retelling through lyrical and dramatic narrative. He lays the foundation for Harishchandra's tragedy in an argument between two great Rishis, Vashishta and Vishwamitra, in Indra's court, about who is the most truthful being on earth. While Vashishta holds up King Harishchandra as such a man, Vishwamitra vehemently disagrees and vows to prove that Harishchandra is a liar. Raghavanka then gives us a picture of Harishchandra's glory, the way he is loved by his subjects. Into this Paradise enters Vishwamitra with his villainy, intent on trapping Harishchandra into an untruth. In an innovative ploy, Raghavanka has Vishwamitra send two *holatis* (low-caste women) to seduce the King. Which they do, but when they ask him to marry them, the King's pride in his family and caste is deeply offended, he becomes violent and drives them out. Vishwamitra, calling the women his daughters, insists that Harischandra marry them. The argument becomes heated, until finally, Harishchandra, provoked by Vishwamitra, says, 'I would rather give up my kingdom than marry these low-caste women'. Fateful words, which cost Harishchandra everything: his kingdom, wealth, his wife and son, his own self, and, finally, even his caste.

In her introduction, Vishwanatha says that Raghavanka brings 'the conflict between the castes centre stage'. In fact, it enters the story when Vashishta calls Vishwamitra a Kshatriya sage (sages were always Brahmins) and an enraged Vishwamitra threatens that Harishchandra would pay for this insult. He does pay—to an unimaginable extent: not only does he lose everything he has, he has to work under a Chandala master in a burning ghat, becomes a Chandala himself, and has to execute his wife as a killer. At this culmination of Harishchandra's tragedy, relief, in the best tradition of all moral stories, comes in the guise of Virupaksha (Shiva), and Harischandra gets back all that he had lost.

Translation, as all translators worth their salt know, is a perilous job. It is like trying to enter another writer's mind, at times even the writer's soul. Translation from an Indian language into English is harder, because the two languages belong to different cultures, each comes from a different ethos. The difficulty of translating a classical text which is 'utterly religious, unabashedly hyperbolic, highly stylised and entirely bound by metrical convention' (the translator's words), specially when done for a contemporary reader, is undoubtedly immense. Fortunately, humans thrive on challenge. Which is how we have this translation of *Harishchandra Charitre*. The translator speaks of the need for tightrope walking between faithfulness to the text and making it accessible to the reader. The fact that reading this text yields unhindered pleasure tells us that the translator has maintained her balance remarkably well. The choices she has made have yielded a happy amalgam of verse, prose narration, and crisp dialogue which give a sense of immediacy and modernity. Shama Futehally, a writer and translator, says that a translation should leave the reader 'astounded and joyful'. Passages from the chapter on hunting do just that. The hunting chapter is indeed a remarkable one, the very words carrying with them the clangour of weapons, the clamour of voices, both human and animal, while the swiftly issued crisp commands give us a sense of ordered chaos and the list of weapons an idea of the professionalism of the hunters. In translating these amazing passages, the translator has matched the poet word for word, phrase for phrase, the words coming, not out of a thesaurus, but the same treasure chest the poet had dipped into. Above all, the translation comes to us as a living story, having almost the same vitality the original has.

In an essay, Vishwanatha has spoken of how, in translating from an Indian language into English, the need is not to bend the original language to fit into English, but to stretch English 'to make it speak the poetry of the original language'. Clearly, she has carried out this idea in this translation. Which is why some words which are untranslatable have been retained. This perhaps is right; what makes one uneasy are the occasional infelicities in the English words used. Like 'fairies' for forest goddesses. Or the 'coquetry' of the brothel. While, thankfully, the translator uses an easy contemporary English, some slang words hurt: Vishwamitra's 'why get mad at me' and words like 'blathering' or 'rattling' for profuse talk. But, as the poets say, even the moon has its spots, though one wishes the editorial eye had been keener and picked up these inapposite words.

One of the problems for a translator, specially of a text of earlier times, is the ideology. Writers write out of the social, political, and cultural world they live in. Clearly another age will find some ideas and beliefs odd, perhaps even abhorrent. As Vishwanatha says, 'I had to fight my visceral resistance to the text's implicit stance towards caste and gender'. Harishchandra's treatment of the women sent to him by Vishwamitra, and his arrogance of caste, will make a contemporary reader cringe. Nevertheless, no translator can impose her ideas on another writer's text. And in fact there are correctives to these offensive ideas in the text itself. (One must remember that Raghavanka came only a short while after Basaveshwara, that great rebel against the caste system.) There is the spirited defence by the women themselves when they ask the King why, when their music, their beauty, and fragrance don't defile him, only their touch does. Ultimately, Harischandra does express regret for his arrogance, his pride in his family and his caste. Though, sadly, not for the way he treated the women. Gender prejudice, it seems, is harder to conquer than caste prejudice.

This translation is, as the words 'largest readership' hint, meant for any interested reader (and reviewer), not only for a scholar or a specialist. It left this reader with the simmering excitement of discovery, of surprise, that a text nearly 800 years old could be not only so readable, but thought-provoking as well. For, it arouses questions not only about caste and gender, but also about the truth. We see that, strangely, in India, truth lies not in words, but in keeping one's word. In fact, whether it is Dasharath, Bhishma, or Sri Ram, all of them adhere to this kind of truth. Whereas, in the story of Job in the Bible, so strangely similar to Harishchandra's, Job's faith is in God. 'The Lord gave and the Lord hath taken away; blessed be the name of the Lord', Job cries out when his wealth is gone and his children die. Max Müller spoke of the Mahabharata's profound 'regard for the truth'. But the word that resounds in that epic is 'dharma'. So is there some kind of ethical principle which embraces both these words, satya and dharma? Something to ponder over.

Classics don't have to be venerated or enshrined. They have to be read. And *The Life of Harischandra* makes it clear that what a language needs are publishers with a vision like the MCL and passionate translators like this one. Fulminating against English and agitating for a classical language status are no substitutes for steady and scholarly work like translating such texts.

(2018)

A Review of *Filomena's Journeys* by Aurora Maria Couto

The two beautiful pictures on the front and back covers of the book seem to convey the essence of the story told within the covers. The young woman on the front cover is looking at the camera with a shy, sideways look, a look which belies the poise and the sophistication she otherwise shows. Contradicts, too, the firm line in which the delicate lips are set. In the picture on the back cover, the same woman, much older, is laughing heartily, released, it seems, from whatever had inhibited her earlier, giving a hint of the journey she has travelled in the years in between.

Filomena's Journeys is Aurora Maria Couto's second book. Her first, *Goa: A Daughter's Story,* was a remarkable book, which, through a mingling of personal and family histories with the larger history of Goa, gave the reader a picture of a Goa most of us did not know. A Goa that, through long years of Portuguese rule, was set apart, both from British India and the areas ruled by local rulers. *Filomena's Journeys* has a much smaller canvas, being the story of Maria Couto's parents and their marriage. Yet, this book, too, by combining the story of two people and their marriage with the history and culture of Goa, goes way beyond the merely personal.

It is hard to write about oneself, about one's family. Harder still to see one's parents as people, to enter that prohibited sacred space of their marriage. For the truth is that all families have their secrets, dark rooms which have been kept firmly shut. Yet, like she did in *Goa: A Daughter's Story* when she unflinchingly told the painful story of forced conversions in Goa, here, too, Maria Couto opens the door to the dark rooms in her family; she tells the truth about Filomena's father's death, a man lying in 'an unmarked grave', she speaks openly of the alcoholism that destroyed a family, and of the gradual disintegration of a marriage. Her great strength is the manner of narration—she is never just telling, she is probing, questioning, trying to understand. And by knitting the story together with memories, surmises, conversations, both real and imagined, and documented facts, Maria Couto goes way beyond the story of two people and their marriage. Her careful detailing of the two families, Filomena's and her husband Chico's, makes it as much a story of contrasts as of conflicts: Chico belonging to a class of people used to inherited wealth and prestige, 'not conscious of hardships and deprivations in their own backyard'; Filomena's family, a rural one, where 'women's lives were connected to the rituals of the Church and the agricultural calendar'; Chico, a pampered and indulged child; and Filomena, who lost both her parents very early, responsible and hard-working. This is also the story of contrasts in Goa, of class and caste differences in a feudal society, a story of those who were afraid that the end of Portuguese rule would mean that they would lose the distinctive culture that Portuguese colonisation had given Goa and who therefore did not want to be part of the new independent India ('Liberation! It was invasion') and of those who fought for liberation.

In telling the story of her parents' marriage, Maria Couto often eschews the personal and speaks of herself in the third person as 'Chico's/Filomena's oldest daughter', keeping herself in the background. The only time she comes out of the shadows is when she speaks of what living in Dharwad, a small town, did to the family, to her specially, opening out a larger world to her than she would have seen in Goa. Otherwise, she achieves a rare objectivity. A remarkable example is the way she brings back a memory of cruelty and violence, telling the story through the eyes of the frightened child she was then, giving an impressionist picture of anger, raised voices, broken plates and blood and of children cowering together fearfully on a bed. Yet, the author's objectivity does seem to desert her at times. 'Why should he deserve understanding?' she asks, speaking of the father. Then quickly adds, 'If she (Filomena) had compassion for him, how can her daughter not?' Her comment, 'Chico is a mystery to be lived, rather than a problem, a tragedy to be explained', is indeed a compassionate one.

Though this is the portrait of 'a marriage, a family & a culture', there is no doubt that this is really Filomena's story. She is the heroine of it. Orphaned early, she married a man full of promise, a man who belonged to one of the elite families of Goa. And yet, within a short time, their life together began falling apart and she had to take on the entire responsibility of the growing family. Maria Couto's unstinting admiration of her mother is always controlled, preventing the book from becoming a hagiography. There is the way she speaks of Filomena's decision to move away from Goa, to settle down in Dharwad for the good of the children's education and for Chico as well—a decision she took despite Chico's violent rejection of the plan. She went alone to Dharwad to check out the place, went on ahead with all the luggage to set up house, and then came back to take the children. Something very unusual for that time when women rarely travelled alone, almost never without a male escort. Yet, this is stated by Maria Couto in a remarkably matter-of-fact manner, as if it was the norm for any woman, and no great achievement.

When Maria Couto wrote *Goa: A Daughter's Story*, it seemed Goa had found its ideal chronicler. Now, with her second book, she has invented an entirely new genre, a mixture of memoir, biography and history, resulting in a fascinating tapestry of human lives and relationships, showing, almost as an aside, how human lives are impacted by historical events. Her painstaking research about the places Chico and Filomena lived in—Raia and Margao—about their families and family connections, about the way they lived, the food they ate, the clothes they wore, gives us a clear picture of their lives. Thankfully, the book does not sag under the weight of the facts it carries, though at times the reader, wanting to go on with the story of Filomena and her Chico, may find some of the details, like the lists (of the food eaten and the music played at parties and during weddings) a little tedious. So too the plethora of families and their names, which at times tend to leave the reader a little confused.

Feminism has questioned the invisibility of women in history. Virginia Woolf, speaking of the Elizabethan woman, says, 'One knows nothing detailed, nothing perfectly true or substantial about her. History scarcely mentions her'. This is true about all women everywhere and at all times. And though it would be unfair to speak of feminism in the context of Filomena's life, or of her daughter's account of it—that was, after all, another era, it was a different world—there is no doubt that Maria Couto gives us certain truths about women's lives: of the difference in the way girls and boys were educated, of the loneliness of the wives of migrant men who went out of Goa to earn money, of women who lived privileged lives but were unable to cope with a changing world, of women like Filomena's mother, who brought up her grandchildren after her daughter's death, as also managed the land that gave them their livelihood. Apart from its undoubted literary value, there is no doubt that in writing this book, and bringing one woman's life out of the shadows, Maria Couto has given us a glimpse of how the chronicling of women's lives can fill a large empty space in history. Long back, Isak Dinesen wrote a short story, 'The Blank Sheet', about princesses whose marriage sheets, with the bloodstains which declared their virginity, were publicly displayed. Only one sheet stood out among all these stained sheets—a sheet which remained white and pure, giving rise to various surmises about what that princess's story could have been. There is no doubt that books like Maria Couto's *Filomena's Journeys*, whether it was the author's intent or not, try to do away with the blank sheet and give women their legitimate place in history.

(2014)

A Review of *Distant Traveller*—a Collection of Attia Hosain's Writing

A tribute to Attia Hosain in her centenary year, *Distant Traveller* is an unusually beautiful production, even the elegant cover conveying a sense of nostalgia for an earlier age. The book contains excerpts from an unfinished novel of Attia Hosain's (*No New Lands, No New Seas*), a number of stories, including some unpublished ones, and a non-fiction piece, 'Deep Roots'—all this lovingly clasped between a 'Foreword' by Shama Habibullah, Attia's daughter, and an 'Afterword' by the writer and critic Aamer Hussain, both of whom have also selected the material and edited the book. Shama's 'Foreword' gives a personal view of her mother and her writing, while Aamer puts the writer in the context of other writers of her time. All of it making the book a satisfying and fitting tribute to an author who needed to be freshly looked at.

In her brief note, the publisher Ritu Menon refers to the feminist enterprise of retrieving and locating women's writing. Attia's novel, *Sunlight on a Broken Column*, and her short story collection *Phoenix Fled* were indeed reissued by Virago (1988) in their Virago Modern Classics series, part of their project of rediscovering classics by women writers. But, as Menon herself admits, Attia would not have regarded herself as a feminist writer. Nevertheless, *Distant Traveller* once again shows that some of

Attia Hosain's best stories are about women. The wretchedness of their lives is at the heart of 'The Loss', 'The Street of the Moon', 'The Daughter-in-Law', and 'Parrot in a Cage'. Yet, the stories are never simple ones of victim and exploiter but bring out the complex nuanced web of human relations. In 'The Street of the Moon', the tragedy is as much that of Kalloo, the cook, as it is of his young wife, Hasina. In fact, Attia's stories are really about the underdog, a word that seems far more suitable than 'subaltern' with its military overtones. Though, in truth, to call the stories as being *about* women or *about* the underdog would be to do them an injustice, because her best stories are, above all, intense and powerful stories. 'The Loss', for example, a story quieter than 'The Street of the Moon' or 'The Daughter-in-Law', which could be looked at as a story of two different classes, is remarkable for the variety of emotions it portrays in the relationship between a man, his foster mother and her real son. The guilt the man feels, because of his money and his privileged position, subtly changes at the end into a sense of loss when he realises that, to his foster mother, the only thing that matters is her son. At the end one is confronted with the question: Whose is the loss? The mother's, who lost her property, or the man's, who lost his sense of being loved?

The unpublished stories in this book do not have the same strength. In fact, 'The Leader of Women' carries the author's note: 'I don't know what I was driving at really. What can I do to this?' It makes one wonder: Does everything that a writer leaves behind need to be published? Does an author, guided by the writer's self-critical instinct, deliberately leave some writing unpublished? Would not the author rather have some early attempts shrouded in silence? But since the editors' desire in *Distant Traveller* was 'to chart the progress of Attia's literary career', as Aamer Hussain says, the inclusion even of her lesser stories makes sense. The unfinished novel *No New Lands* ... is a case in point. It shows the distance Attia had traveled since her first novel, *Sunlight on a Broken Column*. Unlike *Sunlight,* a youthful exuberant novel spilling with colour and energy, this novel (written sometime between the 1960s and 70s) is, from what little one gets to read of it, grey, spare, austere, enveloped in the sorrowful mist of nostalgia and regret. The characters in this novel seem tormented by the anguish of not belonging, bewildered at finding themselves where they are. To read even these few pages is to see the possibility that Attia was, perhaps, charting a new course in diasporic writing, looking at immigrants with a different vision. (She herself called this 'my immigrant novel' or 'my expatriate novel'.) The character Murad Sahib calls Munnay, the Bangladeshi waiter, and his like, 'intrepid explorers ... adventurers who came, like conquistadors, in search of wealth'. The characters, the conversations between Murad Sahib and Munnay, between Murad Sahib and Choudhary, the owner of a restaurant, make for fascinating reading and whet the reader's appetite for more.

Why did she never complete the novel? Shama hazards a guess that 'perhaps the imagined lives she wanted to write about took her into political areas that were dark and pessimistic'.

I have to wonder whether the answer lies in something she says in 'Deep Roots', which, to me as a writer, is the most interesting essay in the book; it is in this piece that she affirms the credo of her writing. She speaks of the 'great and silent gap' that remains between two cultures which words are not adequate to bridge. 'In writing my first novel, I became painfully aware of the inadequacy of the words I was using when I came up against that silent gap'. Attia Hosain's was not the path of the usual expatriate diasporic writer—distanced, an observer rather than a participator. 'I could never have written so truthfully about Britain and the British as I did about India', she says. She had to be an insider. And she abhorred explanations, something which has plagued Indian Writing in English (IWE) since the beginning; in *Deep Roots* she calls explaining a curb on the creative process.

> 'Explain, explain. That is just what I am tired of ...' says Isa in *No New Lands* ... 'What constitutes belonging? That there is no need for explanation.'

Was it her refusal to bridge the silent gap by explanations that made it hard for her to go on writing? And yet, so many Indian English writers have been able to surmount this problem, even without explanations. Perhaps, being part of a constantly changing dynamic society, being knitted into it, helps to make the leap across that gap possible. Would Attia have found a way out of her dilemma if she had continued to live in India and knew where she belonged? As she herself says, belonging means there is no need for explanation.

Reading this book and realising the kind of writer Attia was, one wonders why she is not given the recognition she deserves in India. Why she is rarely mentioned when pioneers like R.K. Narayan, Mulk Raj Anand or Raja Rao are much celebrated. Is it because she did not live in India? Or because she wrote very little? Or was it because she was published in England first and only later in India so that she was not so widely known? (In fact, *Distant Traveller* is the first of her books to be first published in India.)

In truth, the quality of her writing, as well as her concerns, put her squarely among the early Indian English writers. Aamer Hussain speaks of critics who place her in the midst of the multi-cultured writing in England, specially among the women writers born abroad, like Doris Lessing, Jean Rhys, Muriel Spark. But to me, as a reader, she belongs very much to Indian Writing in English. I remember my own excitement when I first read *Sunlight*, an excitement that no other Indian English book has given me, except, much later, Anita Desai's *Clear Light of Day*—and this, not to the same extent. Later as a writer I felt a kinship with her I felt with no other writer of an earlier generation.

Distant Traveller is not only a tribute to Attia Hosain, but a timely reminder to Indian readers of the existence of a writer whose language was elegant, narration nuanced, and whose characters never dwindled into stereotypes. This reminder is very necessary today, when Indian Writing in English is on a self-congratulatory high, with good writing being disdained in the search for bestselling books. Virginia Woolf in *A Room of One's Own*, referring to the early women writers, says, without those forerunners, Jane Austen and the Brontë's and George Eliot could no more have written than Shakespeare could have written without Marlowe or Marlowe without Chaucer.

Yes, we need to know where we come from. And Attia is one of the pioneers who helped to make it possible for English writers in India to write, to move on.

(2013)

A Review of *The Artist of Disappearance* by Anita Desai

Anita Desai's *The Clear Light of Day* (1980) came like a breath of fresh air into the world of Indian Writing in English, dominated at the time by themes of East-West conflict, India's spirituality and mysticism and so on. Anita Desai's novel was not an *Indian* novel, it was just simply a good novel; even today it remains one of her best. Her next novel *In Custody*, equally impressive, confirmed her status as a major novelist in India. The elegance and austerity of her language, as well as the intensity of her writing, set her apart from other writers. By the time she moved away from India in the late nineties, she had a formidable reputation, both in India and abroad. One was curious to know whether the displacement would show in her work, and which way her writing would go after this move; after all, she had clearly stated that she could 'no longer relate to India'. But would she still, like most diasporic writers, continue to write about India? Would she keep going back to what seems to become in time an imaginary homeland, the writers often seeing only the larger picture, unable to get at the dynamics of a swiftly changing society?

Fasting, Feasting and *Journey to Ithaca* disappointingly seemed to follow the trodden path of diasporic writing, but with *The Zigzag Way* she made a break and wrote a novel in which Mexico, not India, was present. Now, years later, she has come out with *The Artist of Disappearance*, a collection of three novellas—

'The Museum of Final Journeys', 'Translator Translated', and the title story, 'The Artist of Disappearance', in all three of which she has gone (come?) back to India. One wishes the book had given the reader a hint of when these stories were written. Are they early unpublished stories, or recently written stories?

These are three very different stories, but all of them are steeped in melancholy, the sense of decay, defeat and loss hanging heavily over them. In the first story, a young man, beginning his career as a bureaucrat, is posted to a small dreary place. He welcomes the chance to get involved in the story of an old zamindar family, when the clerk/caretaker requests that the 'sarkar' take charge of a museum housed in the ancestral home. The family, a mother and son, is mysteriously absent. Almost each article in the museum is described in minute detail, but the museum remains just that, a carefully described place. What could have brought it alive—the mystery of why the son sent these to his mother from his travels, and what happened to the son and why the curios stopped coming—is missing, these mysteries remaining untouched. The story ends with the young man doing nothing about the caretaker's request and being haunted later by the memory of his failure to save the last gift, a living elephant.

'Translator Translated' has (like *In Custody*) the theme of a regional language, of translation and translators. An English lecturer's sudden decision to study Oriya (it is her mother's tongue) leads her to translation. After meeting an English-language publisher, an old schoolmate, she translates the stories of an Oriya (woman) writer. The book is a modest success and, when the writer tells the translator she may write a novel, the lecturer is excited at the thought of translating it. The novel, when it comes to her, is disappointing and she finds herself almost rewriting the novel as she translates it. An interesting theme, but the story is flat, without any conflict whatsoever. The translator is nervous and guilty about what she has done, but there are no repercussions; neither the publisher nor the original writer react as she had feared. She, however, stops translating and goes back to her teaching. In fact, it is surprising how unsurprising this story is, how true to type the characters are: the translator is dull, defeated, the English-language publisher is smart and oozes self-confidence, the Oriya writer is reclusive, nearly invisible. The translator's failure is almost inevitable, one doesn't expect anything else.

The title story is the most rewarding and brings back the Anita Desai one admires. Once again there is a sense of melancholy, with a young man, Ravi, living in the ruins of his burnt-down house. But the life in this story comes from the outdoors, where there is freedom and where 'the spiders spun their webs in tall grass, a spinning you would not observe unless you became soundless, motionless, almost breathless and invisible'. Everything is drawn with the tiny brushstrokes of an artist. There is also an unexpected touch of tenderness in Ravi's relations with the Englishwoman who lived with him until she accidentally burnt the house down, and with Bhola, who unquestioningly looks after Ravi's needs. Into this paradise come the city-people to shoot a documentary about the destruction of the environment of the hills. Familiar characters and one can predict that they will end up by becoming destroyers. Which is what happens; they destroy Ravi's secret garden. Surprisingly, the book (a Random House book!) has the last pages (how many?) missing and one is deprived of the denouement.

In spite of being rather disappointing (one expected more from Anita Desai), these stories are still worth reading for the language alone. In this era of dumbing down of language, of elevating mediocre writing, *The Artist of Disappearance* proclaims that you don't need to be loud to be heard, that you don't have to go to a thesaurus to impress the reader. The use of the right word in the right place, the rhythm of a sentence, the felicity of a phrase—these are enough. In this book, Anita Desai reminds us of the beauty of quietness and of elegant writing.

(2011)

Gulkand and Rose Jam: Gauri Deshpande as Translator

Some two decades or more back, my publisher, the poet P. Lal, sent me an anthology of poems by women writers which he had published. That was the time when women writers in India were happily finding their voices and in this volume I was hearing them for the first time. Though not much of a reader of poetry, I read the book with excitement and, when I had finished, went through the poets' brief biodata with much interest. Among them was Gauri Deshpande, who 'writes poetry in English, short stories in English and Marathi and novels in Marathi'. Unusual though this was, my attention was more caught by the words 'lives in Yugoslavia', which made her in my mind one of those writers in English who live abroad. (I'm very glad I never spoke of this to her. I'm sure it would have brought on a 'gnashing of teeth and balling of fists'—Gauri's own words!) Much later, I met her very briefly in Pune, when her chaste and fluent Marathi almost made me forget the 'writes in English' part of her. We met again in Bangalore, where she came for the release of Saniya's first novel. (Saniya was another Marathi writer, living in Bangalore.) Gauri, hearing from me that I had not read her novels and that I could not get them in Bangalore, sent me the whole bunch when she went back to Pune. After I read them, I realised that here was a writer who was equally creative in English and Marathi—truly bilingual in the best sense. Inevitable then that she should be a translator and, when she told me she was translating a story of mine into Marathi for a magazine, I was very honoured. She has left her mark on this story, 'Lost Springs'. In the course of translating it, she wrote to me that there was some confusion in a certain passage. 'What do you really mean?' she asked me, rather sternly, I felt. I read that bit again and knew she was right; the time sequence was a bit muddled. I rewrote those lines and, when the original English story was published (unusually, the Marathi translation was published first), Gauri's correction was part of it.

But I really came to know Gauri as a translator through a piece she wrote in the *Indian Review of Books* for a special issue on translation. The journal unfortunately had to close down, but I have preserved this issue, an excellent one, with many fine articles by scholars and translators. Gauri's article is, in my opinion, the best in that issue. I've read and reread that piece over and over again and quoted from it so often that, when editing my earlier collection of essays, my editor remarked, 'Too much of Gauri, isn't there? Shall we remove some of the quotes?' This piece, 'Translating Burton's *Arabian Nights*', speaks of translation through her hands-on experience of translating *Arabian Nights* into Marathi. If anyone thought that translation was an unemotional, totally cerebral exercise, she/he has only to read this impassioned account to correct that thought. Unlike the other articles in that issue, it is a very personal one and begins with the matter-of-fact statement (characteristic of her, I think) that she did this translation because she needed the money. However true this was to begin with, I'm sure that what she was paid was no recompense for the ten years of work translating sixteen volumes. And by the time she finished, she had clearly become passionately involved in the task ('I missed Burton for I had lived with him for nearly ten years') and gained some amazingly perceptive insights into translation—all of which come through in her article. Her insights go beyond language into issues like colonialism, gender bias and the translator-text relationship. Questioning, thinking, probing, finding her way through the text she was translating, Gauri admits that she learnt much about translation. This task gave her, she says, 'an awareness of the act of translation, an act I used to perform almost instinctively due to an accident of birth'.

Gauri begins by saying that she was wholly ill-equipped for this task of translation since she knew nothing about Burton, the Arabic language or people, or matters like orientalism, etc. And since she was living abroad or travelling most of the time during the translation and had no help, she had to take certain decisions alone, decisions which she took instinctively. One of these was that she would employ a casual spoken style, keeping in mind the orally transmitted nature of the original, something she says neither Burton nor Chiplunkar, the first Marathi translator, had done. The second decision about language came out of what she calls the 'pervading atmosphere of clandestine sexuality' of *Arabian Nights*. Burton, who was translating for Victorian England, had problems finding contemporary words and therefore turned to Chaucerian or Elizabethan English, when there were fewer inhibitions in the language used. Gauri says it was easier for her, since 'Marathi has enough words to describe everyday bodily functions', words which she had heard the women in her family—grandmothers, mother, aunts—use matter-of-factly in the presence of children. But, Gauri says, 'while I was not looking Marathi had progressed towards Victorian English!' And, therefore, many found the book obscene. Gauri's experience reminded me of another poet/translator, P. Lal's, story of Edward Fitzgerald's translation of *The Rubaiyat of Omar Khayyam*. The famous 'Thou beside me in the wilderness' referred in the original to a male companion. But knowing that Edwardian England, for whom Fitzgerald was translating, would find the idea of a romantic picture of two men unacceptable, he made it a genderless 'Thou'! As Lal says: 'One is translating only for one's contemporaries. Creative writing may be done for hundred years hence, not translation', a statement I'm sure Gauri agreed with after her experience!

But the most important discovery Gauri made during the course of this translation—so she says in this article—is what came out of her observations about colonialism and gender. Though she has a great admiration for Burton as a translator—she called him one of the greatest translators of his times—she found a certain lack in him as she went on translating. In spite of his almost faultless knowledge of Arabian society and in spite of being wholly sympathetic to that world and people, she says there was a 'subtle orientalism' in his translation. For example, she says that it became clear to her that the extravagant opulence *Arabian Nights* repeatedly spoke of—the diamonds, rubies, pearls, emeralds and so on—were really the fantasies of a poor people. Burton would surely have known this, but he too, like all other translators of *Arabian Nights,* including Chiplunkar, emphasised *these* things, because the exotic was the point about *Arabian Nights,* because it was the exotic that the translator was intent on highlighting. Gauri digresses at one point into a very long account of how she tried to find out what the '*sayeechya purya*' (literally puris made of cream—a nonsensical non-existent dish) mentioned in Chiplunkar's translation was and how it turned out that Chiplunkar, as well as some others, used words that would make the dish something extraordinary—never mind if it had nothing to do with what the original word was.

The other discovery she made in the course of the translation was the way women were spoken of. 'I was becoming deeply unhappy about the women in the Nights', she says. And adds, 'How alienated from women a culture must be to base one of its major oral texts on the facts of a woman's sex-crazed infidelity'. But she soon began to realise that the picture of women that *Arabian Nights* presented was as much a fantasy as the opulence and riches it described; these women were no more real than the riches were. These observations led her to making a very important observation about translation, something which she calls 'the next step'. This 'next step' means a deeper understanding of the text which has to go into the translation, it means that you are no longer speaking from the outside, which was what Burton was doing, in spite of his knowledge and sympathy. To be an outsider is to speak of the world you are looking at as a different, a strange world, it leads to explanations, to 'a display and explication of curiosities'. The Arabs and women therefore became 'the other'. This brings on the colonial attitude (that's how those people are!) and the gender bias (women are strange creatures!). Nevertheless, Gauri acknowledges her debt to Burton, 'who made it easy for me a whole century after him not only to take the next step but to feel impelled to do so'.

Clearly Gauri formed many of her ideas about what translating meant in the course of translating this voluminous work. But did she indeed as a translator take the next step? Most creative writers—and translators, too—are impatient of theories; theories emerge out of the actual writing, not the other way round. Actually, writers work by instinct, though their decisions, if later analysed, may yield certain rational connections. And, therefore, one needs to look at Gauri's translations to see whether she did take 'the next step'. For me, as a writer in English, there was an added curiosity about Gauri's translations from Marathi into English. Very early in my writing career I realised that as a writer in English, I was almost a translator, since I was in effect translating our lives here into English, that I was translating from Kannada or Marathi into English. This was not a conscious act, nor was there any conscious decision-making. I would rather use the words of another very eminent Indian poet/translator, A.K. Ramanujan, for this process: 'unconscious agenda'. The main question that underlies this 'unconscious agenda' is: how much does one 'English' the details of our life? There is rarely a definite answer and eventually one works out of some negatives. For example, I knew that some of the things done by writers in English were unacceptable to me. 'Horse radish pancakes' for *mooli parathas*, for example. Or 'rice and lentils pancakes' for *dosas*! Even in my first novel, I kept the Kakas, Kakis, Atyas, etc. as they were. No transformation into 'uncles' and 'aunties', unless the characters were such that they would call a person 'uncle' rather than 'Kaka'. Bigger problems come with cultural and religious rituals and practices, as also women's lives, which are rarely lived in English. '*Sola*', a word in Marathi for example: how do you put it into English and how can you possibly convey the entire truth and the nuances of this most peculiar Brahminical practice which centred round a bizarre idea of purity? My own unconscious agenda dictated that the 'Englishing' should never be obtrusive, that, hopefully, it should not be jarring and that the original word in the Indian language is retained only if it conveys some sense of what the word implies. The idea that lay at the basis of this unconscious agenda was that none of these are strange exotic things; I was writing of things which were a natural and familiar part of my life.

These ideas of mine made me very curious about how a bilingual creative writer/translator like Gauri Deshpande would translate into English. And therefore I read her translation of Suneeta Deshpande's *Aahe Manohara Tari ...* (translated into English as ... *And Pine for What Is Not*) with great interest, specially since I had also read the original in Marathi. It is an easy and comfortable translation and, as a translator, Gauri has made some daring leaps that work delightfully well. 'Peter Pan', for example, for Suneetabais's remark about Shyam, a character in a play, that he was a person who never grew up. Barrie's character Peter Pan, the symbol of everlasting youth, is just the right phrase in English. So too 'Man Friday' for '*harkamya* secretary'. Gauri has even changed some of Suneetabai's English words: 'joke-y' for 'farcical'. Yes, there is a difference in the two words and perhaps, for an adaptation of Gogol's *Inspector General*, 'joke-y' is more apt. I was also very intrigued by the way she has changed the term '*aga*'. This is something that I have had to deal with and, knowing it is impossible to find an exact English equivalent of this term of great intimacy between women, I have left the '*aga*' as it is. But Gauri translates '*aga*' into an actually spoken word—'love': '*kay sundar aahe ga*' becomes 'it is beautiful, love'. Inventive, certainly, but...?

These decisions intrigued me, but some others frankly puzzled me. Words like 'Grandma', 'Grandpa', 'Sister-in-law', 'Mother-in-law' (with the capitals) when referring to an actual person. 'Sister-in-law said ...' or 'Mother-in-law was ...' for example. And 'Cobra Festival' for '*Nag Panchami*' or 'manor' for '*vada*'. (Whereas *munj*, the thread ceremony performed for Brahmin boys, has been retained as it is.) And 'your good self' for the formal address '*aapan*'. 'Good self' is Indian English all right, but does it convey the *desire* to distance oneself that Suneetabai speaks of here? The bracketing also made me very curious, specially since today most translators are trying to do away with brackets and footnotes. Gauri has given the botanical names of flowers and trees in brackets. Was this, I have to ask myself, an editorial decision rather than the translator's? And what about explaining '*gulpapdiche ladoo*' by listing the ingredients that went into it? Why not just *ladoo*? And 'Does' for the two streams that flowed near Suneetabai's village? 'Does'? I was bewildered and had to go to the original Marathi to understand that it means female deer: '*Harni*'. I still wonder: did Gauri deliberately avoid a glossary or was this too an editorial decision? Or why not a translator's note giving us a clue to her decisions? I remember how appreciatively Gauri speaks of Burton's Notes and Annotations; did she think these things were out of place in a book like *Aahe Manohara Tari ...*? A.K. Ramanujan agonises over the need for an Afterword and Notes, but concedes they are inevitable. Did Gauri reject them on principle? All those who write in English/

translate into English have to cope with the problems of how to do these things, each finds her/his own answers. But, somehow, some of these decisions of Gauri's didn't seem to fit into my idea of her as a translator, or as a creative writer.

I got some clues to this puzzle when I went to Gauri's own stories in English, though the collection I read, *The Lackadaisical Sweeper*, initially presented me with a fresh problem. Gauri wrote stories both in English and in Marathi. Clearly, the stories in this collection belonged to both the categories—i.e. originally written in English as well as in Marathi, since the acknowledgements include both Marathi and English magazines and periodicals. Though five Marathi magazines are mentioned, only two stories are admitted to be translations. My arithmetic tells me that this leaves out three other stories which were originally in Marathi. Which were these? 'Maps' for example, one of the finest stories I've read, gives the feeling that it could have been written in no language but English. Was I right? But the two stories which were acknowledged to be in Marathi originally, 'Debt' and 'Insy Winsy Spider'—gave me the same feeling as well. The texture of these stories was the same as the others, which may have been originally in English. Or, had Gauri rewritten in the process of translation? I thought of her words: 'when it is your own work being translated, it becomes very difficult ... I have to sort of curb myself as an author and put on my translator's hat'. She had said it to me personally once as well, that translating your own work became a sort of rewriting. But it's also possible that Gauri's stories lend themselves very easily to translation into English, which is why they don't give the feeling of being translated. 'Debt', an acknowledged translation from Marathi, moves very smoothly into English because the viewpoint is that of an American woman coming to India for the first time. And yet, it is completely different from most of the 'foreign-eye-looking-at-India' stories. (Even Pulitzer Prize winner Jhumpa Lahiri's stories based in India have such an outsider quality.)

Gauri's story is of a woman who comes to India for the first time in rather tragic circumstances and who finds everything strange and frightening; that she is an American is incidental. But how had this story worked in Marathi? I was very curious.

Finally, it was a story titled 'Rose Jam' that gave me the answers to some of my curious questions. I am quite sure that this story was originally in English because it is meant very clearly for the English reader. It is a rather naughty and provocative story which told me much of Gauri's 'unconscious agenda' in translation. Actually 'Rose Jam' is scarcely a story; it does not fit into that slot. It seems more a wholly personal account of Gauri herself, of her own background, which becomes the basis for her ideas about how the West sees India. There is a sharp criticism, a mockery really, of English writing by Indian writers in this story. The title itself, 'Rose Jam', is a deliberate, almost tongue-in-cheek rendering of 'gulkand'—which is actually rose petals preserved in sugar. Something with which so many of us are very familiar. But when you call it 'Rose Jam' it sounds strange and perhaps spells out 'India' to a foreign reader, who expects something strange when it comes from India. Like Gauri says in the story, 'millions of Indians like myself are not in the least exotic and yet are perfectly Indian. And yet many Indians writing in English—specially those living abroad—make it exotic by writing about the special ingredients that went into "Grandmother Goddess-of-Wealth's special curry"'. She has used 'Rose Jam' to show how something as ordinary to us as 'gulkand' can be made to seem exotic.

Tongue-in-cheek though the story seems to be, lighthearted spoofing though it may be, Gauri is saying something serious here which applies as much to writing in English as to translation into English. The whole trend of exoticising India, of the West imposing *its* ideas of *our* reality on us, is a continuing part of colonialism, which Gauri stands firmly against. The tendency to see India as 'the other', to look at it from the outside and to explain it to outsiders is something Gauri is speaking out against in this story. She is saying something that has been part of my thinking as well. 'Read my novel as a novel', I want to say, 'not as an *Indian* novel'. But once you write in English and go out of the country, it becomes an *Indian* novel. And there are certain expectations, which come from preconceived images of India as a mysterious and colourful country. I remember an Indian teacher who was teaching Indian writing in Germany telling me that her students found a character in my novel 'not culture-specific'. This character, Sumi, did not conform to their idea of the Indian woman because she refused to see herself as a victim. It is Gauri's resistance to this kind of colonisation that she speaks of in her article on translating *Arabian Nights* and which she works out in 'Rose Jam'. I think that this refusal to make anything sound strange (no *sayeechya purya*!) accounts for the 'Mother-in-law', 'Sister-in-law', etc. To say 'Sasubai', or whatever, would make it strange in English, it would stand out as an oddity. To use the English word was, perhaps, part of her determination to keep out such a sense of strangeness, a refusal to make her reality seem exotic. Arshia Sattar, who translates from Sanskrit to English, says in the same *IRB* issue on translation: 'Instead of allowing the source language to determine the flavour of the translation, we might be better off using our own language'. I have a feeling that this is what Gauri was doing, the 'own language' in this case being English, because that was the language she was translating into. But I still have some questions: Was she happy with the strategy she was using? Would she have changed at some time when she stopped reacting to this 'exoticisation'? I know how strongly she felt about this 'writing for the Western reader' attitude. I remember her piece on Arundhati Roy's *The God of Small Things* in which she expressed these views with her usual forthrightness.

It is hard to know whether she would have changed her views. But I do know that there is one translation of hers in which she has negotiated with great artistic skill between two languages and found the perfect way. This is Asha Bage's story 'Pankh', translated into English as 'Wings'. When I first read it, I thought it was a wonderful story. A little later I realised it was a translation and understood it was one of the finest translations I have read. The story moves smoothly, without a jerk, and carries the flavour of the original without loudly announcing that it is a different culture. In this story she retains many of the original Marathi words: *bhawla, bhawli, Mangalashtak, akshada, pohe,* etc. as well as relationship names like *Aai, aaji, ajoba, Mama,* etc. A few rhymes are rendered in English with remarkable felicity (after all, Gauri was a poet as well) and, what I admire greatly, music, which runs through the story like a steady humming background, comes through in English with great ease and naturalness. Having written about music in my novel *Small Remedies*, I know it is not easy to write about Indian music in English. But Gauri has done it to perfection in 'Wings'. A perfect story, in my opinion and a perfect translation.

A.K. Ramanujan, one of India's best-known translators, once called himself the hyphen in Indian-American. I think of Gauri as a bridge between Marathi and English, a bridge which was not just a way of getting from one to another, but which was a meeting point of two languages, two cultures. Reading her piece 'Appa, Shakuatya, Sai (ani mee pan)' in a magazine, I came to understand that Gauri was both a creative writer and a translator. It was not just that she 'possessed' two languages in the real sense, she was two selves in one. Not only was English her language as completely as Marathi was, but she also combined in herself, very unselfconsciously and with ease, a Marathi self as well as a Western self. When I read her Marathi novels for the first time, I was conscious of a very 'un-Marathi' sensibility which I had not seen in the few Marathi authors I had read. At the same time, her short story 'Vervain' has a European woman as the main character, whom she presents as easily and naturally as she would an Indian woman. And 'Debt', originally in Marathi, has an American woman as the protagonist and works as perfectly as her stories in which the protagonist is an Indian. When Vikram Seth wrote *Equal Music*, there were murmurs about an Indian writing a novel in which all the characters were Europeans. But if you forget that the author was Seth, an Indian, you get just a very readable novel. In contrast, *A Suitable Boy* is very obviously an *Indian* novel, presenting India to the world; it seems that Seth felt that India was 'the other' which needed to be explained. Gauri differs from Vikram Seth in that, even when she writes in English, she writes the same way as she does in Marathi. The point is that for Gauri it worked both ways. She was equally at home in both the cultures and languages, she was an insider in both worlds. Gauri was a truly international person, but one who was secure in her roots and strongly grounded in her own realities. And therefore her position—that it was not for her to explain anything, but for the readers to make the effort. I can understand this very well, because as a writer in English I feel the same way. Why should I explain myself to a reader? Why should I *presume* a foreign reader because I write in English? The majority of my readers are (hopefully) Indians. And don't I read Russian, American, German, British and many other writers and make the effort to enter into their world? Surely readers can make the same effort and enter into the world I create as well? To presume that we need to explain our culture to others is a kind of colonial mindset Gauri took a stand against; it was a principle both in her creative writing as well as in her translation.

When I began attempting to write something about Gauri Deshpande as a translator, I knew I was eminently unqualified for the task. Gauri, speaking of how little qualified she was to translate *Arabian Nights*, adds that all she had was enthusiasm, necessity and bilingualism. I have none of these, either. Only an admiration for Gauri Deshpande and a sense of kinship with Gauri which began when I read one of her poems in P.

Lal's anthology, a feeling that our thoughts ran on somewhat similar lines. On a more mundane level, sharing a name became a kind of link too, for there were many who asked me whether we were related (we were not). Actually, the publisher of her translated book *...And Pine for what is not* was also my publisher and once even sent me Gauri's royalty! (I imagine that with one Deshpande as the author and another as the translator, they were so confused that they sent the royalty to a third Deshpande!) And so I began this piece fearfully, with a full knowledge of my ignorance. But, like Gauri herself, who came to both knowledge and understanding in the course of her translation of *Arabian Nights*, I too have learnt a few things during the writing of this. One of them is that Gauri was a rare translator, for there are very few in our country who can translate both ways with equal competence. She was not only creative in both the languages, she was also at home in the real sense in both of them. She could travel with as much ease from Marathi to English as she could the other way round. That she was a creative writer adds to her translating skills, because, as she says herself, 'Creative writers are the best translators of creative writing'. There is one problem with creative writers as translators, though: to be a creative writer is to necessarily have a big ego. A translator cannot afford to have an ego, she/he has to learn to submerge it. Gauri could do this; I saw her during a seminar in Hyderabad, where she had taken over the task of translating a Marathi writer, Pradnya Lokhande. When she translated, she was wholly self-effacing, scarcely visible. With all this she was a poet as well, and a poet is one who can handle words with great skill and sensitivity. In an article on translation in the magazine *Miloon Saryajani*, she speaks of the ellipses in all languages which should not be ignored, she speaks of the meaning behind the words to which one needs to be as alert as to their obvious meaning. This kind of an understanding of the nuances of language makes for an ideal translator.

This is the era of translations, and translators are at long last finding their place in the literary scene. I may be wrong, but for some reason I think Marathi has not made its mark in translations as much as some other languages have—Tamil, for example, or Kannada, or Malayalam. I also feel that Gauri is not as much known as a translator as she should have been. I hope that greater note will be taken of her role as translator. I also hope that there will be more translations of Gauri's work into other languages. She has done her share in making Marathi writing known outside the language. It is for others now to make her known through translations of her work. I am sure it will surprise many in its qualities of being postcolonial and gender-sensitive in a way very few so-called postcolonial writers are.

(2004)

On John Steinbeck

I read *Tortilla Curtain* recently, a novel I'd never heard of and written by an author, Coraghessan Boyle, I'd never read. Nevertheless, I had a strong sense of déjà vu as I began reading it. A few pages on and I got it: it reminded me of John Steinbeck's *The Grapes of Wrath*, a novel about the migration of people, mostly small farmers, from the American South West to California in search of jobs during the post-Depression era. Boyle's novel, a contemporary picture of Mexican immigrants coming to find work in California, seems to be taking up where Steinbeck left off. If, in Steinbeck's novel, people were lured by handbills promising them a great life fruit-picking in the orchards, the Mexicans today know the real situation much better; nevertheless they come, ready to face anything as long as they can get work. In both cases, the picture is one of exploitation. (The seamy underside of the golden California we Indians hear of from our software kin!) I don't know how many readers will make the connection between Boyle's book and Steinbeck's, or how many today will even have heard of Steinbeck. And he was a Nobel Prize winner!

That's the curious thing about the Nobel Prize—and I'm speaking only of the literature prize. For some time after the announcement of the prize, there is a spate of publicity about the author and her/his books. Publishers hastily bring out reprints which are prominently displayed in bookstores. And then, after a while, the author and the books are generally forgotten—except, perhaps, in the country they belong to—and the books settle down into that large morass of 'great, but not-much-read' literature. The fact is, the prize is so often given to obscure writers that one gets a feeling that to be popular, saleable and readable is frowned upon. A notable example is Graham Greene, whom many considered worthy of the prize, but who never got it. Of course, one presumes that most winners would be outstanding writers, but the Committee has goofed at times and often created controversies in its choices, since various other factors influence the choice as well. Like good lobbying, for example. Or politics, for after all, the prize is a kind of political statement. Therefore, the politics of nations and the politics of the author also count. Which is why it became more possible for dissident writers behind the Iron Curtain to become strong contenders when the world was divided into two camps—Communists and others.

One wonders what worked for John Steinbeck when he got his prize in 1962. For one thing, he is very readable. And he sold well—which should have gone against him. Some of his novels became successful movies, and one, *Of Mice and Men*, became a very long-running and popular play. Steinbeck had some kind of a political history too, though nothing that marks him out as Nobel Prize winning material. He had been a socialist sympathiser, visited Soviet Russia and was a great advocate of trade unions, which almost amounted to treason in the US at the time. When I read *The Grapes of Wrath*, I didn't know any of this. I had no idea that the book had received the Pulitzer Prize, nor that Steinbeck had won the Nobel Prize. Publicity machines didn't work very hard then, nor was the reach of publicity very long. Which is why I read most books without any context; they were either good novels or bad novels. *The Grapes of Wrath* was just a very good book to me. The long and difficult journey to the West, the dreams of the Joad family, their hardships and disillusionment and the shocking finale, made a deep impression on me. The next

Steinbeck novel I read was *East of Eden*—literally a big novel. My much-read truncated copy is 550 pages! I learnt from his *Journal of a Novel*, which I read much later, that he *meant* this to be a big book, that he set out, in fact, to write a great novel. The journal is a fascinating account, written simultaneously with the novel and within the same notebook in which he wrote the novel; he wrote the notes, which became the journal, on the left-hand pages and the novel on the right. (The journal gives so many insights into the problems, the agonies and the techniques of writing that it should be rewarding reading for aspiring writers.) Like *The Grapes of Wrath*, which is a kind of parable of a journey, *East of Eden* too has clear Biblical overtones; it is a retelling of the Abel and Cain story. And a story of evil as well, evil personified in the character of a woman, Cathy.

Steinbeck was very different from the British writers I was more familiar with. No 'carefully fenced, highly cultivated garden'—as Charlotte Brontë said uncharitably about Jane Austen—in his writing. A sense of vast open spaces, instead. He rambles—none of the Hemingway clipped, terse style for him. He is preachy. There's a hearty optimism in his books which seems slightly old-fashioned. He's sentimental and emotional, often unapologetically going over the top. And yet, it works. Because he tells you a story, a *good* story, about people we get wholly involved with. And what people! One of my favourite characters is Lee, the Chinese servant in *East of Eden*. Wise, philosophical, intelligent. And full of stories. The story of his birth, a few minutes before his gang-raped mother died, stayed with me through the years. Intensely personal and painful, it also gives a glimpse of the history of the building of the railroads in California and of the Chinese men and women who came to work on it to pay off their debts at home. Lee's mother disguised herself as a man to be with her husband, a disguise that was smashed wide open when she went into labour. And then the men in the labour camp, who had not seen a woman for months, fell on her like animals. Lee ends this painful story by saying, 'No child ever had such care as I. The whole camp became my mother'. You see? Unapologetically sentimental. Actually, when he speaks of mothers, he seems perilously close at times to the Hindi movie mushy picture of 'Ma'. But then, Steinbeck also gave us Cathy, the mother who refused even to look at her twin sons. Another wonderful story is about Lee and some ancient Jewish and Chinese scholars setting out in search of the original Hebrew of an English word in the King James translation of the Bible. An exhilarating story with a triumphant ending.

It is the human triumph against all odds that Steinbeck celebrates. Human triumph that has nothing to do with success. In his Nobel Prize acceptance speech, Steinbeck said, 'The writer is delegated to declare and to celebrate man's proven capacity for greatness of heart and spirit—for gallantry in defeat—for courage, compassion, and love'. He put it in less dignified words in *Cannery Row,* whose inhabitants, he makes a man say, are 'whores, pimps, gamblers and sons of bitches'. And then adds, 'he might have said, "saints and angels and martyrs and holy men" and he would have meant the same thing'.

That's what Steinbeck's books are about. The downtrodden. He is at his best when he writes about them. *Cannery Row* and its sequel, *Sweet Thursdays,* are about underdogs and failures. Each one of them a loser. And yet, they are his happiest, liveliest books. I can still remember my joy when I first read them, my enjoyment of the characters, from Doc of Western Biological to Mack and the boys and the whores in the Palace Flophouse. *Cannery Row* ends with Doc reading out a poem to this audience; when he finishes, they are all a little tearful because, 'a little world of sadness had slipped over all of them'. I too was caught in the same enchantment as Doc's audience, caught, like them, by the beauty of the words. For years I searched for this poem, a Sanskrit love poem, *Black Marigolds,* translated by E. Powys Mathers. I finally found another version of the same poem,

Barbara Stoler Miller's translation titled *Fantasies of a Love Thief.* When I read the poems, I was transported back to those magic moments when I first read *Cannery Row* and came across these poems.

Even now,
I remember her,
A fragile fawn-eyed girl ....

A marine biologist, created by an American novelist, had led me to the poetry of a Sanskrit poet, Bilhana, who lived in the eleventh century. This is what great literature does, linking us across time space to other humans, asserting our connections.

(2006)

On Virginia Woolf

Books which have been with you for years tell you much more than what's printed between their covers. I only have to open one for memory to flow in; the name, dates, places and inscriptions on the first page give me back bits of my life. The inscription on this book reminds me that it was a twenty-first birthday gift from my father, and this set of Dickens a wedding gift from a friend. Even more fascinating are the dates of subsequent rereadings. (A habit of mine.) Here's a book with dates that go through four decades, overflowing from the front to the back of the book. With passages marked, sentences underlined, comments, exclamations and interrogation marks in the margin. Obviously a much-read book. Why did I buy this book? It has a beautiful cover, a picture of a woman reading a book. An earnest young woman, wearing a sober grey dress with a high neck, the sleeves coming down to her wrists. Jane Eyre, one imagines, would have looked exactly like this. There is a luminous quality to the picture, which comes from the light on the woman's face. Did I buy the book for the cover? Or for the author? I don't remember; I can only call my buying of the book a happy accident. It was the right time for me to read it; at no other time would it have made such an impact.

The first date on the book tells me I was trying to write my second novel then, struggling, not only with the novel, but to find the time to write in the midst of the busy and endless routine of a mother of two school-going children. And constantly the thought running through my head—*I want to write, please, I want to write*. There was resentment that there was no time. Guilt at the resentment. What was I doing that was so important? Writing something that might never be published, that would never earn me any money. Did I have the right to steal time from my family for this? 'Get off that chair', I told myself at times, 'and go out and earn some money. Or else, give the home and kids 100 per cent of your time'.

And then I read this book. A classic today, a cult book, its title *A Room of One's Own* often used as a catch phrase. And the author, Virginia Woolf, as much known for this book, perhaps, as for all her novels. I turn over the pages, delighting once again in the arguments, the elegance of style, trying to find what was it that had struck home. I come to where she speaks of the 'flaw in the centre' of the novels of early women writers. Novels written with deference to a vision different from their own. Novels that seem to meet criticism by being aggressive, conciliatory, or apologetic. Only Jane Austen and Emily Brontë, Virginia Woolf says, wrote like women write, not like men write. And I think—yes, this must have been my *Aha*! moment, the words like a rap on my knuckles. Making me ask myself: Was I trying to wriggle out of the fact that the novel I was writing was primarily a woman's story? Was I afraid of being slotted as a 'woman writing about women'? But this was *my* novel, it had to be written the way it came to me—in a woman's voice. As it finally was.

Is a writer consciously aware of the fact that her book will influence readers? Does she write with the *intention* of influencing readers? I would say 'no' to both these questions. And yet, as I write this, I have a letter from a reader in another continent who tells me that my book gave her the strength to go through a dark period in her life. I am pleased, gratified. And surprised; I never expected that a reader would respond in this way. I am sure Virginia Woolf would have felt the same. She very clearly says, 'Do not dream of influencing other people'. But, for me, *A Room of One's Own* was like a magic potion; it fortified me. It made me feel that I could, that I *had to* write like myself. Only one other book had this effect on me, Simone de Beauvoir's *The Second Sex.* But Simone's book is heavily weighted with scholarship, whereas *A Room of One's Own*' spoke directly to me, as a woman, as a writer. Told me some irrefutable truths and gave me the courage to go on, gave me the confidence to see myself as a writer.

It is interesting to read Virginia Woolf's opinions about her own work. Like all writers she is full of doubts and anxieties. 'Good or bad?' she asks in her diary about *A Room of One's Own.* And then, what seems amazing now, 'I am afraid it will not be taken seriously'. And adds, 'I forecast, then, that I shall get no criticism, except of the evasive jocular kind'. She also asks, 'A brilliant essay?', modesty affirming itself through the query mark. It *is* brilliant. Reflective, lucid, playful, but never trite, working brilliantly through irony, she moves from argument to argument with the ease of a highly skilled acrobat. I entertain myself with the thought: What if Virginia Woolf had sent this to a publisher today calling it an 'essay'? Essay? The publishers would have been puzzled. It's a forgotten word. We use, instead, the generic term 'non-fiction'. Can this book be called non-fiction then? But so much in it is invention, including the 'I' who is not Virginia Woolf, but could be anyone; in fact, Virginia Woolf herself says, 'lies will flow from my lips'. Besides, the book works, not through information, but through abstract ideas, stories, 'what-if's. (What if Shakespeare had a sister, what if she was as talented as him ...) 'Ma'am', the publishers might have written, 'we are sorry we cannot find a place for this on our list'. Because, they might have added, if they wanted to be honest, it is a book impossible to slot.

Every few years a debate erupts about fiction and non-fiction, as if it is an either/or situation. I recently read a provocative statement by Lee Siegel, an American critic, that the greatest story tellers of our time are the non-fiction writers. 'Tell me their names', I want to say. Instead I go back to *A Room of One's Own* and find something that can put a final end to this debate.

'Write all kinds of books', Virginia Woolf advises young women, 'hesitating at no subject however trivial, however vast .... For', she adds, 'books have a way of influencing each other'. Her statement, 'if you consider any great figure of the past, like Sappho ... like Emily Brontë, you will find that she is an inheritor as well as an originator', made me aware of the great truth, that there is a chain of writers, and all of us are inheritors as well as originators.

A Room of One's Own is that rare thing—a wise book. How can a book like this, written, as Virginia Woolf confesses in her diary, with ardour and conviction, not influence readers?

(2010)

On Professor P. Lal

It was my father, a writer himself, who told me to put my published short stories together in a collection when I had a sufficient number of them; otherwise, he said, they would be lost. Being wholly ignorant at the time of the literary world and even more of the publishing world, I would not, perhaps, have gone beyond the intention of publishing. Then someone recommended that I write to Prof. P. Lal of Writers Workshop; he, I was told, was sympathetic to new writers. I wrote to him and soon got a businesslike reply. 'Yes', he wrote, 'do send your stories'; but, he said that he was pressed for time and would go through the stories as soon as he could. I didn't have to wait too long. Soon after this letter I got another, saying that he would publish the stories, adding that he was impressed by their 'artless fluency and humane nuances'. A first manuscript submission, a first acceptance—I was walking on air. Not only the acceptance, but the words of praise. Just four words, but they showed perfect appreciation. I knew little about publishers then, but I know now how rare it is for a publisher to give an author such words of praise. It was an unforgettable moment for me. Even better, he wrote again to say that he would write a small blurb to the book himself, something that 'I normally never do'. And one more letter after that, saying that one of the stories would be read at the Sunday morning meetings in his home. I can honestly say that I had never had such appreciation and encouragement before—nor have I had it since. After that time, there was a steady correspondence between us, all of it relating to my work, all of it giving me steady encouragement. Encouragement was something I badly needed then, for I was, after all, 'only a housewife', as they say, sitting at home and writing, having no contact, either with the academic or the literary world.

In the years since I first got to know Prof. Lal, I came to understand that there were two things that defined him. One was his passion for literature, for good writing; he never hesitated to push writing that he thought was good. The other was a great generosity, which made him so openly and fulsomely praise a new writer; I know now how rare this is among writers, how little inclined older writers are to praise new writers. His generosity worked in other ways as well. I have received so many books from him that I now have a veritable Writers Workshop library at home. Books which I have read, enjoyed, profited from, books which have added immeasurably to my understanding and writing. I had read very little of Indian writing in English. And so when I read *Hers*, an anthology of women's poetry in English, I was overwhelmed; I was hearing women's voices, Indian women's voices, for the first time. I specially valued his books on Sanskrit texts. I had grown up among Sanskrit books since my father had been a Sanskrit professor, I had loved the plays and read many of them in translation. But it was through P. Lal's work, his translations (sorry, transcreations) and his essays on the works, that I got access to the texts in a different and an infinitely better way than the literal clumsy translations I had read until then. I have used many of his ideas in my own writing, specially in non-fiction, and in my talks. Once again there was the same generosity. For instance, when I asked for permission to use some words from his translation of the Dhammapada as an epigraph to my novel *The Dark Holds No Terrors*, after first giving me the permission to use the lines, he wrote:

> Please feel free to use whatever quotations you like, in as much quantity you like, whatever you like, without referring to me, assuming permission as given. It is an honour to have one's work remembered and utilised sensitively.

I have made full use of this blanket permission. I used the words from his translation of some verses of the *Rig Veda* as an epigraph to my novel *Small Remedies*—words which, like the epigraph to *The Dark Holds No Terrors*, seemed amazingly appropriate. I have used a story from the Mahabharata translation to illustrate a talk. I have used his theory of Indian culture as the starting point of a talk I gave in Amsterdam. I could go on and on with this list.

The list of writers he has published is like a who's who of Indian English writers: Ruskin Bond, Keki Daruwala, Kamala Das, Nissim Ezekiel, Jayant Mahapatra, Vikram Seth and many more. As Jed Bickman, an American who came to India on a fellowship to work with, and on, Writers Workshop, says, 'Because he has developed a system that is not dependant upon market forces and popular tastes, he can publish a bewilderingly broad range of writers' (*A Literal Journey in India: Encountering Writers Workshop*). However, the truth is that most writers inevitably soon moved on to bigger publishers. Prof. Lal told me of a young writer he had published and who soon found a major publisher. He went for her book launch, but, he said, 'she did not see me. She had stars in her eyes'. I could almost see an invisible resigned shrug of the shoulders accompanying his words. It was a matter-of-fact statement, holding no rancour. P. Lal was that rare thing in the literary world, a man who held no grudges against writers who left him for other publishers. When I asked for permission to have my stories republished by Penguin, I was gently rebuked. 'You know we don't do things that way. The stories are yours'. And once, when there was some delay in publishing some of my stories, he wrote, 'if you can find another publisher for them, please go ahead ... There's no compulsion to stick to WW: it'll be wonderful if they can get a wider exposure than WW can give them'.

There is some talk of the vanity publishing he did. I must speak of my experience, which makes his stand clear. His acceptance letter to me asked me whether I would buy a hundred copies from him, in addition to the fifty he would give as royalty. I wrote back and said I could not buy any copies, because, while I had no problems not earning money from my stories (after all, I had already been paid by the magazines for them), I would not spend any money on my writing, either, except for paper, ink and postage. He never referred to the matter again. In fact, he was always very apologetic about the delay in publishing subsequent volumes of my stories, saying that he was short of cash and would publish them as soon as he got some royalties, or money from his lecture tour in the US. I have no doubt at all that it is I who owe him a great deal, for the exposure I got through my published stories was huge.

He was a great defender of Indians writing in English and on the side of what he called 'home-grown writers' as opposed to the expatriate variety. A letter after I got the Sahitya Akademi award praises the Akademi for 'not running after expatriate excellence'. During my first visit to his home, as I was leaving, he gave me two books written by a much-admired-in-the-West Indian, adding, 'you need not return the books'. Which told me what his opinion of the books was! Many of his statements on IWE can't be bettered. 'If we look after the honesty of our feelings and the skill of our craft', he says, 'the Indianness will look after itself'. Words that should be chanted by an IWE writer every day before beginning writing. For him, Indianness meant, above all, an understanding of our myths and a sensitive use of them. In a letter about two of my stories based on the epics for which I could not find publishers, he wrote, 'most of the editors of popular English magazines in India are sufficiently alienated from the Indian myth background not to really know what you are writing about. Secondly you are using the first person singular and the stream-of-consciousness and both frighten off low- and medium-brows ... unless you thoroughly archaically jargonise the dialogue, they'll never believe it's authentic'. Then he added, 'See pages 7–8 of *Great Sanskrit Plays* [his own book] for the kind of thing they want'.

I looked it up and found it hilarious. The translator of Kalidasa's *Shakuntala* has Dushyanta saying: 'O thou, with-thighs-like-the-outer edge-of-the-palm-of-the-hand'.

At the end of the letter, he very practically suggested journals and magazines to which I could send these stories. And added, 'when all else fails, you know that Barkis is willin'. I run a bimonthly Miscellany and I will be happy to use both'.

It is a great pleasure to me that, when, finally, I decided to bring out a volume of my short stories which came out of the epics, it was Prof. Lal who published them. *The Stone Women* is a very beautifully produced book. The perfection gives me a glimpse of his pleasure in the stories.

I think it is a great pity that P. Lal's work in translations and his views of translation are not as much known as they should be. To read him on translations is to get a deep understanding of what the process means. He had strong views on translation of the Sanskrit texts. He unequivocally and bravely states that 'an Indian is better equipped to translate India's sacred works than a foreigner', giving examples, like the one above, to prove his point. His comments on the various translations of the Kunti-Karna episode in the Mahabharata, which he calls a 'tight and poignant piece of drama, carefully constructed, near-perfect in its delicacy, brevity, simplicity and intensity' are brilliant. 'The haunting Karuna rasa, the flavour of compassion in this episode, needs a sensitive translating approach'. I wish more translators would read him on translation.

His theory that 'One is always translating for one's contemporaries. Creative writing may be done for a hundred years hence; not translation' was one that he regularly put into practice. This translation of a Sanskrit poem of unknown date shows how well he did it:

Oh yes, I'm good at stitching and darning
And half my life's
Spent giving good dinners to guests who come
without warning
–I am a wife

'Touché!' one is tempted to cry out. And there is this one, from his transcreation of Sanskrit love lyrics:

On that rich night, bright with lamplight,
We made love, slowly; but all night,
The bed creaked ...

Ageless eroticism indeed!

It will be long before we realise the extent of Prof. Lal's voluminous and varied contribution to the literature of IWE (Indian Writing in English). He speaks of IWE having begun in 1947 with a group of undergraduates in a Calcutta college who wrote in English. One does not know who the others were, but Lal went on to becoming an institution himself. He was not only a pioneer of IWE, he was a phenomenon. The only other person I can think of who has this stature is Nissim Ezekiel. Ezekiel was also a great teacher like P. Lal, and again, like him, always a great source of encouragement for young writers. But he was no publisher. P. Lal was a publisher as well; he has to get the credit for the fact that so many writers would have languished unread if not for him. (If there are some compromises in the quality of the writing, it seems to me important to remember that good writing can emerge only out of a large volume of writing.) And he wrote. He wrote poetry, essays, criticism, and above all translations—or rather transcreations, the word he coined himself. There are transcreations of the two great epics, of the

Gita, the Dhammapada, the Upanishads, the *Rig Veda*, of Sanskrit plays, of little-known Sanskrit verses, of Tagore, Premchand and much more. I have a great many of the books with me, some I asked for, many sent by him with great generosity, with heart-lifting inscriptions on the fly leaf written in his beautiful hand. His letters too were marvels of brevity, beautiful language and handwriting, treasures worth preserving. It is amazing to see the punctiliousness with which he punctuated his writing—the commas, the colons, the semicolons are all exactly where they should be. I look with awe at his absolutely correct use of the hyphen in 'low- and medium-brows'. And this in a letter! There was also his puckish sense of humour. His letter congratulating me on the Akademi award ends with, 'And be humble', since the local paper had referred to me as 'Anil Deshpande'!

I was fortunate to visit his home in Calcutta a few times. The first time was a visit with my husband and younger son, and I remember that he found some comics for the child to browse through. The last time I visited him was in 2005. He was to have launched my new novel *Moving On* (I was looking forward to this very much), but poor health prevented him. When I visited him with a friend, he looked extremely frail. But to see him sitting among piles of books, to hear him talk, was an experience I will never forget. He gave us a brilliant exposition of Keats' 'Ode to a Nightingale' and I could see what a wonderful teacher he must have been. When we were leaving, he gave me a book written by his grandfather in 1817, a chance discovery, he said. In the preface to the book he writes, 'It is not always one finds a lost ancestor with lotus-feet worthy of being touched. Good karma, I suppose'.

All Indian English writers should say 'Good Karma' too for having a literary forebear like Prof. P. Lal.

(2011)

www.ingramcontent.com/pod-product-compliance
Lightning Source LLC
Chambersburg PA
CBHW071143130626
46553CB00004B/1495
9789357764605